**Human Action
and its
Psychological Investigation**

Human Action and its Psychological Investigation

Alan Gauld and John Shotter
Department of Psychology, University of Nottingham

Routledge & Kegan Paul
London, Boston and Henley

First published in 1977
by Routledge & Kegan Paul Ltd
39 Store Street,
London WC1E 7DD,
Broadway House,
Newtown Road,
Henley-on-Thames,
Oxon RG9 1EN and
9 Park Street,
Boston, Mass. 02108, USA
First published as a paperback in 1980
Set in V.I.P. Times by
Western Printing Services Ltd
and printed in Great Britain by
Unwin Brothers Ltd
The Gresham Press, Old Woking, Surrey
A member of the Staples Printing Group
© Alan Gauld and John Shotter 1977

British Library Cataloguing in Publication Data

Gauld, Alan
Human action and its psychological investigation

1. Human behavior
I. Title II. Shotter, John
150   BF131

ISBN 0 7100 8568 0(c)
ISBN 0 7100 0589X(p)

Contents

Preface

The authors of this book, though differing in outlook and interests, have this in common. We began to study psychology during a period – the second decade after the war – in which it seemed to many that an experimental science of human behaviour, a science that would meet the canons laid down by Mill and subsequent philosophers of science, was well under way. For a while we were inclined to share this optimism. Though the fundamental inconsistencies of Hullian behaviourism had been devastatingly exposed by Koch (1954), the twin stars of information theory and artificial intelligence shone with increasing lustre upon multiplying devotees. But before long we were seized by all manner of doubts – doubts about the applicability to psychology of ideas drawn from an out-of-date physics; doubts about the relevance of the findings to real-life psychological problems; doubts, above all, as to whether, should we devote ourselves to the study of, say, two-choice reaction times, or nonsense syllable learning, or bar pressing in rats, we would be able to look back upon lifetimes of modest progress in rewarding intellectual endeavour.

Such doubts remain, and this book is one of the outcomes. In part it represents some of the reasons for our doubts, but its main purpose is constructive – to work towards a form of psychological endeavour less drab and less encapsulated than that lately predominant, while at the same time less crazy than that advocated by the more extreme 'humanistic' psychologists. We do not pretend to do more than suggest, and in a preliminary way discuss, a possible conceptual framework for such a psychology, and to illustrate in little the sort of empirical enquiries which might be undertaken within that framework. Our principal target is the honours psychology student; and if we can dissuade a few such students from wasting the years which we were foolish enough to waste, and induce them instead to explore, more deeply than we, the problems we have touched upon, we shall be content.

Specifically we are concerned to explore a framework within which we can think about man as an agent, as a being himself responsible for at least some of his actions. Part I of the book gives the gist of our views. In part II certain key conceptual and empirical issues are taken further, though still in a relatively non-technical way. We have, whenever possible, centred our discussions upon recent books and articles. We hope thus to illustrate the relevance of our proposals to contemporary issues, and to provide the student with sign-posted avenues for further exploration.

The gist of our approach is contained in chapters 1, 6 and 13. Students coming to these issues for the first time may find it helpful to begin by reading just these chapters.

The enquiry is not of academic interest alone. For, unlike material objects, people seem able to act upon the basis of mere beliefs. Thus it is only too easy for our beliefs about ourselves – that we are, say, complex machines or information processing systems or bundles of reflexes or the puppets of unconscious libidinal forces – to become self-fulfilling prophecies. To some extent at least we can act as if we are complex machines or whatever it may be. The belief that that is what we are is then legitimated by the empirical 'proof' science is thought to provide, and we are off into a vicious spiral.

The spiral is doubly vicious because how we act towards one another is affected by what kind of thing we believe we are. Curiously enough this view is shared by B. F. Skinner (1972), the most eminent surviving behaviourist. Skinner holds that the science of 'behaviour control' must be applied in solving the problems that face us in the world today. It is, in his estimation, our old concept of ourselves – as autonomous agents with inner selves, possessed of freedom and aspiring towards dignity – which must be obliterated if society is to survive. To this we can only say, in the words of Kurt Vonnegut, Jr,

> We are what we pretend to be, so we had better be careful about what we pretend to be.

Acknowledgments

We would like to thank our colleague Dr R. B. Joynson for reading the first draft of this book in its entirety and making some very helpful comments. We would also like to thank Professor Michael Argyle for permission to reproduce Figure 2 and Professor Jerome S. Bruner for allowing us to quote him at length in chapter 13.

AG and JS

Note added in proof: Neisser's new book, *Cognition and Reality* (U. Neisser, San Francisco, Freeman, 1976), came to our notice at the proof stage in the production of this book. As his *Cognitive Psychology* (Neisser, 1967) has been taken by many as setting the scene and defining the aims in recent experimental psychology, we felt it worthwhile to add a comment about his new book here. For in it, we feel, he takes great strides away from the mechanistic approach we criticize, towards a position with some features similar to our own.

In *Cognitive Psychology* Neisser grasped only partially the nettle of *agency*, proposing the idea of an 'executive agent' which from a position in the centre of our affairs 'selects and uses stored information' (p. 293). Thus he left open the possibility that the peripheral processes providing the information initially could be of a mechanical kind; and it was these which as computer 'routines' or 'programs' could be studied by experimental psychologists. Now he repudiates all that: it is not just at the centre of our affairs that we are agents but at the periphery too. We actively direct our own perceptual processes, he suggests, in the course of conducting a 'perceptual cycle' (p. 21). And, he says, 'when perception is treated as something we do rather than as something thrust upon us, no internal mechanisms of selection are required at all'. Instead, what people can do is a matter of what they try to do and their skill at realizing their intentions. And 'practiced subjects can do what seems impossible to the novice as well as the theorist' (p. 92).

While we find his treatment of man as an agent interesting, his treatment of him as a social agent is entirely inadequate. But we shall have to continue this 'conversation' with Neisser elsewhere.

AG and JS

Part I

1
Approaches to the Study of Man

In this chapter we shall distinguish two broad approaches to the study of human behaviour, the natural scientific, and the hermeneutical. To understand the former it is necessary to look back to Descartes. The view presented by Descartes, and accepted as at least a starting-point by many subsequent philosophers, was that man is essentially a thinking subject, an extensionless rational soul, set over against the extended physical world, and only contingently related to it. However, if we rightly use our capacity for rational thought, he suggested, we may in time achieve control over the material world of which we are the detached observers, for

> by knowing the force and actions of fire, water, air, the stars, the heavens, and all other bodies that surround us . . . we should be able to utilize them for all the uses to which they suited and thus render ourselves masters and possessors of nature.

Masters and possessors of nature we have increasingly become. By conceiving the physical world as made up of elementary and separable particles of matter in blind but lawful interaction, and by developing methods of controlled experimentation with which to investigate them, we have greatly increased our power to control at least certain aspects of that world. But in what terms are we to conceive and understand the knower whose knowledge has been so strikingly advanced, the 'rational soul' whose intellectual activities, directed upon that natural realm of which he is not a part, yet have rendered him master and possessor of nature? The spirit of our times permits only one answer. Scientific knowledge in the Cartesian tradition has grown to be the ideal of all knowledge, and we are now attempting to bring within its confines what Descartes quite explicitly left out – the thinking mind, the scientist himself. 'While therefore, most modern thought has continued to divide human beings sharply from the natural phenomena around them', remarks Broadbent (1961, p. 11), 'an attack upon this division has been quietly growing in strength.' This stance is also assumed by contemporary psychologists who, like Milner (1970, p. 1), want to treat questions about any natural entity 'as if they had been asked about some man-made object like a radio or motor car'. It is assumed by all those psychologists who discuss human activities in terms of incoming stimuli and subsequent responses, and then immediately reduce these to mechanical categories.

The wheel has indeed come full circle when the Cartesian 'rational soul', the non-material observer of the material world and discoverer of the causal relationships which traverse it, has itself been dissolved into a nexus of cause and effect relationships. And yet is such a dissolution plausible? Is it even logically consistent? If the scientist is himself no more than an arena within which inevitable causes produce their inevitable effects, how could he have discovered the causal laws which his own behaviour is supposed to instantiate? A scientist practising his craft must assume himself to be a free agent; a being capable of arbitrarily manipulating his corner of the universe. The effect of his manipulations must be to destroy any chance regularities among phenomena, leaving the real, i.e. causal, regularities to show themselves. But if the scientist's intervention is itself causally determined the possibility must always remain that his intervention did not destroy a fortuitous regularity, but was the upshot of an antecedent state of affairs which also caused the disruption of the regularity.

> Thus in this case, as in others, man can only have a true view of the universe and the laws of nature by excepting himself from their sway, and considering himself over against the universe, not as part of it, and not subject to its laws (Lucas, 1970, p. 63).

It is far from clear that a reflexive psychology, one which embraces as it must the psychology of the practising psychologist, can coherently be formulated within the natural scientific tradition.

. . .

The term 'hermeneutics' comes from the Greek *hermeneuo*, I interpret, explain, make clear. It was at one time in use among scholars to denote the science of the elucidation of the meaning of texts. More recently the term has been widened to include the interpretation of 'text-analogues' (see especially C. Taylor, 1971). A text-analogue is, roughly speaking, any sequence of human activities, or set of the products of such activities, to which, or to items within which, one can assign a 'meaning' in the somewhat broad sense we are about to touch upon. It has been proposed that the psychological and social sciences are essentially hermeneutical, that the proper task of the psychologist is not to formulate the laws of human behaviour, but to elucidate the 'meanings' of pieces of human behaviour. What are we to make of this proposal?

There is a vague but familiar sense of the term 'meaning' in which 'meanings' can be assigned not just to words or sentences or other textual items, but to all sorts of non-linguistic entities or events. The event or entity concerned has 'meaning' for someone if it, so to speak, carries him in thought beyond it to some other entity or event to which it is empirically or conceptually related. In this sense of 'meaning', the dog's bark 'means' to his master that the postman is at the gate. None the less it would be incorrect to speak of *the* meaning of the dog's bark. The dog's bark may 'mean' one thing to one person ('the postman is here') and another thing to another ('that dog has not been properly trained'). There is no question of one of these meanings being *the* meaning, or a permissible or possible meaning, and so there is no question of interpreting the bark. And this is clearly because the dog itself meant nothing by the bark.

It is only when we come to human *actions*, pieces of behaviour which we bring about rather than find our limbs executing, that it becomes possible to speak of interpretation, of the elucidation of meaning. For some human actions (and we are talking still just of non-linguistic actions) have 'meaning' not just in that they happen to induce persons present to think of some related event or circumstance, but in that the agents knowingly carry out those actions to fill a place in some wider scheme of things. Someone might draw down the blinds as a gesture of respect to the dead; or to protect carpets from the sun; or as the prelude to a crime. To ask for the 'meaning' of the drawn blinds, or of the drawing of the blinds, would be to ask what other than the drawing of them the agent had it in mind to accomplish. And to the extent that this 'meaning' was not patent, to the extent that the agent failed, so to speak, to stir corresponding thoughts in an onlooker, it would be appropriate for that onlooker to seek further elucidation, to seek an interpretation of what he had witnessed.

Sometimes the meaning of an action may, as it were, be negotiated between the agent and onlookers who are in a way participants. Suppose, for example, that someone is ceremonially planting a tree. He throws a spadeful of earth on to the roots. This action, which any gardener might do, is not straightforwardly horticultural. The agent understands that in that context his action is an initiation or commemoration of something not immediately present, that it has a ceremonial meaning which no mere shovelling of earth could have. And he understands further that it has that meaning only because the audience agrees that it shall have it. One might say that it is his understanding of this situational and social meaning that gives his action the meaning it has for him. But the audience in its turn must assume that the agent's action does have the appropriate meaning for him, for if it did not he could not in the relevant sense 'plant' the tree at all. The 'meaning' of this action is thus not simply 'up to' the agent, or 'up to' the audience, but depends upon mutual understanding and agreement between all parties involved.

The affinity between this kind of action-meaning and the meaning of words and sentences, i.e. of texts, is readily apparent. One might as a very crude first approximation say that the reader of a text has grasped the 'meaning' of a text or text item when he is led by perusing it to conceive some state of affairs which the author of the text intended through the performance of conventionally agreed actions to bring his readers to conceive.[1] And the conventional significance of these actions must be grasped by both sides, and is indeed in a sense a matter for negotiation between them.

We conclude, therefore, that it is perfectly sensible to speak of certain pieces of human behaviour, viz. 'actions', having 'meanings' much as texts and text-items do, and to speak of the elucidation of those meanings in cases of obscurity.

Now just as we may say of a word, phrase or sentence, 'Why is that sentence there; what is its function in relation to the rest of the text?' so we may ask about a man's action, 'Why did that action occur, what is its function in relation to his other actions?' Elucidating the meaning of an action commonly tells one why the agent came to do it. We ordinarily explain why an agent did what he did by pointing on the one hand to the goals, desires, purposes, moral principles, etc., which he then had, and on the other hand to the bearing of the situation as he then conceived it upon those goals, desires and so forth. He opens his umbrella because he wishes to stay dry and he believes it is starting to rain. He genuflects because he wishes to remain in the good graces of the Almighty, or because he has adopted principles which make genuflection incumbent upon him, and because the present situation is one in which genuflection seems appropriate. Now a full elucidation of the 'meaning' of an action has to include an account of the intentions, desires, etc., from which the agent acted. The action of a man who absent-mindedly flaps his umbrella or bends his knee has no 'meaning'; he did not carry out the action to fill a slot in a scheme of things already conceived by him. Only when it becomes apparent that what he did he knowingly did under a description which invested it with a place in a framework of thought relevant to his then situation as he saw it can we begin to talk of 'the meaning' of his action. And to the extent that 'the meaning' of his action has been elucidated in these terms, his action has been explained – the motives, purposes, principles from which he acted have been brought into the open, and so have his beliefs about his then situation, and about its bearing upon his goals, etc. We shall call this kind of action-explanation 'hermeneutical explanation', explanation by the elucidation of the meanings of actions.

We have now characterized two kinds of approach to the study of human behaviour, the natural scientific and the hermeneutical. It will be convenient at this point to list some of the ways in which these two approaches may be contrasted with each other. We shall list them with a minimum of comment, since most will be discussed again later.

(1) The subject-matter of the hermeneutical approach is human behaviour *regarded as action*. Now the concept of action is inseparable from the concept of an agent. The concept of an agent is, prima facie, the concept of a being who is, at least sporadically, free to interfere with the sequences of causally related happenings which go on in the world; a being whose behaviour is not itself completely determined by antecedent events in the external world. Many natural scientists would find such an assumption at variance with the whole spirit of natural scientific endeavour.

(2) The concepts which figure in hermeneutical explanation –

agent, action, intention, purpose, desire, belief, rule – are alleged to differ in at least one important respect from the concepts generally thought admissible in natural scientific endeavour. For the latter concepts to be correctly applied in making valid judgments of empirical fact, certain publicly determinable conditions must be satisfied. For the former concepts ('psychological' concepts) to be correctly employed in making valid judgments of empirical fact, it is not in all cases necessary that publicly determinable conditions be satisfied (cf. S. C. Brown, 1965). In other words, you can make valid judgments or statements about certain intentions, desires, etc., viz. your own, regardless of whether or not a given physical state of affairs obtains. Some would say that this fact reflects fundamental differences between the natural and the hermeneutical sciences; that the objects of knowledge, and the kind of knowledge obtained, differ in the two cases.

(3) Interpretations are always relative to a conceptual system – the conceptual system within which the interpreter supposes the author of the text or text-analogue to have operated. You can only understand the meaning which a text or an action had for the author or agent if you understand the way he conceived the world and his position in it. Furthermore, interpretations of actions always involve psychological concepts – the 'meaning' of an action has in part to be elucidated by reference to the agent's intentions, hopes, rules of conduct, etc. We tend to assume that whereas people's conceptual systems may vary pretty much from one culture to another, the psychological categories which we must invoke in explaining their behaviour are constant. This assumption may not be completely correct; the conceptual systems within which people operate in their everyday transactions with the world, and the psychological concepts which are required to specify their psychological states and attributes, may not be independently characterizable, so that psychological concepts vary to some extent from one culture to another. C. Taylor (1971, pp. 12–13) gives the following example of this interrelatedness:

> An emotion term like 'shame', for instance, essentially refers us to a certain kind of situation, the 'shameful', or 'humiliating', and a certain mode of response, that of hiding oneself, of covering up, or else 'wiping out' the blot. That is, it is essential to this feeling's being identified as shame that it be related to this situation and give rise to this type of

disposition. But this situation in its turn can only be identified in relation to the feelings which it provokes; and the disposition is to a goal which can similarly not be understood without reference to the feelings experienced; the 'hiding' in question is one which will cover up my shame; it is not the same as hiding from an armed pursuer. We can only understand what is meant by 'hiding' here if we understand what kind of feeling and situation is being talked about. We have to be within the circle.

Let us adopt the term 'hermeneutical circle' to denote the whole complex of a person's conceptual systems and psychological make-up, a complex by reference to which the 'meaning' of his actions must be elucidated. We may now note the following apparent contrast between the natural and the hermeneutical sciences. The natural scientist stands apart from his subject-matter and is free to try out upon it whatever conceptual systems he pleases. The hermeneutical scientist must himself be within the hermeneutical circle. Only someone who is a participant in that hermeneutical circle can understand the meaning of that agent's actions, for that meaning is given by the *agent's own* conceptual and psychological systems, and cannot be adequately captured within any other systems. And it is impossible for anyone to come to share the agent's own conceptual and psychological systems by applying the methods of natural science to his behaviour, by observing that behaviour in detached fashion and trying to frame laws setting forth or explaining physical regularities detectable in it. The possession of concepts and conceptual systems, and of intentions, desires, beliefs, etc., does not manifest itself in any physically specifiable regularities in behaviour.

(4) It has frequently been proposed that hermeneutical explanations are different from, and irreducible to, the causal explanations which are said to be characteristic of the natural sciences. In an hermeneutical science an action is explained when it is made apparent that the agent did it, as it were, to fill some slot in a scheme of things conceived by him in advance of action or in the course of ongoing action – he did it for a purpose, from a principle, from a desire, as the outcome of calculation. And the relation between purposes, desires, calculations, etc., and the actions which arise out of them, has been held to be non-causal on two grounds, (a) that the relation between the antecedent state or event and the consequent

action can be understood without reference to any general causal statement of the 'A is always followed by B' kind, and (b) that the link between intentions, purposes or desires, and the actions which arise from them, is non-contingent, and cannot be established by empirical observation; for if the actions were not carried out, the intention or desire-ascription would, *ceteris paribus*, have to be withdrawn (cf. chapter 9).

(5) Be that as it may, there would be considerable agreement that within hermeneutical sciences we cannot expect to find the universally applicable generalizations of which the natural sciences have given us so many. There is an obvious reason why this should be so. The 'hermeneutical circles' in which the members of one culture participate will often be vastly different from those participated in by the members of another culture. How could general laws and cross-cultural predictions be formulated under these circumstances? Situations which arise within one 'hermeneutical circle' may very well have no analogue at all within another. And there is a further dimension to the problem which is expressed as follows by Charles Taylor (1971, p. 49):

> man is a self-defining animal. With changes in his
> self-definition go changes in what man is, such that he has to
> be understood in different terms. But the conceptual
> mutations in human history can and frequently do produce
> conceptual webs which are incommensurable. The entirely
> different notions of bargaining in our society and in some
> primitive ones provide an example. Each will be glossed in
> terms of practices, institutions, ideas in each society which
> have nothing corresponding to them in the other.

(6) Finally, we should perhaps note that the phenomena which form the background to the hermeneutical scientist's whole endeavour – actions, intentions, desires, beliefs, etc. – are 'intensional' phenomena. This is said to mean (roughly speaking) that it makes sense to talk of these phenomena as being 'directed upon' objects which do not exist ('intentions' are thus only one class amongst those phenomena which can be called intensional). Thus one can believe in fairy gold (which does not exist) and intend to obtain some (which one never will). It is further alleged that none of the phenomena in which the physical scientist trades possess this property.

It is thus apparent that, at first glance, hermeneutical accounts of human behaviour are in many ways contrasted to natural scientific ones. The question therefore arises, are these two kinds of account in conflict with one another, and if so which must give way? Now one line that has not infrequently been taken, and has as frequently been opposed (Melden, 1961; Peters, 1958; Warnock, 1963; Ayer, 1964; Flew, 1965; Fodor, 1965; MacIntyre, 1966; Sher, 1973; Crowell, 1975), is to claim, following Waismann (1953), that language contains a number of 'strata' or 'realms of discourse' each carrying a 'logic' of its own which determines the meaning of its basic terms. Talk of actions regarded as movements determined by causes belongs to one such stratum, and talk of actions regarded as carried out intentionally by rational agents operating within an hermeneutical circle belongs to another. According to Melden (1961, p. 201), 'absolutely nothing about any matter of human conduct follows logically from any account of the physiological conditions of bodily movement', and Ayer (1964, p. 24) draws an analogy: 'the fact that to talk about wave-lengths is not to describe colours is not an objection to the science of optics'.

Let us consider again the example of someone genuflecting at the sight of the unveiled cross. Prima facie this piece of behaviour lends itself very readily to explanation in terms of certain neo-behaviourist paradigms. For here is someone making a simple movement in response to a simple stimulus. No doubt the response has been 'reinforced' on many occasions in the past. By contrast, an upholder of hermeneutical explanations would probably say that the *agent* genuflected as a matter of conscious policy because his beliefs had led him to adopt certain rules of conduct which might in some sense be rationally derived from them, or (more crudely) because he desired happiness in the after-life, intended to obtain it, and thought genuflection in that situation an action which would further that intention. These two kinds of explanation might each seem appropriate in different cases. Perhaps the behaviour of an ancient peasant woman who was whipped as a child for failures in her religious observances, and given sweets for good behaviour, might fit into the stimulus-response paradigm. Without doubt the genuflections of an intellectual Catholic would seem susceptible of hermeneutical explanation. But could both these kinds of explanation simultaneously and without conflict be supposed to account for the same physical occurrence, viz. the limb movements involved in the same action of genuflecting? Surely not. For it is clearly essential to an hermeneutical explanation that the agent's intentions and so forth, his 'reasons' for acting, are not superfluous; i.e. that had the agent not had the intentions and so on which he did he would not have genuflected and the limb movements involved in genuflection would not have taken place. Thus, the movements cannot *also* be fully explicable in behaviourist terms. Similarly stimulus-response theories claim to explain the occurrence of the movement without making any reference to the agent's beliefs, intentions, etc., or indeed to his *acting*. The validity of one of these kinds of explanation appears to put the other kind out of court. Certainly they cannot co-exist in totally insulated language strata; for there are events (limb movements) of which *both* purport to provide an explanation.

It appears, therefore, that so far as the explanation of, at any rate, paradigm cases of human action is concerned, one of these kinds of explanation has to give way to the other. Which has it to be? Mechanistic explanation has one enormous initial disadvantage as compared to everyday or hermeneutical explanation – it cannot as yet even begin to cope with the phenomena to be explained. But even if we set aside this point, it remains inconceivable that hermeneutical explanation should have to give way.

Let us again consider the central case of those everyday action-explanations which explain actions by reference to the further intentions which the agent had in acting. Someone who wanted to uphold mechanistic explanations of the same actions would have to argue that the conscious intentions of an agent who believes himself to be planning, directing and controlling the movements of his body so as to bring about some state of affairs antecedently conceived by him are in fact quite without influence on the initiation and course of those movements. The intentions would be like the bubbles on an incoming wave, which accompany it but do not influence its course.

This would be an extraordinary position to have to defend. It puts all agents who suppose themselves to be consciously exercising their power to plan and direct their own activities rather in the position of a passenger in a wind-blown conveyance who can predict its direction of travel and who suffers from the delusion that he is steering it in accordance with his own plans. The problem then arises, how could this particular delusion have come into being when *ex hypothesi* no one has *ever*, in the relevant sense, implemented any of his plans? In ordinary delusions and illusions of perception, memory and so forth, or in paranoiac delusions of grandeur, persecution and so forth, one can at least suppose that the delusions are derived from acquaintance with non-illusory or non-delusory instances. In the case which we are now considering there are alleged to be non-illusory or non-delusory instances, so we appear to have examples of notions (those of intention, action, and their relatives) to which nothing in the world corresponds and which could hardly have arisen from any experience of the world.

In fact the whole of one's effective practical understanding of one's own and other people's behaviour is based on the belief that they plan and direct the movements of their bodies to fulfil criteria conceived by them. The belief that intentions – 'phenomenological intentions' (Turner, 1971) – are mere epiphenomena is not one anyone could consistently hold and act upon. There would be no point in the holder of such a belief trying to plan his behaviour. A sort of behaviouristic quietism would be his logical policy. Yet even this would be a policy for action, which, according to his hypothesis, would necessarily be without avail. To adopt it would be to admit its erroneousness. We have here a belief which, if held, cannot be consistently embodied in practice because according to it there is no practice. If acted upon it must be false.[2]

Can we therefore at once rule out the natural scientific approach to human behaviour, and devote the rest of our space to examining the hermeneutical? Unfortunately things are not so simple. For so far we have implicitly assumed that natural scientific explanations are ones which do not and cannot find a place for the central concepts of hermeneutical explanation – action, agent, intention, desire, belief and so forth. If that were the case natural scientific explanations would be non-starters. But we have not yet confronted the possibility that the leading concepts of the one sort of explanation might be au fond translatable into the terms of the other. In that event it would be in principle possible for one sort of explanation to incorporate the other. Hermeneutical explanation might then emerge just as a subspecies of mechanical or natural scientific explanation, a position which is maintained for example by Nagel (1961), Goldman (1970) and Locke (1974a).

We shall tackle the issue as follows. In the next chapter we shall attempt to define in its most general form the nature of a 'mechanistic system', and shall ask what limits there may be upon the kinds of phenomena which could be explained in terms of the operations of such systems. In the two subsequent chapters we shall briefly analyse some notions of central importance in hermeneutical explanations – especially the notions of concept, action and intention – and shall enquire whether a mechanistic system could in principle be designed whose behaviour could properly be characterized in terms of these notions. We shall ask, in effect, whether a mechanistic system is possible which could truly act, possess concepts, have intentions, etc.

2

The Generalized Machine

Mechanistic explanation in psychology has taken many forms. If one lumps them together one risks being accused of over-simplification. Fortunately it is possible to make some general points in terms of a framework of thought within which the leading features of them all may be represented. This is the framework of what (following Ross Ashby), we may call the 'machine in general'. A 'machine' is to be thought of, in Ross Ashby's words, as 'that which behaves in a machine-like way, namely, that its internal state, and the state of its surroundings, defines uniquely the next state it will go to' (Ross Ashby, 1962, in Buckley, Ed., 1968, p. 111). A 'finite-state machine' is a machine which at any moment is in one of a finite number of discrete possible 'internal' states, and which has a finite number of possible 'input' states and a finite number of possible 'output' states.

	M_1	M_2
I_1	O_1, M_1	O_2, M_1
I_2	O_1, M_2	O_2, M_2

Figure 1

The functioning of any such machine may be described in terms of 'machine-tables' which specify for any given 'internal' state of the machine what 'output' will result from a given input and what internal state the machine will move to next. Thus the machine-table in Figure 1 specifies what Minsky (1967, p. 20) calls a simple 'memory' machine. Here I_1 and I_2 represents inputs, O_1 and O_2 outputs, and M_1 and M_2 machine states. The table indicates that if at time t the machine is in state M_1 and receives input I_1, then at time $t + 1$ it will emit output O_1 and remain in state M_1; and so on. Since the output at $t + 1$ tells one what state the machine was in at time t, and this in turn tells one what the input was at time $t - 1$, the machine is said to 'remember' its inputs of two units of time ago.

Machine-tables of this kind can be expanded and diversified indefinitely. They have their place within the mathematical theory of automata, and it has been claimed by such theorists as Ross Ashby that the functioning, not just of any man-made machine, but also of all or very many natural systems, may be represented in this generalized form. This issue is too large to be dealt with here. It does, however, seem to be quite clear that the mechanistic psychological theories which we are considering could all (in so far as they are internally consistent) be in essence expressed in machine-table notation. In fact S-R theories, macromolecular theories and computer 'programme analogies' simply *are* at root specifications of 'machines' as defined above.

Any system whose functioning can be specified in machine-table form can in principle be paralleled or 'embodied' on a digital computer; that is to say a digital computer can, in theory even if not in practice, be programmed in such a way that the outputs and state-transitions with which it responds to inputs formally correspond to those specified by the machine-table. Digital computers may thus be regarded as 'generalized machines' (GMs), machines which can be so organized as to mirror the functioning of any other 'machine'.

In the last decade or two psychologists have taken a good deal of interest in the computer 'simulation' of behaviour. This has been not only because S-R and other traditional theories lend themselves to representation on a computer, but because it is in digital computers, if anywhere, that we find inorganic physical systems capable of 'intelligent' behaviour – capable, it is said, of doing arithmetic, solving logical problems, playing chess, draughts, nim and tic-tac-toe. Thus psychologists have come to study and utilize digital computers because they hope that the ways in which computers are programmed or organized to carry out 'intelligent' functions will provide clues as to how the human brain is organized to the same end. It should be noted that the 'same' programme or organization (in effect the same machine-table) may be embodied in computers of which the actual circuitry is quite different. A leading 'cognitive' psychologist has gone so far as to say (Neisser, 1967, p. 6),

> The task of a psychologist trying to understand human cognition is analogous to that of a man trying to discover how a computer has been programmed. In particular, if the program seems to store and re-use *information*, he would like to know by what 'routines' or 'procedures' this is done. . . . He wants to understand its *utilization*, not its incarnation.

For immediate purposes, however, there are two important points about the GM as a tool in psychological inquiry. The first is this. The limitations (if any) of the generalized machine, the ultimate theoretical constraints upon what it can do, show us the limitations of mechanistic theories in general. To any possible 'machine' as the term was defined above there corresponds a machine-table. Any machine-table can in principle be embodied in or programmed into a generalized machine. Therefore, if it can be shown that a human agent can do things which it is in principle impossible for a generalized machine to do, it will *a fortiori* have been shown that mechanistic explanation in psychology, at least as that sort of explanation has generally been conceived, breaks down at a certain point.

The second point is a corollary of the first. If the term 'cause' is given the neo-Humean sense which has come to dominate modern thinking on the subject, then GMs are causal systems *par excellence* and the laws of their operation are paradigm examples of causal laws. It is impossible here to examine the neo-Humean view of causality in any detail, but its leading features may be summarized as follows: (1) An event A may be called the cause of a subsequent event B if events like A are, in circumstances like those which obtained, regularly followed by events like B, and if, further, the non-occurrence of an event like A is in circumstances like those which obtained, regularly followed by the non-occurrence of B. In other words we can call A the cause of B if we can assert upon the basis of observation that if A had not occurred B would not have occurred. (2) It must be in principle possible, though it may not always be practicable, to characterize A and B independently of each other, for otherwise they would be non-contingently related, i.e. there would be a relation between them for the ascertainment of which empirical investigations would be superfluous. (3) A 'causal law' is simply a statement of observed sequential regularities among events, observed regularities which lead us to suppose that if A had not then occurred B would not then have occurred, and so forth. Any system of whose behaviour a full account can be given in terms of such causal laws can receive a representation in machine-table terms; and any consistent machine-table can be embodied on a GM. From this it follows that any system whose behaviour *cannot* be fully represented on a GM would be a system whose behaviour is not fully describable in terms of causal laws as conceived above. Any 'understanding' which we might achieve of the behaviour of such a system would not be, or would not entirely be, the sort of understanding which comes from a comprehensive grasp of the relevant causal laws, i.e. of the relevant observed sequential regularities.

To say this is not to say that the system concerned would, in part, necessarily be a non-physical system. We are not asserting that all physical systems are mechanistic or causal systems as above defined. Indeed it seems to us likely that certain of the physical systems hypothesized in the frontier regions of modern physics are *not* representable on a GM. But the physical systems which psychologists advance as possible analogues of the central nervous system and its functioning are almost all of a mechanistic kind.

It will perhaps help both to clarify the notions of mechanistic system and generalized machine, and to introduce the topics of the succeeding chapters, if we turn briefly aside at this point to discuss an argument which has in recent years been several times advanced in an attempt to show that certain aspects of human behaviour are refractory to mechanistic explanation. This is the so-called argument from Gödel's theorem (see, for example, Lucas, 1970; Turner, 1971, chapter 5). The issue here is somewhat technical, and, though the essential points can be outlined quite simply, it will first be necessary to say a little about computing automata in general and about a special class of discrete-state machines in particular.

A central concept for the theory of computing automata is that of an *algorithm*. An algorithm is, very roughly, a list of instructions specifying a sequence of operations which will yield the answer to any problem of a given type. Constructing algorithms and proving their validity requires a high order of mathematical gifts. But once an algorithm has been found, it can be used by a person who has no idea of its purpose. An idiot operating quite mechanically can solve any problem of the kind for which the algorithm has been devised. We might say that in so doing he acts 'like a machine'. And in fact he could be replaced by a machine. These days he would tend to be replaced by a digital computer. The algorithm for solving the class of problems concerned would be incorporated into the programme governing the running of the computer.

It is widely agreed among mathematicians that any algorithm can be given in the form of a machine-table specifying the operations of a discrete-state computing automaton of the class called *Turing machines*. Turing machines are expository devices rather than assemblages of actual hardware though they can be represented on digital computers (GMs).[1] Each machine-table specifies a different Turing machine (just as in effect each new programme makes a digital computer into a 'different' machine), but we can also specify a 'universal' Turing machine, which can imitate any other Turing machine.

It is also widely agreed among mathematicians that if there are classes of problems no Turing machine can solve (i.e. which are algorithmically insoluble) no computing machine can solve them. And there are indeed various classes of algorithmically insoluble problems; for instance no Turing machine can compute which formulae are in principle computable by it.

We can now state the outlines of the argument from Gödel's theorem. In a celebrated paper, Gödel (1931) proved that within the system of elementary arithmetic we can show to be true certain theorems whose truth cannot be arrived at by algorithmic methods from the basic axioms of the system. From this it follows that if you embodied the axioms and rules of the system in a generalized machine, it would be unable to generate these particular theorems. However, human mathematicians can show them to be true by invoking a metasystem, a system which takes the original system as its subject-matter. It has been argued (though not by Gödel) that this shows that human beings can do something which machines cannot do. If it be replied that we can embody *both* system *and* metasystem in a GM, the answer is that in the new enlarged system there will be theorems which we will be able to prove in a meta-metasystem, but which will be beyond any machine embodying the system and the metasystem. Thus men will always be one jump ahead of the machines.

J. J. C. Smart (1963, pp. 119–20) has proposed a way by which a computing machine of sufficient complexity might catch up on us. For we can conceive a machine programmed to observe its own behaviour and to induce therefrom the rules of its own operation. Such a machine might (Smart supposes) convert itself into a machine embodying its own original rule-system plus a metasystem of which the original rules are, so to speak, the object.[2]

To us the controversy surrounding the argument from Gödel's theorem is of interest less in itself than as providing an arena in which certain issues of more general significance become plainly visible. One of these issues is as follows. Human mathematicians can be *creative*. For instance, Gödel created the metasystem within which the refractory arithmetical theorems can be proved. Once a creative step of this kind has been taken, a machine can be programmed to execute any resultant algorithms. But it cannot take the initial step. Smart's suggestion (though unworkable) is clearly intended as indicating a way of endowing a machine with the creativity which it would otherwise lack. (There are, of course, cases in which a machine, following its algorithm, may be 'creative' by producing a result not foreseen by its programmer; but this is not the sort of creativity we are concerned with.)

One might, however, go further and remark that machines lack not just mathematical creativity, but mathematical *understanding* and the *capacity to reason* mathematically (or in any other way). Let us first take up the issue of mathematical understanding, for to a large extent the issue of reasoning capacity hangs upon it.

The input to any computing automaton, the 'problem' confronting it, will be, say, holes in a length of tape. The resultant output, the 'solution' to the problem, will be holes in or printed marks upon another tape. The mathematical interpretation of these holes or marks is put upon them by the programmer. The mathematics exists in *his* eyes. And the operations the machine goes through in transforming input into output are 'mathematical' only in virtue of the programmer's mathematical interpretations. What would we have to add to a computing machine's repertoire to make us agree that it really does do mathematics as distinct from rattling through a sequence of state-transitions the inception and upshot of which the programmer invests with mathematical meaning? To put it in its simplest terms, we should have to make the machine *understand* *what it is doing*.

Now a human being would not be said to understand what mathematics is, or is about, or indeed to be capable of doing

mathematics at all, unless he possessed at least in embryo a variety
of complex and exceedingly abstract concepts; for example logical
concepts like 'not' or 'and', the concept of number, the concept of
implication, the concepts of problem, proof and solution, geometri-
cal and arithmetical concepts, the concept of an equation, and so on
more or less indefinitely. One's activities, whatever they were,
could not be regarded as, for instance, proving a theorem in number
theory unless one had to an extent grasped such notions as those
of number and proof. In fact doing mathematics can, from a
psychological point of view, only be regarded as the process of
exercising such concepts in a systematic and directed manner, in
accordance with rules not separable from the concepts themselves,
and in order to accomplish a certain purpose. Someone who possessed none of these concepts could not be said to do mathematics.
He might go through motions, blindly following some algorithmic
routine, on which someone else could put a mathematical interpretation; and then he would be in the same situation as the computing
machine into whose operations the programmer reads the solution
of a mathematical problem. Thus no machine which could not be
said to possess mathematical concepts, could possibly be said to be
capable of doing mathematics. So it is possession of mathematical
concepts which we should have to add to our machine. We should
have to design a machine which could not merely work through
prescribed or permitted 'mathematical' moves, but could, for
instance, realize the affinity between these moves and comparable
moves in other routines, think discursively about mathematics and
talk intelligently on mathematical topics (including novel ones). It is
certain that no such machine has as yet been invented.

Precisely analogous remarks might be made about so-called
'games-playing' machines. Michie (1974, p. 135) says, 'Hubert
Dreyfus, a professional philosopher, pronounced a few years ago
that no computer could play even amateur chess. He was challenged
to play against the Greenblatt chess program and was ignominiously
defeated.' But Dreyfus's logic may have been better than his chess.
For machines will not *play chess* until we can properly attribute to
them possession and exercise of such concepts as 'rule', 'move',
'piece', 'strategy' and 'game'. And certainly no machine as yet
designed could, as Smart supposes, induce its own rules from observation of its own behaviour; for such induction would require it to
possess the concept of 'rule'.

The issue of whether or not machines (in the sense of the term in which a digital computer is a 'generalized' machine) could possess and exhibit mathematical (or other) understanding, could, in short, do mathematics or 'reason' at all, partly resolves itself into the issue of whether or not it is in principle possible to design a 'machine with concepts'. And *mutatis mutandis* so does the problem of whether or not it is possible to design a games-playing machine. At this point we re-connect with our main line of argument. For (as we pointed out at the end of the previous chapter) a central issue in the problem of whether or not the leading features of hermeneutical explanation can be re-interpreted in mechanistic terms is bound to be whether or not a mechanistic system can in principle be designed to which it would make sense to attribute the possession of concepts. An agent invests his actions with 'meaning' in the relevant sense only when he carries them out *as* actions of such and such a kind or description, when he conceives them as having a place within some project or scheme of things already, though perhaps dimly, envisaged by him.

3

Concepts, Rules and the Generalized Machine

No term has figured more frequently in modern philosophy, and few in modern psychology, than 'concept'. None the less there is considerable obscurity as to its meaning – so much so that nearly fifty years ago McDougall (1928) argued in a forceful article that it should be dropped from the psychologist's vocabulary, while Mundle (1970, pp. 91–109) has recently criticized the laxity with which it is used by contemporary philosophers. Few philosophers have made any extended attempt to discuss the concept of concept (Nowell-Smith, 1967; Adler, 1967; and Cassirer, 1923, are exceptions), and while there is no shortage of definitions by psychologists, these are mostly tailored to the needs of some grossly over-simplified theoretical framework. We shall therefore have to build up an account of our own.

It will perhaps be helpful if we offer a few preliminary remarks on the character of our account, and on the purposes it may serve. An answer to the question 'what is it to have a concept?' may either detail, in everyday language, the behavioural or intellectual capacities possession of which would ordinarily lead us to ascribe such and such a concept to someone, or it may consist in an attempt to explain within some wider theoretical framework the fact that he exhibits that behaviour and those capacities. Our answer to the question will be of the former kind. We shall suggest that to attribute possession of a concept to someone is to attribute to him various kinds of intellectual and behavioural capacities. This will constitute a mapping of the territory which any explanatory theory of concept-possession must cover.

We do not claim to reduce concept-possession to a list of capacities, each individually non-conceptual, but adding up when juxtaposed to concept-possession. All we shall do is try to draw out the main features of concept-possession. We shall not proffer a componential analysis. In fact we shall suggest that the various kinds of capacity involved are so interrelated that none of them could exist without the others. Thus there is a certain unity among the capacities which make up possession of a concept, and this is a fact which any explanatory account of concept-possession will have to consider.

In order to simplify the problems involved, we shall begin by treating concepts of everyday perceptible objects, and shall for the most part neglect the distinction between the accepted or official definition of any particular concept and each person's individual variations on that theme.

The first and most obvious capacity which enters into concept-possession might be described as the capacity to lump objects together in thought. (Some writers think that this capacity originates from one's capacity to lump them together in practice.) At the most elementary level this capacity perhaps takes the form of directing a passing thought to some heterogeneous and probably transient collection of objects which happens to meet one's gaze – as when, for instance, one wishes that one's child would clear *those things* away. But more commonly, one thinks not of *those things* but of things *like that*; one groups things together in virtue of their possessing a certain characteristic or a set of interrelated characteristics. At a more advanced stage of development one may group things together on the basis of, for example, their being different from rather than similar to some other thing, or because they can be serially ordered in some way, or because they stand in almost any relation to each other or to something else. One can think, for instance, of all those people who possess the worldly goods one lacks, of the series of odd numbers, of all the inhabitants of the Isle of Wight and so on. One's thus lumping certain things together in virtue of their possessing a common location or set of characteristics or certain relational properties could be said to amount to one's establishing a principle of classification or division by means of which to simplify one's handling in thought and action of the objects and events which surround one.

It might be said that in order to give an analysis of what it is to possess an object-concept we have assumed the prior possession of attribute-, or characteristic-concepts, that we are saying in effect that one is able to group all red objects together in thought because one antecedently possesses a concept of redness. We shall, however, suggest in chapter 8 that to group red objects together on the basis of a perceived characteristic similarity is not necessarily to possess a concept of 'redness'.

We can now amplify our initial over-simplification very slightly, and say that the first mark of concept-possession is the capacity to bring a principle of classification to bear on the objects which one encounters in one's transactions with the world, and to make judgments or decisions about, formulate propositions concerning, and so on, all the objects which one thinks it covers, or any one of them considered as instantiating the principle; and to do so both in the presence and the absence of a member of that class.

An obvious corollary is that one must understand the principle of classification with which one is operating. One could not be said to mark out, to think of, make judgments about, or formulate propositions concerning (let us say) dogs considered as dogs, as objects falling under a common classificatory rubric, unless one could be assumed to know (at least in some minimal sense) what the accepted defining characteristics of dogs are. Suppose one judged, thought or affirmed that dogs eat bones, and it then transpired that one apparently also believed 'dogs' are vegetarian, live under water, and lay eggs. It would be quite clear that whatever one's initial judgment may have been about, it was not about 'dogs'. It is a matter of definition that dogs breathe air and are viviparous. Unless one's judgments, statements and actions showed that one appreciated this point, one could not be said to be able to make judgments about 'dogs' *as such*. One's 'dog' judgments must either have been about the members of some eccentric class of one's own specification, or else have been symptoms of total classificatory confusion.

The question now arises, what is it to understand a principle of classification, what is it to know what 'dogs' are? There has been a tendency to answer in terms of certain stimulus patterns coming through processes of association to arouse certain expectancies, so that if one glimpses a dog-shape one knows that one will shortly hold truck with a vertebrate animal that has fur, sharp teeth, etc. This analysis is so wide of the mark that it is hard to see how it could be entertained for a moment. However strong the expectations which a dog-shape aroused, the disappointment of these expectations could *per se* provide no grounds for anything except surprise.

Understanding what dogs are does not involve one's being surprised at the absence of a certain characteristic in a particular context, but rather one's appreciating that it *necessarily* follows from what one has just observed or failed to observe that the object before one is *not a 'dog'*. If an object is to qualify as a 'dog' it must possess certain characteristics, and these characteristics may be positive (to be a dog an object must have a backbone) or negative (no dog has wings), and may be related to each other conjunctively (a dog is a mammal *and* a vertebrate *and* . . .), disjunctively, etc. Understanding what 'dogs' are, grasping the principle of classification upon which the class is founded, involves one's knowing most of the defining characteristics of dogs and also appreciating the logical relationships by which those characteristics are definitionally linked.

We may therefore say that a second capacity involved in concept-possession is that of understanding the principles of classification in accordance with which class membership is assigned; and that this capacity in turn involves the ability to understand, in however rudimentary a manner, the logic of conjunction, disjunction, negation and so on.

The further claim is sometimes made that having the concept of a certain kind of perceptible object or event *necessarily* involves the ability to recognize specimens of that object or event. At first sight this seems to follow directly from what has just been said. Involved in possessing the concept of dog is understanding what 'dogs' are. If someone whose senses and faculties were in working order failed to recognize dogs as dogs when he came across them we should have strong presumptive evidence that he did not know what the defining characteristics of 'dogs' are. Therefore understanding what 'dogs' are would seem to involve the capacity to recognize dogs as 'dogs'. However, things are not as simple as this. It is prima facie possible for someone to have the concept of a kind of perceptible object, instances of which it might be impossible for him to recognize. For example, most of us have some concept of 'Martian', but none of us could recognize a Martian. The concept of 'Martian' appears to be wholly parasitic upon other concepts. The most, therefore, that we can claim is that a prerequisite of being said to possess the concept of any one kind of perceptible object is that one should be able to recognize an instance of that class of object or of other related classes of objects.

There is accordingly a rather weak sense in which some kind or extent of recognitory capacity is a necessary mark of the possession of object-concepts. It is perhaps also worth very briefly considering the reverse issue, namely, is someone's ability to recognize objects as of certain kinds *sufficient* for his being said to possess the corresponding concepts? It does not seem inconceivable that one should be able to recognize as what they are objects which one could not make judgments about in their absence, so that one could recognize a dog as 'dog' without exhibiting the capacities mentioned above as the initial and most obvious mark of concept-possession. It might perhaps be replied that possession of the ability to recognize dogs as 'dogs' requires that one should understand what 'dogs' are, and that understanding what 'dogs' are involves one's being able to make judgments or formulate propositions concerning the class of dogs. One must realize, for example, that all dogs, past, present, future, real and imaginary, possess internal bony skeletons and suckle their young, and realizing this involves one in passing altogether beyond any scene with which one may be immediately confronted. If one's abilities were confined simply to judging 'dog' whenever one was confronted with some individual animal one could never satisfactorily make manifest one's grasp of these general principles.

To summarize: among the capacities which one must have if one is to be said to possess some simple object-concept are: (1) The capacity to mark out in thought and to think of, contemplate, make judgments about, formulate propositions concerning, and so on, the whole class of dogs, or any individual dog in so far as it instantiates that class. (2) The capacity to show that one understands what 'dogs' are, that one knows the defining characteristics of dogs. (3) The capacity to recognize dogs as 'dogs' when one meets with them. These capacities seem to be logically inseparable from each other.

We have so far dealt only with possession of concepts of everyday perceptible objects. Possession of concepts of qualities or attributes, for example redness or bitterness, could probably be handled in analogous ways. And it seems likely that somewhat similar analyses could be given of possession of some more complex concepts, or that analysis may often usefully begin by pointing to the differences between these cases and the relatively straightforward ones which we have examined. Possession of social and moral concepts, for example, appears to be susceptible of a somewhat similar analysis to the one we have offered for possession of object-concepts. Someone who is to be said to possess such concepts as 'honesty' or 'patriotism' or 'game' must obviously be able to think about honesty or patriotism or games, and about particular persons, events or transactions as honest, patriotic or a game; he must have at least some rudimentary understanding of the relevant defining characteristics; and he must be able to recognize instances.

Our account of what it is to possess a concept has been rather 'intellectualized'. We may have given the impression that we think concept-possession the special prerogative of the detached thinker of abstract thoughts. Nothing could be further from the truth. We must emphasize, and shall emphasize again, that a person's conceptual capacities develop and diversify in and though his encounters with his environment, not least his social environment. Concepts, one might say, are for coping. There is, however, a reason why we have chosen to orient ourselves by somewhat intellectualized examples. A perennial temptation for psychologists has been to over-simplify such phenomena in order to accommodate them within some popular theoretical framework, e.g. that of stimulus-response learning theory. It is correspondingly important that one's initial delineation of the problem should make clear its complexity.

We shall accordingly adduce fairly complicated examples of rule-possession, which is the topic we shall consider next, though more briefly. Indeed, it has sometimes been suggested (for example by Fisher, 1974, pp. 254–5) that concept-possession is a species of rule-possession. To have a concept is to be able to divide up the world in thought in accordance with such rules as, if this has characteristics c_1, c_2 and c_3 it is an x, if it has characteristics c_4, c_5 and c_6 it is a y. And this of course leaves us with the problem noted on pp. 24–5 above, namely whether the recognition of characteristics c_1, c_2, c_3, etc., requires possession of the concepts of c_1, c_2 and c_3. Hence, according to another way of talking, concept-possession is a prerequisite of the ability to appreciate and act in terms of rules. Rules can only be understood by someone who possesses appropriate concepts, for rules are framed in terms only comprehensible to those who possess the relevant concepts. Consider, for example, the Ten Commandments, the rules of a monastic order, the rule for extracting a square root. In these cases to adopt a rule is, roughly speaking, to frame in terms of concepts already possessed a standing intention with regard to the nature and conduct of one's own future actions or activities. Further, there are intermediate cases where comprehension of rules, of chess, say, requires possession of certain concepts, yet possession of these concepts, of pawns, etc., consists in part of having grasped the rules governing their moves – 'constitu-tive' rules (Searle, 1969).

The problems seem to us terminological ones: for convenience we will talk of 'rules' only when an agent applies conceptual capacities to his own actions so as to promote a certain consistency among them. Thus we shall *not* say that someone who distinguishes cats from cheetahs on the grounds that cats have retractable claws but cheetahs do not, is following a rule, for the conceptual capacities he applies there do not have his own actions as their objects. Whereas we *shall* say that someone who is extracting a square root or being polite to his aunt is following rules; rules for the *activities* of extracting square roots and of being polite to aunts, i.e. following them involves exercising conceptual capacities which, in part, are directed upon one's own actions or activities as *one's own*.

A problem which arises with regard to both concept-possession and rule-possession and which perhaps merits some brief remarks, is this. We suggested above that possessing the concept of x involves knowing what x's are. Similarly rule-possession, and action in accordance with rules, would generally be supposed to involve knowledge of the rules acted upon. But the facts are that people can very often sort x's from y's and identify x's, without being able to list the defining characteristics of x's and that they not infrequently act upon rules or rule-systems which they could not state and of which they have no systematized awareness. Grammatical rules are the rules most often cited here. In order to bring to explicit conscious-ness the principles of categorization that one commonly applies, or the rules that one regularly follows, one may have to conduct 'thought experiments' and ask oneself, 'What would I say or do if. . .?' In short, people seem often to have a kind of 'knowledge' of rules or principles of categorization which is neither verbalizable nor propositional, but is rather a kind of 'being versed in' the rules or principles concerned (see Fisher, 1974, or Berlin, 1976).

Some people have tended to talk here of our possessing an implicit or unconscious knowledge of the rules or principles (Chomsky has done so in connection with grammatical rules), or have supposed that there must be in our brains analytic mechanisms operating beneath the level of consciousness which have the relev-ant rules or principles built into them. But is there really any need to talk in these mysterious ways? Let us draw an analogy with certain well-known perceptual phenomena. We all of us can and, frequent-ly, do such things as recognize the face of someone whose facial characteristics we could not a moment before have described; recognize a passage of Beethoven without being able to say in detail how we know it is Beethoven; realize that something in a room or scene has changed and even pinpoint the locus of change without being able to describe how things previously looked. In all these examples successful performance could be said to depend upon some kind of 'knowledge'; and yet the performer may well be ignorant of what it was he 'knew'. Mechanistic speculation here tends to be cast in terms of underlying analytic mechanisms selectively sensitive to features of the input but operating below the level of consciousness. The results of the analysis alone are fed into consciousness. But why should it not be the case that we are directly sensitive to patterns *per se*, and recurrences of patterns, without our nervous systems having to decompose the inputs into elements in order to tell us whether or not a given pattern has occurred before? Under these circumstances one might very well become familiarized with a recurrent pattern for whose overall or general characteristics one has sufficient 'feeling' to sense changes, but whose features one cannot analyse or recall in detail. Now let us suppose that something analogous to this may happen in the development of one's awareness of the ways of categorization conventionally adopted in one's society, and of the linguistic and social rules therein followed. The members of one's society draw one's attention to instances in which the jobs of categorization or of rule-following have been properly carried out, and to instances in which they have not. Gradually one acquires, say, a 'feeling' for the grammatical 'patterns' to be found in accepted linguistic usage, though of course these 'patterns' are not specifiable in physical terms – the 'elements' of the patterns are 'noun phrases', 'verb phrases', etc., and what a 'noun phrase' is or a 'verb phrase' is cannot be pinned down in terms of physical characteristics. One becomes able to distinguish deviant from acceptable instances, and even to transform the former into the latter, without needing or being able to formulate and consider grammatical rules. Why, therefore, should one suppose that a 'knowledge' of such rules is somehow built into one's nervous mechanisms at a level of operation below that of conscious awareness? Why should one not simply say that grammatical practice is based on a general and direct (i.e. non-analytic) grasp of the grammatical 'patterns' to be found in speech, an awareness for which Chomsky's term 'intuition' would seem appropriate. Explicit formulation of grammatical rules would then be derived from intuitions concerning practice, i.e. it would overlie rather than underlie it. At least we may say that if the arguments of this chapter and the next are correct, one's 'intuitive' recognition of the grammaticality of spoken sentences, and one's capacity to produce grammatical sentences, cannot depend upon underlying analytical mechanisms into which is built a 'knowledge' of the relevant rules. The rules are not susceptible of embodiment in a mechanistic system.

We shall now attempt to show, in a preliminary way, how implausible it is to suggest that a GM could be so programmed as to exhibit capacities which might induce us to agree that it could properly be said to possess concepts or to manifest rule-guided action. We shall argue that no generalized machine could be so programmed as to duplicate the behavioural capacities of a concept- or rule-possessing human being, however limited that human being's intelligence might be. We shall deal here only with concept-possession. Rule-possession as we have defined it may be regarded as a special case of intention-possession (which in turn of course necessarily involves concept-possession) with (at least in more advanced cases) the additional complication of reflexivity. A person could not be said to be following a rule unless he understood that he was acting as he did *because he regarded those actions as required by the rule*. Understanding and following a rule involves one's possessing, at least in embryo, the concept of a rule.

In order to simplify the ensuing discussion we shall for the time being make one major (and quite unjustified) concession to the machine theorist. We shall allow that if a person, or an organism, or a machine, can make just one consistent response to all the members of a given class (for example saying 'dog' when confronted with any member of the class of dogs), that person or machine shall be admitted to possess the relevant concept. We shall begin by arguing that even on this minimal definition of 'concept-possession' (one in fact adopted by many behaviourists and machine theorists) there are many commonplace concepts possession of which could not be built into a machine.

These are concepts which, to adopt a term from Watson (1958), we may call *stimulus-neutral*. A 'stimulus-neutral' concept is a concept of a class of events, objects, characteristics or entities whose members share no common physical characteristic that they do not also share with an indefinite number of objects or events which are *not* members of the class; to possess such a concept is to operate in terms of principles of classification among which physical properties, however general, do not figure.[1] All persons of even moderate sophistication possess very many stimulus-neutral concepts. Here are a few examples of such concepts: patriotism, leadership, game, accident, articulateness, politeness, justice, honesty, deviousness, generosity, perfidy, propriety, bargain, action, cleverness, piety, profit, double, co-operation, crime, oddity, liberty, organization, retribution, property, novelty, courtesy.[2] It could hardly be maintained for a moment that all the members of each of these classes share some special physical property, either qualitative or relational. Thus there is no perceptual situation of an everyday kind which could not under some conditions be rated as an instance of honest behaviour and none which could not under some conditions be rated dishonest. Someone might steal something simply to return it to its rightful owner; and someone might pay his debts only in order to perpetrate an even bigger swindle. What makes a piece of behaviour honest or dishonest are relevant aspects of the background circumstances – whether a debt is involved, whether all is straightforward, above board, fair, honourable, whether a future misdemeanour is intended, what rules are being kept or broken. And these relevant background circumstances, or most of them, can by and large only be understood in terms of concepts which are themselves stimulus-neutral. Again 'games' do not constitute a class of situations definable in terms of special shared physical characteristics, whether qualitative or relational. If American football has any such features in common with postal chess, or kiss-in-the-ring with nine men's morris, we should like to know what they are.

The following simple argument may now be put forward. We cannot analyse possession of stimulus-neutral concepts in terms amenable to embodiment in a machine-table. For there is no physically delimitable class of input-classes to all the members of which and to those alone the output 'game' may appropriately be linked; and similarly for 'honesty' and for every other term we have considered. Thus we could not write a machine-table to represent the behavioural capacities of a person who can 'recognize' games of all sorts of (physically quite different) kinds; one cannot sort out the relevant inputs to which to attach the outputs.

There are two lines of reply which, though obvious, may be immediately ruled out. The first is to say that whether or not a given input is or is not responded to as, say, an 'honesty' input can be made to depend upon some previous input, which in effect reveals whether what is now being witnessed is the payment of a debt or the extortion of blackmail. A machine can be so programmed that dependent upon which class the previous input belonged to, the machine will pass into internal state M_d or internal state M_b. Then when I_p comes in, the output, depending as it does upon the machine's current internal state, will be 'honest' if the antecedent circumstances indicated debt-paying, and not if they indicated blackmail. Thus the fact that there is no special (physically definable) class of 'honesty' inputs or of 'game' inputs does not *per se* preclude one from writing machine-tables to represent the behaviour of a person who possesses the concept of 'honesty' or the concept of 'game'. However, this argument will not do, because (1) it presupposes that the machine can recognize situations in which debt-paying is imminent and situations in which blackmail is imminent, i.e. that the machine already possesses stimulus-neutral concepts, and (2) it does not help us with the difficulty that the number of input-classes, members of which could, *in appropriate circumstances*, be responded to rightly with the output 'honest', is indefinitely large and not delimitable in physical terms. All it does is force us to complicate our machine-table with an equally refractory class of *'appropriate circumstance'* inputs and the changes of internal state that result from them.

A second line of reply might be to propose that those input-classes to which responses of 'game', 'honest', etc., are appropriate could in principle be exhaustively enumerated so that theoretically each could have the appropriate output attached to it. This line of reply, besides being open to all the objections that we are about to offer to a 'compromise' version, leaves one quite without an account of why all 'games', all 'honest deeds' and so forth, were in the first place lumped together in the same classes.

The 'compromise' version referred to above can apparently handle that problem. It goes as follows. Games are a family of which no two members necessarily bear any special physical resemblance to each other, but of which each member does clearly resemble at least one other. Thus, shuffleboard physically resembles darts, and darts physically resembles clock patience, but clock patience does not resemble shuffleboard. Hence to call certain events a 'game' is just to say that they physically resemble at least one subclass of the events already called 'games'. It would not be difficult in principle to design a machine which would 'recognize' all the 'games' of the family, and which would be able to extend its application of the term to new games resembling the old, and to new games resembling the newer ones. Boden (1968) attributes this kind of ability to the 'pattern-recognition' programme of Uhr and Vossler (1963).

None the less this 'compromise' suggestion is not plausible. In the first place, many activities which are not games physically resemble some game or another as closely as many games resemble another game. In order to build a 'game-recognizing' machine we would have to agree upon the precise physical respects in which an activity must resemble some extant 'game' in order to be itself classed as a 'game'. But this involves us in agreeing upon the defining physical dimensions of the class of games, and the 'family resemblance' approach collapses. In any case, of two situations which are physically identical – for example a gun is being waved – one may be a game-situation and the other not; likewise of two situations in which a pound note is being tendered and accepted, one may be an instance of honest behaviour and the other an instance of dishonest behaviour. What is happening in these cases can only be decided in the light of antecedent circumstances; but as remarked above the relevant aspects of the antecedent circumstances can themselves only be grasped in terms of stimulus-neutral concepts.

In the second place, the 'compromise' solution implies that one could neither invent a 'game' which bore no distinctive physical resemblance to some already existing game, nor recognize such an invention as a 'game'. Similarly, there could be no such thing as being 'honest' in physically novel circumstances. But it seems quite obvious that we could all of us recognize physically novel instances of games and of honesty, and that we could do this without any special further training (except perhaps that involved in learning the language and customs of some culture other than our own). Indeed failure to recognize novel instances would count as evidence that one did not possess the relevant concepts.

In short there is no possibility of analysing possession of stimulus-neutral concepts in a manner that could be formalized on a machine-table. For the behavioural capacities involved in possessing such concepts cannot be pinned down in terms of inputs of physically definable classes eliciting outputs of physically definable classes, and furthermore any normal human being can extend (and correctly extend) his application of such concepts to an indefinitely large number of physically novel instances.

We shall now attempt to establish a somewhat analogous conclusion with regard to concepts that are clearly *not* stimulus-neutral in any simple sense, viz. concepts of everyday kinds of perceptible object. An obvious preliminary point is as follows. Many kinds of perceptible objects which have physically definable features in common and which are classed together partly on that ground could none the less only be 'recognized' in the fullest sense by persons in possession of stimulus-neutral concepts (Gauld, 1966). For instance, a pound note could only be perceived *as a pound note* by a person who possessed such concepts as 'monetary value', 'exchange' and 'legal tender'. A 'missionary' could only be recognized *as a missionary* by someone who possessed some very complex religious concepts. An example of particular interest is that of letters of the alphabet. Machines have been built which can 'recognize' letters of the alphabet in the sense of reacting consistently to them despite considerable minor variations in their physical properties. But to be able to recognize them *as letters of the alphabet* the machine would have to possess such exceedingly high-level concepts as: 'word', 'meaning', 'sentence', 'communication', 'intention to communicate'. These considerations should at least serve to put 'pattern recognition machines' in perspective.

We shall not, however, pursue these points, but shall advance arguments independent of 'stimulus-neutrality'. In so doing we shall withdraw our concession to the machine theorist that the making of a consistent discriminatory response to all examples of a class of objects shall be deemed sufficient for the attribution of a concept. We pointed out earlier that if a man is said to 'possess' some concept, for example that of 'dog', it is not enough that he should consistently discriminate between dogs and other objects. He must in addition show us that he has grasped the definition of the class 'dog'. He must demonstrate that he knows, for example, that if something lacks an internal bony skeleton it cannot be a dog. But the behaviour by means of which such an understanding can be manifested cannot in any way be delimited or set bounds to. For example, part of what is involved in knowing what 'dogs' are is understanding that if a thing is to be rated a dog it must be a vertebrate. This understanding could be manifested, in similar sorts of circumstances and also in quite dissimilar ones, by, let us say, a nod of the head, a shake of the head, by saying one thing, by saying another thing, by waving the hands excitedly, by raising an eyebrow; and so on and so on indefinitely, dependent upon what intelligent appreciation of novel situations required. And analogous problems would arise in regard to possession of the concept 'vertebrate'. No finite list of machine-table entries could exhaust the limitless possibilities. Nor could we accept some limited subset of such entries, as canonical, as defining possession of the concept. For (1) if someone's behaviour were in fact sharply limited to that prescribed by the entries we should tend to say that he had merely learned parrot-fashion and should deny him possession of the conceptual capacity. (2) Any such list of 'canonical' entries would be wholly arbitrary. (3) Such a list could always be criticized as not adequately representing the conceptual capacity, but such criticism would only be possible for people who possessed a concept not susceptible of being pinned down in terms of the list. (4) Different people exhibit their possession of the same concept by means of quite different behaviour, yet in terms of the present proposal they could not be said to possess the 'same' concept.

Special problems for the machine theorist would arise over the acquisition of new concepts. Let us suppose that someone's conceptual equipment has been completely embodied in a generalized machine. Then it is always possible that the machine should 'acquire' new concepts. Let us suppose that the definitions of 'quark' and of 'quasar' are fed in. If the machine acquires these two concepts and already possesses an adequate concept of 'dog', it ought to be able to show us that it 'knows' that dogs are not quarks or quasars, and this will involve its exhibiting a range of additional behaviour. Behaviour suggesting that it does *not* 'know' that dogs are not quarks or quasars will necessarily reflect doubt upon its possession of the concept 'dog'. Now with respect to its gaining the potential to exhibit these new behaviour patterns there are only two possibilities. Either (1) the machine had to have further input-output linkages built into it; and in this case it did not in the first place possess the concept of 'dog'. No one who fully grasped the defining characteristics of doghood could fail when introduced to the notions of 'quark' and of 'quasar' to realize at once that dogs are not quarks or quasars. Or (2) the machine did *not* have to have further input-output linkages built into it, and in this case it could not belong in the class of GMs; it would need capacities beyond those of a GM. For *ex hypothesi* it did not already have the necessary linkages, and a GM could *neither* create its own linkages in accordance with the concepts (this would imply that concepts are anterior to linkages, and in any case GMs cannot *create* linkages), nor yet act appropriately without such linkages.

It could perhaps be replied that although the concepts of 'quark' and of 'quasar' might be new to the machine, when these concepts were acquired they would emerge as 'subconcepts' within the framework of such 'superconcepts' as 'fundamental particle' and 'celestial object'. Since the relationships of the superconcepts to the concept of 'dog' would already be established, the relationship of the concepts of 'quark' and of 'quasar' to the concept of 'dog' would be laid down in advance. But even if we waive the question of what, in machine-table terms, the assimilation of the new subclasses to the old superclasses would consist in,[3] this answer is still unsatisfactory. For in the first place it is regressive, and in the second place only new subconcepts readily assimilable within old superconcepts already standing in the appropriate relations to the concept 'dog' could be handled in this way. And there does not seem to be any reason for supposing that all new subconcepts could be thus assimilated.

It is not only the 'acquisition' of new concepts, but what may be described as the creative recombination of the old that presents problems to the machine theorist. Someone who possesses an ordinary repertoire of concepts can in general combine any one of them with almost any other. He can think of dogs, dog-breeders, dog-lovers, dog-eaters, trisected dogs, daft dogs, celestial dogs. He can utilize his concept of 'dog' in limitless ways, no matter how absurd. And if he could not do this, his possession of the concept might be called in question. Someone whose 'possession' of a given concept could manifest itself only in a sharply limited set of responses to a sharply limited set of stimulus situations could not be said to possess the concept at all. If someone is to be said to possess concepts, he must display this kind of intelligent and wide-ranging creative and combinatorial ability. Indeed, the process of combination is likely to be genuinely creative. Suppose someone had a concept of 'dentist' and that his behaviour in this respect could *per impossibile* be represented by a finite set of machine-table entries, and suppose that he had a similarly delimited concept of 'chair'. If he were then introduced to the notion of 'dentist's chair', his construction of the idea would involve his intelligently extending his concept of chair *in the light of* his concept of dentist, and the result could certainly not be represented by a subset of the old 'dentist' machine-table entries plus a subset of the old 'chair' machine-table entries.

Thus possession of a concept, involving as it does intelligent understanding of the defining properties of a class of things, can manifest itself, and indeed *must* manifest itself, in behaviour which cannot be reduced to a finite set of input-output rules of the kind which may be embedded in a GM.[4] Conceptual capacities are open-ended. They can be manifested behaviourally in ways which diversify and multiply without limit, and which elude complete codification into a machine-table. Furthermore, *even if* the behaviour in which possession of a certain concept manifested itself were sufficiently circumscribed to admit of representation on a machine-table, the machine-table would not reveal why the relevant entries 'belonged together'. It could not be the case that the entries 'belonged together' as being a list of the input-output concatenations obtaining when and only when the machine was in a certain internal state, for the various internal states of a machine are partly defined in terms of the machine's being liable to exhibit this, that or the other set of input-output concatenations. In other words, a 'unitary' machine-state is partly constituted by *de facto* association of certain inputs with certain outputs, and cannot be the source of a 'unity' among the set of input-output concatenations. While it remains trivially true that if the whole of a man's behaviour could be recorded from his birth to his death, a machine could in principle be programmed to reproduce his entire outward history, it is equally but less trivially true that no machine-table could possibly represent his conceptual *capacities*.

We have tried in this chapter to show that two of the leading concepts of hermeneutical explanation – the concepts of concept and of rule – cannot be translated into the terms of mechanistic explanation. Since we have already argued that unless the concepts of hermeneutical explanation can be translated into the terms of mechanistic explanation the latter must give way to the former, it appears that mechanistic explanation must give way. We shall, however, discuss the issue of translatability further in the next chapter, in connection with two more of the central concepts of hermeneutical explanation, viz. the concepts of action and of intention.

4

Actions, Intentions and the Generalized Machine

What is an 'action'? Although in the last couple of decades many philosophers[1] have shown interest in the nature of human action and of our knowledge of it, there is as yet very little consensus as to what 'an action' is.

A preliminary problem is that the term 'action' is used in a wide variety of contexts, many of them far removed from that of human behaviour. One talks of the action of a drug, the action of water on rock, the action of acid on metal and so on. The sense of the term with which we are concerned is of course the somewhat narrow one in which 'actions' are ascribed to agents rather than to agencies, so that one can talk of 'his' action and 'my' action or say *'he* did that'. The word 'act' is nearly, though not quite, synonymous with 'action' over the relevant part of the latter's range; and some of the differences in their customary usage may perhaps be set down to considerations of euphony. 'Act' has also uses more or less special to itself; we speak, for instance, of 'mental acts' but hardly of 'mental actions'. We shall be principally concerned with behavioural acts, though it may of course be that behavioural acts have an inward or mental aspect which will require consideration.

A second initial difficulty is that a good deal of our behaviour is not readily classifiable as either 'action' or 'movement' – we neither bring it about ourselves nor yet find it merely happening to us. Changing gear on a hill or taking off one's hat on entering a house are actions which, with repetition, may harden into 'habits' which are almost like reflexes; such activities as biting one's nails or twiddling one's thumbs constitute a no-man's-land between actions, habits and neurotic symptoms; one may suddenly discover that one is beating time with one's foot, and behaviour which one *discovers* oneself carrying out can hardly qualify as action – yet surely it is not mere movement either. Again there are activities, like breathing for example, which normally, as it were, run themselves without any attention being paid to them, but which may none the less under some circumstances be deliberately controlled or modulated; and sometimes one may refrain from acting in such a way that one's inaction may be counted as a mode of 'action'.

Still, we none of us doubt that there are pieces of our bodily behaviour which we ourselves bring about and pieces of our bodily behaviour which merely happen to or are inflicted on us and that we have no difficulty in discriminating between them. Thus Penfield (1966, p. 413) says of patients in whose limbs he induced movement by placing electrodes on their cerebral cortices:

> There is no evidence of any awareness of stimulation
> excepting awareness of the movement, and the patient will
> often say in the end, 'you made me do that'. He recognizes
> the fact that it is not a voluntary movement of his own.
> I never had a patient say 'I just wanted to do that anyway'.

Indeed so compellingly clear and so practically and socially important is the distinction between what we deliberately do and what merely happens to us that it is doubtful whether any considerations whatsoever could obliterate it from our discourse.

Although many recent writers have discussed how the term 'action' might be defined, there is little agreement except as regards what actions are not. Thus everyone agrees that it is hopeless to seek a definition of 'action' in terms either of the overt physical characteristics of the behaviour involved or of special sensations supposed to accompany that behaviour. There is also a wide measure of agreement upon the unsatisfactoriness of two other proposed kinds of definition, viz. H. L. A. Hart's endeavour (1949) to pin down 'action' as behaviour for which 'responsibility' can be ascribed, and various attempts to pin down actions as movements having certain sorts of causes.

The latter view has been extensively discussed. The writer most frequently pilloried is the nineteenth-century jurist, J. Austin. Austin held that actions are definable as bodily movements caused by 'volitions'; the arguments are, however, much the same whatever brand of causal antecedent one selects.

The commonest argument against those who hold that actions may be defined as bodily movements with certain kinds of causal antecedents is as follows. Of any proposed causal antecedent in the body or mind of an agent we may enquire, was it something that he brought about? If it was, we are landed with a regress, and the term 'action' remains unanalysed; if it was not, no action has as yet been carried out. This argument presupposes that anything which an agent *does*, and which might serve as the 'cause' of a piece of his bodily behaviour, must itself be an 'action'; and this could be debated. However, it seems to be widely agreed that the movements of our bodies which we regard as 'actions' are not regularly preceded by any image, act of the will, yearning or choice;[2] nor do we know of any state of the brain or the muscles or the unconscious mind which regularly occurs prior to such movements. From that it follows that our concept of action *cannot* be one of antecedent state of the body or mind of the agent, followed by a bodily movement as consequence.

Some writers (e.g. C. Taylor, 1964; Malcolm, 1968) who admit that actions cannot be defined as movements caused by certain kinds of states or events in or of an agent, have instead tried to define them as movements springing from antecedents non-contingently and hence non-causally related to their consequents, especially such antecedents as intentions and purposes (cf. above, p. 10).

Now it is true that in certain contexts the intention with which an action is carried out may be held to characterize or identify that action. But it seems fairly clear that an 'action' cannot usefully be *defined* as a movement arising out of an intention. For an intention can only be an intention *to act*. The concept of intention cannot be elucidated without reference to the concept of action.

In short it seems that all attempts to analyse the concept of action into elements which are not themselves actions have failed. This has led some writers (see especially R. Taylor, 1966) to propose that what makes a given bodily movement 'an action' is that 'an agent' caused it in a sense of the term 'cause' different from the conventional neo-Humean one. 'Agent causality' is a power exercised by agents in virtue of which it is 'up to' them whether or not a given movement of their bodies (or effect thereof) occurs. It is not further analysable, and neither, therefore, is the concept of action.

The idea of 'agent causality' has been extensively criticized (see for example Thalberg, 1972, chapter 1; Locke, 1974a, pp. 27–31) and acceptance of the notion does seem to lead to one serious impasse. If an 'action' is simply an exercise by an agent of his unanalysable 'agent power' to 'cause' a movement of his own body, and an 'agent' is simply an entity which possesses this unanalysable power, there does not seem to be anything else one can say about the notion of action, or for that matter the notion of agent. Yet whether or not the concept of 'action' is analysable in any reductive way, it clearly possesses various aspects or facets each of which is essential to the whole, and each of which must be elucidated if our grasp of the concept is to be made firmer. Thus, for an action-term to be legitimately applied, at least the following must be the case:

(1) There must be a movement, or the cessation or alteration or inhibition of a movement, of an agent's body.

(2) The movement must be initiated and/or guided or controlled by the agent. It is possible to re-describe almost any action, though in a roundabout and cumbrous way, by using such expressions as 'he initiated, directed and controlled a set of bodily movements of such and such a type, tendency or outcome'. These phrases are *synonyms* for action expressions. One could claim a movement as one of one's 'actions' only if one could truly say that one had initiated or directed or controlled it. To deny that one had done at least one of these things would be to deny that one had acted. Now prima facie the initiating, guiding and controlling are processes over and above the mere occurrence of the movement, for the movement *could* have occurred, for example as the result of stimulation of the nervous system and the 'agent' been a mere spectator of it. So, prima facie, there are involved in any action processes which look suspiciously like antecedent causes of the movement involved. A moment ago we cast doubt on the regular occurrence of any such antecedent factors. Are we now changing our minds? We shall dodge this issue for the time being, and shall return to it later.

(3) If we reflect on the verbs 'direct' and 'control' which figure in the action-synonymous phrases proposed above, we can at once see that actions must have a direction, a goal or a prescribed course. A person could not properly be said to be directing or controlling something unless he were shaping its destiny, or maintaining its progress, along one path rather than another. *Actions must have criteria of success or failure*. And this appears to be a most important feature of the concept of action.

It is worth noting how diverse are the criteria which may be involved. The criterion for the success of an action may be narrow, as when one sets out to jump a fence or to sink a put; or vague and broad, as when one tries to do something useful; it may demand a movement of part of one's body or of the whole of it, for instance flexing one's biceps or cutting a caper; it may specify a change which is to be wrought in one's surroundings by no matter what muscle movements; it may require of the action that it fulfil certain aesthetic or ethical norms or rules, for example being graceful or honest and so on and so on. Many, perhaps most, actions are liable to assessment in terms of more than one criterion – often interrelated, as when one sets out to switch on the light with a flick of one's forefinger.

(4) Now if one's behaviour is rightly to be characterized as action, it is obvious that one must oneself 'possess' the criterion which one's behaviour may fulfil or not. Acting involves understanding what would constitute completion of the act and what failure. A man who, while his limbs were in motion, did not know where they were supposed to go, or what they were supposed to effect, *could not* be directing their progress; he would be a mere spectator of his own movements. Possessing and applying some criterion or another is a necessary prerequisite of being said to act at all.

At this point the question naturally arises, what is it to possess and apply a 'criterion'? (The term 'criterion' will be discussed again, in a different connection, in chapter 10.) It is clear that if an agent is to direct his limbs so as to fulfil a criterion he must in some sense 'know' that criterion before it is actually fulfilled, i.e. must have the ability to think of it, make judgments about it, formulate propositions concerning it, regulate his conduct in relation to it, and so forth, before it is actually fulfilled. (This is not to say that the criterion cannot become more determinate as the action or activity proceeds.) Someone who was unable to think of, contemplate, set up before himself, make judgments or decision about, formulate propositions concerning, or otherwise indicate an object, event or state of affairs in its absence could not be said to 'possess' or have 'applied' a criterion in the regulation of his behaviour. Possession of these abilities is therefore among the prerequisites of being said to possess or apply a criterion for an action; but, as we argued in chapter 3, it is also among the defining characteristics of possessing a concept.

If it is indeed the case that applying a criterion involves possessing the capacities to think of, make judgments about, and so on, the state of affairs envisaged by the criterion, both in the presence and in the absence of that state of affairs, then it follows by arguments similar to those set forth in connection with concept-possession, that possessing and applying a criterion involves some understanding of the defining characteristics of the state of affairs demarcated by the criterion, together with the capacity to recognize that state of affairs. The conditions of being said to possess and apply a criterion turn out to be thus far the same as the conditions of being said to possess and apply a concept, and the obvious conclusion is that the 'application' of a criterion is simply a specialized 'exercise' of those capacities which go to make up 'possession' of a concept. From this it follows that no entity which did not possess concepts could act; the exercise of a concept is intrinsic to action.

(5) This does not, however, give us the whole story. For as one moved one's limbs (or one's tongue or one's ears or for that matter altered one's heartbeat by biofeedback) one might apply to the movements all kinds of criteria additional to those by which one judged the success or failure of the action. A man at an auction nods to express conventional agreement with his neighbour, and suddenly realizes that he may also have fulfilled the conventional criterion for making a bid. Accepting a criterion as *the* criterion (or one of *the* criteria) by which the success or otherwise of an action is to be measured involves not just applying it to one's directed movements, but as it were *committing oneself* to fulfilling it, guiding one's self-expression in accordance with its requirements. How exactly this committal-of-self is to be analysed is a question indeed, but it can be shown to be an essential ingredient in action, to be indeed that which distinguishes the engagement of an agent in action from the detached observation of action by a passive spectator. If one notices that the movements of one's body fulfil or fail to fulfil criteria other than what for the moment we may call the 'primary' ones, one may esteem it a bonus or a nuisance or simply an uninteresting and irrelevant fact, but it is not essential to one's acting. If one realizes that one is fulfilling or failing to fulfil the 'primary' criteria one esteems one's directing of one's movements not just successful or a failure but *one's* success or *one's* failure. Such successes and such failures fulfil or frustrate one in an indescribable and peculiarly intimate way. If there were no criterion whose fulfilment one would regard as *one's* success and whose non-fulfilment one would regard as *one's* failure, *one* would not be acting, would not be *involved* in the events one watched. If one *could not* in this

way commit oneself to the fulfilment of a criterion one would not be an agent at all.

(6) It has often been remarked that the notion of action involves that of an agent and vice versa, but the point is seldom enlarged upon. We can, however, perhaps begin to glimpse some facets of the concept of agent and of its relations to the concept of action (the concepts of self and of agent will be investigated further in chapter 11). In action a conceived criterion is brought to bear upon an incipient or ongoing bodily activity and used in the guidance or modulation of that activity. The concept of agent is the concept of that which unifies these different aspects of action, hence of that which makes action *possible*. One cannot guide someone else's activity in the same way as one can guide one's own; one cannot guide one's activity in accordance with someone else's conceived criterion unless that criterion becomes part of one's own conceptual equipment. Activity, guidance and concept must, so to speak, be brought together.

(7) Closely linked with the preceding point is this. Although it is only by observation of one's bodily movements or of their consequences that one can know whether or not one's action has been successfully completed, one cannot learn by observation that a given movement of one's body was one of one's actions. There is no publicly observable aspect of an action that one has to notice in order to be able to say that one did it. Thus the concept of action appears to be essentially linked *both* to what S. C. Brown (1965), following Griffiths (1963), calls a-concepts, i.e. concepts which are correctly applied in making judgments only when certain publicly determinable conditions are satisfied, *and* to what he calls b-concepts, ones which, like psychological concepts, may be correctly applied in making judgments regardless of whether or not any publicly determinable conditions obtain. Many philosophers would refuse to recognize the existence of b-concepts, and a good deal of effort has been expended by philosophers and psychologists in attempts to prove that b-concepts are either totally confused or reducible to a-concepts. On the other hand, attempts have been made to mark out the domain of psychology in terms of the applicability of b-concepts (for example Gauld, 1972), and such attempts have at any rate the merit of suggesting why actions and their explanations are so obviously in part a problem for psychology.

It remains for us to consider again the question which we raised a few pages back, the question namely of what we are to say of the fact that it seems necessary in attempting to elucidate the concept of action to refer to processes of the initiation, guidance and control by the agent of movements of his own body. On the face of it, reference to such processes, besides encountering the objection that they are not empirically detectable, involves us in a regress, since the processes concerned themselves sound very much like actions. We have already touched upon these objections (pp. 40–1 above) and they may conveniently be studied at greater length in R. Taylor (1966). Accordingly we shall now give a brief account of the counter-arguments developed by some recent writers, especially by McCann (1974, 1975) and Ripley (1974).

Both of these writers argue that action is to be distinguished from mere bodily movement in terms of a 'volition' present in the former and absent from the latter. 'Volition' seems to be a blanket term for the processes of initiation, guidance and control of which we have been talking. Thus Ripley says (p. 143): 'A volition is a conscious or mental act which initiates and guides the physical change that is brought about deliberately in a physical act.' Whether the adoption of this battle-scarred term is altogether wise might be debated.

Both Ripley and McCann argue that, despite what some writers have asserted to the contrary, processes of initiation, guidance and control are distinguishable, or sometimes distinguishable, aspects of our experience of action. Ripley says, 'Ordinary arm-movements are accomplished with ease. The mental effort they require is so minimal that it escapes the notice of the normal agent; in order to discover its presence we must have recourse to abnormal cases.' As 'abnormal cases' he cites examples of persons who think that they have moved anaesthetized limbs when they have not, and of persons who are able to 'move' phantom limbs. Such persons are, in Ripley's view, performing the acts which on happier occasions would have initiated and guided limb movements. More commonplace examples are perhaps provided by movements which are not fully controllable. When, for example, one endeavours to move a limb which has 'gone to sleep', or to overcome the effects of fatigue or alcohol on one's movements, the experience of initiation and guidance rises into prominence. An infant's experiences may be largely of this kind. It is to be noted, however, that a skilled adult may carry out intricate actions or activities or unified action sequences, for example those involved in tying a shoe-lace, with virtually no experience as of 'guiding' the movements he has initiated. He might even be stumped, as expert typists and pianists sometimes are, if he were asked to make the movements in slow motion, i.e. in a 'guided' manner. Actions or action-sequences which have been much practised become habitual and are run off as a whole. 'Guidance' here is reduced to mere 'modulation'.

Like Ripley, McCann (1975) cites certain pathological cases, and the views of both authors are supported by Whiteley (1973) who writes (p. 56):

> Among philosophers who have considered the topic of Volition, I personally have the unusual advantage that, following an attack of poliomyelitis, I have become familiar with the experience of willing to move my arm and finding that it did not go up; I can assure doubters that there is such an experience, and that it is possible to try to do something which you are convinced you cannot do.

McCann (1974) attempts to meet the charge of regressiveness by the following line of argument. For any bodily action of a human agent we may define what may be called its 'result'. A 'result' is a state of affairs which (logically) must obtain if an action of the kind in question is to have been carried out. For example if one is to be said to have 'shot' somebody it is necessary that a bullet from one's gun punctured his skin; if one is to be said to have moved one's finger it is necessary that one's finger moved. (In cases of successful action the 'result' of the action will accord with the criterion which the agent had in mind in acting.) However, the occurrence of a 'result' is never sufficient for the occurrence of an action; one's gun may have discharged itself through a faulty mechanism, or one's finger may have twitched through nervous irritation. The problem of what makes the 'result' the result *of an action* McCann calls the 'action-result' problem, and in his view the missing element is a 'volition', where a volition is a member of the class of 'thoughts' having the peculiar characteristic of causing a particular bodily movement. (Ripley thinks the relation may not be a 'causal' one if the term 'cause' is used in its neo-Humean sense.) Volitions are not themselves 'actions' in the same sense as bodily actions for, like all thoughts, but unlike all 'actions', they do not have 'results'. For example there is no event or state of affairs which one brings about which is logically required for the mental act of thinking of the number one. The content of thought (the number one) is not an event or state of affairs at all. Nor can one's act of thinking of the number one be reckoned its own result. Results are not sufficient for the occurrence of bodily actions, but thinking of the number one is sufficient for thinking of the number one.

None the less, volitions, like all thoughts, possess a certain indefinable action-quality, and it is in virtue of the part played by volitions in causing bodily actions that the latter are looked upon as 'brought about' by the agent. The volitions themselves do not have to be brought about by antecedent volitions, for it is the job of volitions to cause bodily movements, not to cause further volitions. To introduce volitions to explain volitions would be 'rather like supposing that if we explain the wetness of a wet street by saying there is water on it, we must explain the wetness of the water by postulating further water' (McCann, 1974, p. 472).

At least three advantages are claimed for this way of tackling the problem. The first is that it accounts for the fact that the concept of action is, at least in part, a 'b-concept'. For volitions, which impart action-quality to bodily movements, are 'thoughts', i.e. are 'mental', and it is characteristic of mental concepts that they are b-concepts. The second is that it provides us with ways of distinguishing intentions from volitions, and also of relating them. For intentions are intentions *to act*, whereas in volition 'what is willed must be that a change or sequences of changes of certain types occur. These are the projected results of the actions the agent undertakes to perform through the volitional act' (McCann, 1974, p. 467). Volition serves as a conscious executive act with respect to intention and desire (McCann, 1974, p. 469):

> What is willed is a result of just the kind needed for an action of the intended sort to occur. If such a change occurs as expected, the willing will have served as the causally basic act by means of which the intended action is performed. It will therefore, both belong to the process of the action occurrence and be the conscious activation of the agent's intention or desire.

The third is that since 'volitions' are described as 'thoughts', the affinity of 'volitions', and hence of actions, with other conceptual phenomena is made manifest.

Whether or not the proposal of Ripley and McCann prove in the end satisfactory, we may say in summary that any attempted elucidation of the concept of action must take account of the following points:

(1) Actions involve the occurrence, or the continuance or the suppression, of movements of the agent's body.

(2) Action terms may be paraphrased into expressions such as 'he initiated, directed and controlled a set of bodily movements of such and such a type, tendency or outcome'. Prima facie, therefore, actions involve processes of initiation, guidance, etc.

(3) Actions must have criteria of success or failure.

(4) The criteria must be 'known' to or 'possessed' by the agents concerned; possession of the criteria is or involves a form of concept-possession.

(5) The agent must, in a sense hard to express, be *himself* 'committed' to the fulfilment of the criterion.

(6) The concepts of action and of agency are inseparably related.

(7) The concept of action is, in part, a b-concept.

We must now turn our attention from action to the explanation of action. We touched on the subject in chapter 1. There we remarked that a common form of everyday action-explanation is 'hermeneutical', is cast in terms of the 'meaning' of the actions concerned. Actions may be looked upon as bodily movements directed by an agent towards the fulfilment of some criterion conceived by him. It is not uncommonly the case that an acting agent supposes that if he fulfils his current criterion some further state of affairs, or set of states of affairs, will ensue; and when, additionally, it is the case that he has embarked on fulfilling his present criterion in order to bring about the further state of affairs, we have an explanation of his actions in terms of his intention or purpose. To ask for the 'meaning' of an action is to ask for this sort of explanation. It is to ask what envisaged scheme of things the agent hoped to further by initiating that action. It is, in short, to ask what was the agent's intention in acting as he did when he did. And this brings us face to face with the issues of what we mean by the term 'intention' and of how the relationship between an intention and the consequent action is to be visualized.

These issues will be discussed at greater, though still insufficient, length in chapter 9. In this chapter all we shall do is make some preliminary points about intentions, and discuss some of the things that intentions are *not*. Our preliminary points are these:

(1) Some writers, and especially C. Taylor (1964), have represented explanation in terms of intentions as a subspecies of a

wider sort of explanation which they call 'teleological' explanation. The basic form of 'teleological' explanation is as follows: 'In a system S which tends to a goal G, when the state of the system S and the environment E is such that event B is required for the attainment of G, B will occur' (cf. C. Taylor, 1964, pp. 9–10). Event B occurs because it is 'required for' G, and to explain the occurrence of B we simply point out that the system has a perfectly observable 'natural tendency' towards G, and that the state of the system at the relevant time was such that B was 'required for' G.

This account of teleological explanation is of importance because some writers, for example C. Taylor himself and Malcolm (1968), have used it in an attempt to show that teleological explanation, including explanation in terms of intentions and purposes, is incompatible with mechanistic explanation, while others, for example Locke (1974a), have used it in an attempt to show precisely the reverse. We shall argue (a) that there is not, and could not be, any system whose behaviour would require 'teleological' explanation, and (b) that the behaviour of a system which possessed intentions and carried out actions in accordance with them could not be explained 'teleologically'.

(a) C. Taylor defines teleological laws as laws in which events occur because they are 'required for' other events or states of affairs. He defines (1964, p. 9n) 'being required for' in such a way that if an event is required for a state of affairs it is both necessary and sufficient for that state of affairs. He adds that for his present purposes he need not consider instances in which one of a *set* of possible events is necessary for the attainment of the subsequent state of affairs.

Now it simply cannot be the case that one empirical state of affairs is in an absolute sense necessary for another. It is logically possible that any one state of a physical system could be reached from any other state of system via any one of an infinity of possible intervening states or sequences thereof. The system *might* transform itself in any one of a limitless number of ways. Before we can say that one move in a system is 'necessary' for the system's passing from a certain state to a certain other state we have to specify the possible states of the system and the transitions between them which do *in fact* occur. And the states of the system could not for such purposes be described in such terms as 'state requiring B for G', because it is the definition of 'required for' that is in question. We would have to define the states of the system in ordinary physical terms, and to list exhaustively the causal laws governing the succession of those states. But if we could do this we should have shown the supposed teleological laws to be spurious.

(b) Teleological explanations of human action, involving as they do such antecedents of action as intention, purposes and desire, cannot be subsumed under Taylor's schema. For as Taylor himself points out in the intention-action case what determines whether B occurs is not whether B is in fact necessary for G, but whether the agent *believes* it to be necessary; and what constitutes the 'goal' of the system is not the end-state towards which the system 'naturally tends', but the goal which the agent has in mind in directing his endeavours. Now it can readily be seen that being believed to be required for something is not a subspecies of being required for that something, and that having a goal in mind is not a subspecies of there being a state of affairs to which one's behaviour is 'naturally' gravitating. One might believe that burying a nutmeg by the light of the full moon is necessary for the curing of one's quartan ague; but in fact it is quite ineffectual. A skier may take standing upright as his goal; but the 'natural tendency' of all his efforts may in fact be towards his falling over. Thus it seems quite impossible to represent the explanation of actions in terms of intentions, etc., as a subspecies of 'teleological' explanation.

(2) Let us divide intentions in a rough and ready way into short-term and long-term. Short-term intentions are ones which an agent forms and immediately implements with no thought beyond them. Long-term intentions are ones in which a relatively distant goal is pursued either through a series of actions each of which is regarded as a step on the road, or through a single action which is expected to have a certain sequence of effects. The 'meaning' for the agent of such action will be very complex, for it will involve the relation of a given action to all the other envisaged actions or events in the sequence.

We can now make a point which, though obvious, needs to be borne in mind. It is that long-term intentions are only possible for rational agents, for persons who have built up complex and relatively coherent conceptual frameworks through which to handle the world, and who are capable of moderately sophisticated reasoning. For example, in M. R. James's story *The Stalls of Barchester Cathedral*, the Rev. Dr Haynes, an ambitious clergyman and precentor in the cathedral, is kept from becoming archdeacon of the diocese by the longevity of Archdeacon Pulteney, the present holder of the position. He overcomes this obstacle by bribing a maid to remove a stair-rod on Archdeacon Pulteney's steep and dangerous staircase. In order to frame and implement his murderous plan, Dr Haynes had (a) to possess certain physical, medical and ecclesiastical concepts, and be able to interrelate them in certain ways, and (b) to understand arguments such as 'Old men who fall down staircases are likely to be killed. Loose stair-rods cause falls down stairs. Dr Pulteney is an old man. Therefore, if I bribe a servant to remove a stair-rod on his staircase, he is likely to be killed.' Had Dr Haynes not possessed these or other concepts and this reasoning capacity, he could not have formed this or any other long-term intention (and would, in the end, have been far better off).

(3) We pointed out in chapter 1 that there has been a good deal of controversy as to whether or not intentions can properly be described as the 'causes' of the actions to which they give rise. We shall touch on this issue in chapter 9. Here we shall merely remark that it is somewhat misleading to put the question in this form. The problem is not whether intentions 'cause' actions, which makes it sound as though intentions pass through people and cause movements rather as electric shocks pass through them and cause muscular spasms. The problem is whether, when an agent brings about an action in order to promote a state of affairs which he intends, his intending can properly be regarded as the cause of his so acting.

(4) Of course, even when a particular action has been explained, when its 'meaning' for the agent has been made clear, his intention in carrying it out made manifest, many problems remain. How did he come to have that intention? Did he frame it because there was something linked to the fulfilment of the intention that he desired for its own sake, for example fame, knowledge, the taste of haggis, or did he frame it because of his values, because he had adopted, for ethical or religious reasons, rules of conduct which made the formulation and pursuit of such intentions incumbent upon him? How did he arrive at the details of the plan? Did he work them out for himself by processes of discursive thinking, did he read them in a book, were they whispered in his ear by his dark angel? Such problems ramify in all directions, and each *kind* of problem is a subject of study in its own right (cf. chapters 6, 8 and 9).

(5) It would be possible at this point to bring forward arguments to show that the concepts of intention and of agency are inseparably linked. But these arguments would be closely similar to those

advanced above in connection with action and agency, and so we will refrain.

We have given some account of two more of the concepts central in the hermeneutical explanation of human behaviour, viz. the concepts of action and of intention. We must now consider the question of whether or not these two concepts are translatable into mechanistic terms, i.e. are capable of representation in machine-table form. For, according to the arguments we advanced in chapter 1, if the major notions of hermeneutical explanation are not translatable into the terms of mechanistic explanation, mechanistic explanation must give way to hermeneutical explanation. Now prima facie we have already shown that the notions of action and of intention are not so translatable. For we have pointed out that no one can be said to act and to have intentions unless he possesses and exercises conceptual capacities; and we have argued that the possession of conceptual capacities cannot be represented on a machine-table or embodied in a GM. However, to diversify our attack a little, and also to anchor our discussion to some recent psychological speculation, we shall consider an attempt by Turner (1971, chapter 6) to show that explanations making use of the notion of intention are 'essentially equivalent' to explanations in terms of the 'S-R paradigm'. This will be of relevance both to the present discussion and to our remarks about the nature of intention in chapter 9.

Turner's proposals are as follows. The paradigm of explanation in terms of intention is $Sx Ix \supset Rx$. This means that the 'phenomenological intention' (presumably the experienced or conscious intention) is, in conjunction with antecedent situational factors, sufficient for the response. Now we might, in accordance with behaviourist and reductionist dogma, attempt to eliminate all reference to the 'phenomenological intention'. Then we would have to analyse possession of an intention in terms of the subject exhibiting a certain behavioural disposition, i.e. having a tendency to emit certain responses to certain stimuli. Intention would emerge as a behavioural 'construct', a fact which can be expressed by means of Carnap's formula $Sx \supset (Cx \equiv Rx)$ (the construct is exactly equivalent to the range of responses made to a certain range of stimuli). However, this procedure, Turner holds, makes C, the dispositional construct, simply a matter of quite arbitrary S-R linkages. For (p. 158)

S-R translations of dispositional terms such as desires and intentions are clearly problematic. Our evidence for their formulation, the occasions for stipulating the particular dispositional terms, are other than the S-R observational states themselves. Etiologically, the evidence is the intention, the internal non-objective state of the organism, a mental state if you will; and it is only through knowledge of that state, a living through it, so to speak, that we can set about defining the dispositional predicates which are appropriate to the situation.

Why should we not, Turner suggests, incorporate into the behavioural dispositional construct only those S-R contingencies which we know from the 'phenomenological intention' belong together? The 'objectivist' need not disavow such grounds provided that they do not figure in the statements of his developed science. The dispositional construct now has the form $Sx \ Ix \ \supset (Cx \equiv Rx)$.

The methodological behaviourist need not, perhaps cannot, deny the factor of phenomenological intention. But this means only that there has been some heuristic source, some private support, for his deriving and adopting the dispositional terms he finds sufficient for the task of explanation. By and large, this differs very little from how a methodological behaviourist would proceed in developing dispositional translations of the construct intelligence. . . . (p. 160)

To explain a given piece of an organism's behaviour is, according to Turner, to exhibit it as exemplifying one of the set of S-R laws which make up that organism's current 'behavioural disposition' as above defined. We must, therefore, enquire whether or not intentions can be translated into, or represented as, such behavioural dispositions. And on the face of it Turner's position is an impossible one. For there are many kinds of intentions which it is impossible to 'translate' into lists of S-R concomitances of finite length or indeed into lists of S-R concomitances at all. The following examples may serve to illustrate the point.

(1) One's intention at time t may be too vague to be reduced to a list of S-R concomitances. Consider the child who murmurs, 'Mummy, I intend to be famous one day.' The child's intention would be totally misrepresented if turned into a list of specific S-R concomitances. The child intends to be famous-in-general one day, and this intention embraces his acting in ways as yet unspecifiable in

circumstances which he cannot at the moment conceive or envisage. It involves his intending in year y to act in whatever way seems necessary to obtain a certain goal in circumstances which will not arise until year $y + 2$ and which he will not be able to foresee until year $y + 1$. A similar example is that of the painter, confronted with a blank canvas, who may have a general idea of the sort of picture he intends to produce, and yet be initially quite uncertain as to the details he will put into it.

(2) There are a good many sorts of intentions which cannot be translated into S-R lists of finite length, and which cannot therefore be said to be susceptible of 'translation' at all. It is probable that a good many commonplace and quite definite intentions could be exhibited as of this kind once the number of possible circumstances which could re-route the intention without barring its fulfilment is taken into account. But the easiest examples are perhaps intentions whose goals can only be expressed in terms of what earlier on we called stimulus-neutral concepts – concepts possession of which cannot be reduced to tendencies consistently to make responses from physically definable response-classes in the face of stimuli from physically definable stimulus-classes. Here belong such things as the intention always to be polite, always to be scrupu- lously honest. There is no finite list of S-R concomitances which exhausts what is involved in the intention always to be honest. There is no limit to the wiles of Satan, to the forms which temptation can take. Hence one cannot lay down in advance what actions an honest man may have to take in order to stay honest, and in what circumstances. And even if one were able to complete the list of today's temptations, tomorrow will always bring fresh possibilities.

(3) Somewhat similar to the above are negative intentions, for instance, the intention never to smoke another cigarette. The relev- ant behaviour cannot be represented as a list of S-R concomitances, for *ex hypothesi* the fulfilment of the intention consists in what is not done rather than in what *is* done. Could not we then 'translate' the negative intention as a series of negative S-R relations, $Sx \supset \sim Rx$, etc? This will not do, because it fails to distinguish intending not to smoke from not intending to smoke. For the propositions $Sx \supset \sim Rx$, etc., characterize both these kinds of behaviour patterns. It is true that the 'phenomenological' sources for the formulation of the lists differ in the two cases, but *ex hypothesi* it is not the sources but only the resultant S-R lists which are to figure in the developed science.

In any case statements of negative form, of what does happen under certain circumstances, would look very odd among the statements of a putative science. For scientific law-statements are usually statements of what does happen under specified circumstances. The list of what does not happen under any given set of circumstances would presumably in all cases be infinite.

We have mentioned three kinds of intention, translation of which into S-R terms appears to be a very ambitious undertaking. We might further ask, with special reference to Turner's ideas, to what extent a 'phenomenological' intention may be regarded as a source for delivering up to the investigator 'translations' of that intention into a list of S-R concomitances. When one intends to bring about some state of affairs one's disposition is not to execute certain Rs to certain Si; it is to do *whatever* seems at any moment the sensible thing to do in order to bring about the fulfilment of the intention. One explains an action done in pursuance of an intention not by pointing to an entry in a list of S-R concomitances but by exhibiting that action as the logical thing to do given one's intention and one's beliefs about the relevant circumstances. Now which specific actions appear reasonable will change as one's beliefs about and understanding of the situation change and develop. What is implicit in the 'phenomenological intention' is in many instances just this openness to change and development as one's understanding of the situation develops; this absence, if you like, of any cast-iron, hard-and-fast commitment to make only responses from a delimitable set of S-R concatenations.

It might, of course, be proposed here that to talk of intentions developing, becoming more detailed, is misleading, that what we have with each development is a new and somewhat different intention. The consideration which we have just advanced would then be beside the point. It might even be suggested that the limited set of S-R concatenations of which each 'intention' consists could be identified with the set mediated by a given internal state of the organism (to be equated with a 'machine-state' in the machine-table paradigm), thus giving the set a certain non-arbitrary 'unity', 'phenomenological' or otherwise. However, to these proposals we should reply as follows: (a) The problems of accounting within a S-R framework for the transitions between each such 'intention' and the next would be just as refractory as the problem of accounting for the development of an intention as intentions are ordinarily conceived. (b) The new proposals are 'phenomenologically' wrong

– we do not look on our intention or purpose as having changed when we discover new means to effect it. (c) The idea that the input-output relations mediated by a given 'internal state' have *ipso facto* a certain unity was criticized above (p. 38).

Let us, however, once again waive all these arguments, and assume that Turner is right and that we have produced, presumably by utilizing a 'phenomenological source', a translation of some moderately complex intention into a list of S-R concatenations. The question will still arise, can we *really* incorporate the behavioural dispositions, which, so to speak, represent intentions, into the framework of a behaviourist science? These lists of S-R concatenations will manifestly be of no use if, from the point of view of S-R theory, they are wholly arbitrary, i.e. if they cannot be related to or derived from some neo-behaviourist theory. Now there seems, prima facie, every reason to suppose that the lists of S-R concatenations representing intentions would always have to remain thus arbitrary. For consider what we have just been saying about how, implicit in an intention, is the undertaking of such courses of action as the agent has reason to believe may lead to the fulfilment of the goal in question, and about how the behavioural implications of an intention may change and develop as the agent's understanding of the situation and grasp of what it is rational for him to do changes. On the face of it what determines the initial behavioural possibilities here, as the agent sees them, and how these envisaged possibilities change and develop, is not responses acquired by the agent in accordance with the postulates of behaviour theory, but the agent's ability to understand the implications for action of his own changing beliefs and constant longer-term intentions, his being able to see what it is rational for him to do under the new circumstances. No one has as yet succeeded in giving in S-R terms any acceptable or widely accepted account of processes of reasoning (cf. chapter 8). In fact reasons might well be advanced for claiming that no such account can ever be given. Unless and until such an account is either given, or else shown to be unnecessary, the lists of S-R concatenations are bound to remain wholly mysterious and anomalous from the point of view of S-R theory itself.

The objections which we have voiced to Turner's attempt to show that intentions may receive an analysis in behavioural-dispositional terms could, with modifications, be applied to *any* attempt to represent the notion of intention in machine-table terms, and hence to any attempts to programme a GM so as to simulate the possession of an intention. For Turner's 'lists of S-R concatenations' are essentially equivalent to a machine-table. Thus we can rule out *ab initio* any such mechanistic account of intention as that given by Miller, Galanter and Pribram (1960). According to Miller, Galanter and Pribram an intention is 'the uncompleted parts of a Plan whose execution has already begun' (p. 61). A 'Plan' is, for an organism, 'essentially the same' as a programme for a computer. It is 'any hierarchical process in the organism that can control the order in which a sequence of operations is to be performed' (p. 16). Boden (1973) develops the closely related notion of an 'action-plan' or 'procedural schema'. 'An action-plan is an internal representation of possible action that functions as a model guiding intentional behaviour. It is closely analogous to the sets of instructions comprising procedural routines within a computer program . . .' (p. 24). Boden's notion of a 'model' will be criticized in chapter 7.

We have now argued with respect to four of the main concepts of hermeneutical explanation – the concepts of concept, rule, action and intention – that they are not capable of translation into the terms of mechanistic explanation. And this, we shall suggest, is sufficient to show that *none* of the concepts of hermeneutical explanation is so translatable, for all these concepts are interrelated in a way which makes their separate translations impossible.

We may begin by noting that many of the psychological phenomena which the concepts concerned embrace are, as it were, essentially directed towards an 'object' (cf. chapter 7). You cannot have a desire or a belief, or an intention, or a hope, that has no 'object', that is merely a desire . . ., an intention . . ., and so forth. Desires, beliefs, intentions, hopes, are always that something is or shall be the case. But the object (the 'intensional object') of the intention, belief or what have you, *need not exist* in order to be such an object. In other words it is a conceived rather than an actual state of affairs. It thus appears that there is an essential link between intending, believing, desiring, hoping and so forth, and the conceiving of various possible states of affairs. Furthermore, the link here is not a merely contingent one. We could not separately identify on the one hand hopes, fears, intentions, etc., and on the other conceivings of states of affairs, and then lay down a causal law correlating the two. The hopes and so forth could not exist independently of the conceivings. A hope, an intention, a belief, stripped of its 'intensional object', of its relationship to the conceiving of some state of affairs, would disintegrate; nothing would remain behind which would differentiate the residues from each other, or leave them as distinguishable rafts within the stream of consciousness. There are no special sensations or images or feelings whose presence *is always* linked, shall we say, to the presence of a hope rather than a desire, or to that of an intention rather than a belief.

These non-contingent links exist not just between on the one hand intentions, hopes, fears, beliefs, desires, etc., and on the other hand conceivings of states of affairs. They also exist between the intentions, the hopes, the beliefs, the desires, etc., and also between conceivings of different states of affairs. A central example is perhaps that of the relationship between intending and believing. If someone said that he believed he could retract his fingernails or extinguish the sun, and that he intended to do so, we should either assume that he believed such things possible, in which case we would doubt his sanity but not his intentions, or else credit him with a belief in their impossibility, and set him down as a liar or a humorist. We could not attribute to him *both* the belief that such things are impossible *and* the intention to bring them about. And once again we might say that this is not a matter of contingent fact. It is inconceivable that there should be a universe in which intention-states are not thus related to belief-states. If one discovers that one's settled intentions have been framed within a realm of fantasy, that their objects are illusory and unattainable, one's intentions necessarily evaporate. They could not be intentions *to do* anything, and an intention is *nothing* if it is not an intention to do something. This perhaps relates to the suggestion we shall make in chapter 9 that there is an element of committal about intention. When one has framed an intention one is, in a sense not easy to elucidate, committed to a course of action; one commits, as it were, one's energies and resources to it, as such committal can be only within the world as one believes it is. 'Committal' within a fantasy world could only be a kind of adventurous day-dreaming parasitic upon genuine committal.

One could multiply comparable instances almost indefinitely, and further relevant material will be touched on in chapters 9 and 11. We have already remarked how conceptual capacities are inter-linked. These capacities cannot stand on their own – they are in part constituted by their relationships to other such capacities. Again relationships of this non-contingent kind hold between (to take examples almost at random) desire and intention, belief and surprise (cf. Price, 1969, pp. 275–9), hatred and the desire to do harm, remorse and the wish that one had not done harm. Many emotions are intrinsically linked to ways of conceiving the present situation, for example fear and the realization of danger, and are pregnant with what may be called action promptings without which they would be wholly emasculated. Consider, for example, this brief passage in which Macmurray is talking about the relationship between love and anxiety or fear (Macmurray, 1961, p. 62):

> Now the positive motive of the mother's caring is her love for the child; it contains, however, and subordinates a negative component of fear – anxiety for the child's welfare. The negative component is essential, since it provides the motive for thought and foresight on the child's behalf, and for provision in advance against the danger to its life, health and welfare, both in the present and in the future. Without it love would be inoperative and ineffectual, a mere sentimentality and therefore unreal.

These questions are extraordinarily difficult, and we do not claim to have done more than show that they arise. It is, however, important to be clear what we are suggesting. We remarked that the links between, say, intention and belief, or desire and the conceiving of the desired state of affairs, are 'not contingent', i.e. not such as could be discovered by observing correlations between phenomena of separate and independently characterizable classes. But we do not mean by this that the relations between them are non-contingent in virtue of a conventionally established definition (as is, for instance, the relationship between a 'carnivore' and its preferred diet). We mean that the phenomena concerned are, in part at least, constituted by their relationships, and would totally disintegrate, be written out of the universe, if the relationships were obliterated; not just *de facto* out of this universe, but necessarily out of any *possible* universe. Their relationship is one of 'internal' or 'intrinsic' inter-relatedness in something like the traditional (and highly contentious) sense (cf. Rorty, 1967; Blanshard, 1939, chapter 32). A given individual's intentions, desires, beliefs, hopes, conceivings and so forth would thus be better described not as a number of distinct phenomena, but as different aspects or phases of the same phenomenon,[3] a phenomenon which would vanish like a ruptured bubble if any important aspect were torn away.

·   ·   ·

Concl.

①

From the above arguments three conclusions may be drawn. The first is the one we set out to demonstrate, namely that the major concepts of hermeneutical explanation are so interrelated that if any one of them is not capable of translation into the terms of mechanistic explanation, none of them is, for they are concepts of intrinsically interrelated phenomena, of phenomena constituted by their interrelationships to one another, and hence are concepts which can only be expounded in terms of each other. The second,

②

correlated, conclusion is that if we are to admit any one of the concepts of everyday psychological explanation, for example the notion of intention, into our psychological framework, we have to admit the whole apparatus of everyday psychological notions. Thus, if our argument in chapter 1 that the notion of intention cannot be extruded from the explanation of actions is correct, then psychology is stuck with all the other everyday concepts as well. (This is not, however, to say that everyday psychological propositions or pieces of proverbial wisdom have any special claims upon us.) The third

③

conclusion is that we have here a perfectly general reason why psychological phenomena cannot be represented on a generalized machine. For relations of 'intrinsic interrelatedness' are impossible to represent on a GM. One can in principle simulate on a GM the behaviour and the internal relationships of any system the laws of whose behaviour are determined by the laws governing the behaviour of its elements. In the system we are concerned with there are no laws governing the behaviour of the individual 'elements' and no relationships between the 'elements', because it is impossible to sort out any 'elements' which can be characterized independently of each other. As Clarke (1971, p. 524) says:

if we accept the Humean dictum that there are no logical connections between things, events or states, then this feature of our mental life, namely that thoughts logically require predecessors to give them their identity, suggests that mental structure is more closely analogous to a formal than a physical structure.

5

Two Alternative Approaches within the Established Framework

The mainstream psychological establishment is not exactly at one with itself. All seem agreed that psychology is the study of behaviour (rather than of action), and that people should be studied as behaving objects, as mechanisms (rather than as agents). And further, all agree that explanations of behaviour are to be sought by experimental analyses (rather than by enquiry into the 'meanings' which actions have for the agents who perform them). However, there is dispute on the one hand as to whether it is appropriate to seek abstract 'cognitive' mechanisms and 'cognitive structures' (Neisser, 1967; Broadbent, 1971), or whether it is necessary to study people's physiology as a root determinant of their behaviour. On the other hand there is also dispute as to whether laboratory conditions are 'artificial' and give misleading results and as to whether it would not therefore be better to try to test hypotheses in real life, or at least in simulated real-life situations.

We propose to examine now two recent alternatives to or departures from the standard approach. While their authors for different reasons both feel that seeking 'cognitive mechanisms' by an experimental investigation of people's behaviour in laboratory situations is unsound, they none the less still share all the basic metaphysical commitments of the standard approach. They still regard themselves as conducting a 'behavioural science' as behavioural scientists understand that term. In exploring these two accounts, we shall try to indicate some particular applications of our more general criticisms of mainstream psychology; to show that those who have doubts about this psychology would do better to leave it altogether than to palter with it; and to drop some preliminary hints as to the shape of the alternative psychology of action which we shall outline in chapter 6.

The two approaches are: (1) Weiskrantz's (1973) physiological psychology which stays in the laboratory but suggests that the nervous system is simply not put together in the way that abstract models of it have suggested. 'Cognitive' psychology can only be carried on in association with the physiological study of the 'real' nervous system. (2) Argyle's (1969) 'new look' in social psychology which suggests that laboratory experimentation in the past may have given incomplete, exaggerated or simply wrong results and that instead we should study less artificial sequences of social interactions.

(1) **Weiskrantz's Physiological Psychology**
Weiskrantz begins his paper by suggesting that the task of psychology is to understand why we and our fellows behave as we do. Most of us, he feels, would agree that we behave as we do because of what is going on inside us. But of three types of such explanation commonly offered, only one, he believes, is fundamental. The three types of explanations are: first, introspective; second, explanations based on abstract theoretical constructions; and, third, explanations which refer to actual physiological structures and their mode of operation. Clearly, he mentions introspection only for good measure, for he does not treat it as a serious contender. The approach he does attack is that of using abstract theoretical constructions. He points out (a) that 'we have all too many examples in psychology of two logical models starting from quite different, even contradictory, assumptions, and yet fitting the empirical facts equally well',[1] and (b) that 'it is possible for a structural model to make some correct predictions but in the end be fundamentally wrong because it ignores the details of internal bodily events'.

In regard to this second objection Weiskrantz refers to the theories of pattern perception produced by 'theorists' over the decades. He points out that some of the models work well, within their self-imposed limits, but that it is now clear that the 'real nervous system is different from any model previously put forward' (p. 512). No model suggested so far has the correct logical structure. Recent research shows that the cells of the visual cortex are 'tuned' to unique features (Hubel and Wiesel, 1962) or to spatial regularities (Campbell *et al.*, 1969) in the retinal image, and that coding is not, in these at least, a spatial-temporal transform. We could not have known this, he suggests, without having delved into the nervous system itself.

One cannot, however, Weiskrantz points out, conduct the investigation purely in physiological terms. A reference to psychological things is essential. For even when the physiologist has some idea what functional category his observations are relevant to, there is a difficulty in establishing whether they are either necessary or sufficient for that function without studying the creatures as a whole. In fact, there are great methodological difficulties in this area and Weiskrantz does not try to minimize them. This being the case it is interesting to find him remark that increasing numbers of people are turning to this form of psychology, as 'they find it even more frustrating to try to understand how we tick by alternative routes' (p. 516). For he says, in contrast to 'theoretical' psychology, information is gradually accumulating in physiological psychology (p. 516).

> As we accumulate more and more information in physiological psychology certain explanations become more and more compelling. And the way in which they become compelling is when there is a perfect consistency between our observations with the brain as a dependent variable and with the brain as an independent variable. . . . When it is found that certain emotional states cause changes in firing patterns in a particular region of the brain, *and* when those same firing rates, if artificially imposed on that region by electrical driving, can cause just the same emotional states, we can reasonably infer that we have isolated a control mechanism for that type of behaviour.

Weiskrantz concludes with an account, not of the theoretical problems he hopes to solve with his approach and a sketch of how he expects that they will be solved, but with remarks on some of its practical benefits. We will not go into these here. We would now like to turn to a critical examination of Weiskrantz's position. We shall consider in turn his two central claims, viz. (a) that through Hubel and Wiesel's discovery of cortical cells uniquely tuned to features in the retinal image we have learned something of the mechanism of visual coding that we could not have otherwise have known, and (b) that appropriate experimental work with the brain as dependent variable and also with the brain as independent variable may enable us, for example, 'to conclude that we have located an important control centre and can begin to investigate its properties'. With regard to the former claim we shall suggest that we could very readily have discovered without physiological investigations of the brain that coding mechanisms are unlikely to be spatial-temporal transforms and indeed are quite likely to have a wide variety of forms. With regard to the latter claim, we shall remark that Weiskrantz has apparently no better terms in which to conceive a 'control centre' than the entirely inappropriate ones of the conventional mechanistic psychology which he has criticized.

(a) Weiskrantz's comments on 'coding'. Weiskrantz suggests that while principles of 'coding' in the nervous system may not be at all simple, we will certainly not get to know them without delving into the nervous system itself. If, however, people are (as we shall suggest) just as much agents in making sense of what they see and hear, as in all their other activities, it is difficult to see what help physiological investigations could be in discovering such principles, or that they are needed for us to learn that the simple proposals of abstract theorists are mistaken. If people are agents in the matter, scientists will search in vain to detect patterns in brain events paralleling in any consistent manner the patterns of 'meaning' and 'significance' with which agents invest external events. If one's making sense of one's world is not something that happens to one, but is something one must do for oneself, then, presumably, the sense one does make of one's world is a matter of how one goes about trying to do it, not a matter of any pre-established logic.

Bohm (1965) has discussed the problem of how we might abstract what is *relatively* invariant in the structure of what we encounter or interact with in the world. He points out that nothing is seen without movements and variations on the retina of the eye. The eye is in constant motion and the characteristics of its motions must play some part in determining the structure of what is seen. The relevant data, he suggests, are extracted from the *relations* between the movements and their consequences. So we do not at any level perceive simply what is in front of our eyes; what we perceive contains 'structural features which are not even on the retina of the eye at a given moment, but which are detected with the aid of relationships observed over some period of time' (p. 203). Bohm goes on to argue that in fact the attempt to base our idea of perceptual processes upon some physical time-order of events can only lead to confusion for 'the order of signals (may not be) essentially related to the order of time' (p. 201) – it is not, for instance, in the interpretation of a television picture. The 625 lines which constitute a frame follow one another in temporal succession, and if an image is to be extracted from them parts of the image occurring at quite different points in time have to be selected and integrated. But there is no logical or predetermined relation between the selection of the parts and the extraction of an image – indeed, what the image is determines how the parts should be selected and integrated. Bohm suggests that the situation is similar in perception, a view propounded long ago in Dewey's (1896) account of 'acts of seeing'. What seems to matter in perception is the way that a person *relates* his movements with their consequences, and to some extent that is up to him, i.e. he is an agent in the process.

Thus, for Bohm, perception is an act; it is something that people have to try to do. And while we may not do it deliberately, knowing the reasons for our actions, it is none the less something in which we can intend a consequence;[2] it is an act of ours.

Bohm's comments apply also, of course, in speech perception: extracting an image from a verbal description of a scene also necessitates selection and integration of parts in the speech signal occurring at quite different points in time – and the same scene may be described in many different ways. There is thus little reason to believe that in the comprehension of speech there are any principles of natural logic at work in 'coding' our perceptions for us. If we are in any sense agents in processes of perception, it is no wonder that simple 'spatial-temporal transforms' have not been discovered, for agents may 'construct' the 'content' of signals in ways which bear no relation at all to the temporal order of events in the signal. Agents may, presumably, construct contents in relation to their own needs and interests.

(b) Talk of 'control centres' in the brain gained currency most especially in connection with such matters as the regulation of food intake. It has been established by experimental work on animals that stimulation or extirpation of small and circumscribed areas in the hypothalamus can increase or diminish food intake to a most marked degree. It is not difficult to think of crude, and perhaps misleading, mechanical analogies here, for instance the operation of thermostats and other simple regulatory devices. It has, however, become not uncommon for psychologists to speculate about control centres in the human brain regulating, say, linguistic behaviour, to extrapolate this way of talking far beyond the reach of any effective mechanical analogy. Weiskrantz does not indulge in such speculations. He confines himself to mentioning 'control centres' for food intake and for emotional behaviour, both in animals. However, his programme for physiological psychology is such that the problem of control centres for 'higher-level' activities, for activities which we should ordinarily regard as *controlled by the agent*, must inevitably arise for him.

It appears that Weiskrantz looks upon the workings of his putative 'control centres' in pretty much the same general terms as do his opponents, the psychologists who formulate abstract 'structural' models (in the form, perhaps, of 'flow-charts') of the mechanisms underlying behaviour; or that even if he does not quite see eye to eye with them, he none the less thinks of control mechanisms in terms of, for example, the routing and re-routing of nerve impulses or the chemistry of complex molecules or other processes in principle representable on a GM. Now if the arguments of our preceding chapters have any weight, it is clear that an agent's control of particular areas of his own behaviour, for example of his linguistic or sexual or emotional behaviour, cannot be represented on a GM. Such control involves the exercise of rules and concepts in a directed and purposeful manner, and, as we have seen, concept- and intention-possession cannot be analysed into machine-table terms. Thus if the workings of the brain are conceived in ways which could be formally paralleled on a GM, there could not be in the brain a 'control centre' whose operations were equivalent to the 'control' exercise by an agent over some aspects of his purposeful and intelligent behaviour.

A further and related problem which could arise for anyone who sought to locate 'control centres' for 'higher-level' activities is this. How would he know when he had discovered such a control centre? Not by finding certain structures. The functioning of a control centre could not be related to its observable structure as, say, is the functioning of a steam engine to the way it is built. You could not examine the structure and work out its probable mode of functioning. A human being in pursuit, for example, of his sexual goals reacts *intelligently* to the environment's reaction to his previous actions; and he controls his behaviour, makes his next move, accordingly. In other words we cannot delimit the behaviours which the control centre will need to instigate. We cannot, therefore, expect it to have a structure specially suited to the performance of a certain limited set of functions, because its functions cannot be laid down in advance.

Weiskrantz shows himself well aware of such problems, and he points to the advantage of having several different lines of empirical investigation zeroing in on the behavioural function of a particular anatomical locus. However, two kinds of reply might be made here. The first is that no anatomical locus or functional system has been properly shown to be a control centre until we have evidence as to *how it exercises its control*; in the absence of such evidence we cannot rule out the possibility that the observed effects of stimulation or extirpation of that locus have some other cause. The second is that in the case of the 'higher' activities of human beings there is very little evidence even for the existence of 'control centres'. What there is evidence for is loci, interference with which grossly impairs an agent's capacity to control his linguistic activities, thinking, planning, etc. (cf. Delgado, 1969, pp. 193–5). And this is not the same thing at all.

We suggest, therefore, that Weiskrantz, like most other physiological psychologists, conceptualizes and hence investigates the brain in terms which, if they continue to dominate physiological psychology, will make any serious advances in our understanding of 'higher' brain processes impossible. What, then, are we to make of Weiskrantz's reiterated implication that he and his colleagues are studying 'the real nervous system' and 'the nervous system itself', and of his hints that abstract 'structural' models are commonly propounded by persons reluctant to weary themselves with the details of cerebral anatomy and to dabble their hands in blood and juices? 'Real' is a very slippery word – something can be 'real' only within a framework of thought which permits it to be contrasted to what is 'unreal'. If a practical chemist were to claim that only he and his colleagues study 'real' matter, and that mathematical physicists, who never risk burning their fingers with acid, do not, we should have to dismiss the suggestion as merely a roundabout way of commending a certain approach to physical science.

(2) Argyle's 'New Look' at Social Psychology

Superficially at least, Weiskrantz's approach and Argyle's approach seem so far removed from one another that it seems incredible that both are to be found under the same roof in a university department of psychology. For whereas Weiskrantz insists that painstaking laboratory research into individual nervous systems is necessary if we are to discover 'what makes us tick', Argyle suggests that not only are our relations with others the most important part of human life, and that the most essential human characteristic cannot be manifested by a person in isolation, but that a laboratory study of such relationships is inappropriate. He feels that social psychology has suffered both by restricting itself too narrowly to 'social psychology' experiments and theories, and by isolating itself from other groups of scientists studying social interaction with other methods. In those areas in which 'social psychological' experimentation has flourished, Argyle feels that (a) little remains to be done, and (b) nothing very exciting has been found out. Experimental research requires working with situations which are 'simplified or stripped down, which may lack some essential features of the original situation, and which may produce types of behaviour that would not normally occur' (Argyle, 1969, p. 17). 'New look' research in social psychology attempts to study social interaction in more naturalistic settings. It is a 'new look' in more than just this feature though, for, besides recognizing the importance of 'cognitive processes' in behaviour, it emphasizes both the importance of intentional and unintentional communication, and the importance of 'physiological motivation' – Argyle believes that much of what we do is 'driven' by our basic biological processes. Central to his whole approach is the idea that 'social interaction can usefully be looked at as the operation of a serial motor skill, in which each interactor is trying to manipulate the others in order to elicit certain desired responses' (p. 179). It is his 'social skill model' that we would like to examine here. One thing that we shall find, strangely, is that although Weiskrantz would surely place Argyle among the 'theorists' who produce inaccurate structural models of our inner workings, at a deeper level Argyle does not differ from Weiskrantz.

Argyle diagrams his social skill model as in Figure 2 (p. 70).

There are five major components. First, Argyle suggests that people interact in order to obtain goals, and he gives examples of such goals for people in professional situations: conveying knowledge, information or understanding (teaching); obtaining information (interviewing); changing attitudes, behaviour or beliefs (salesmanship, canvassing, disciplinary action); etc. Such aims, he suggests, are linked in turn to more basic motivations connected with work. In everyday non-professional social situations the actors are motivated, too, but by the more basic motivations of affiliation, aggression, sex, etc. Thus 'Each person wants the other person (in an inter-action) to respond in an affiliative, submissive or dominant manner, according to his own motivational structure' (p. 181). Second, performers have to learn to notice cues appropriate to the conduct of their skills – among others, cues about their own perfor-mance, as Argyle suggests that one of the goals of interaction is to present oneself to others in a good light (Goffman, 1956). Third, he

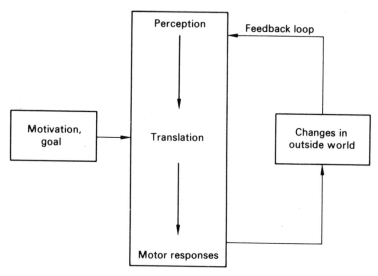

Figure 2   Motor skill model upon which Argyle's social skill model is based

suggests that 'there has to be some central store of "translation" processes in the brain, which prescribe what to do about any particu-lar perceptual information' (p. 183). Some of these special proces-ses may be learned in the course of socialization, but 'Social interac-tion is to a great extent pre-programmed by innate neural structures which result from natural selection, and by cultural norms, which represent past collective solutions to the problems of interaction' (p. 25). The function of these central processes is to *plan* – Miller, Galanter and Pribram's (1960) discussion of plans, and the struc-ture of behaviour, is seen by Argyle as relevant here. Fourth, he discusses what sets the appropriate performances in motion. 'Commands', he suggests, 'go from the central translation system to the muscles, producing a pattern of movements' (p. 184). The apparent advantage of the Miller, Galanter and Pribram scheme is that 'plans' (see above, p. 58) do not, once initiated, run themselves off regardless of environmental conditions; motions are continued until particular test criteria are attained, and only then is the execution of the next part of the plan initiated. When conditions have stabilized, though, performance may become 'automatized' – 'that is, freed from . . . continuous sensory control' (p. 185). Fifth, Argyle emphasizes the function of the *feedback*. 'Feedback provides information for corrective action, which makes allowances for variation in the conditions or materials and for error in the initial plan of response. The social skill performer corrects in a similar way' (p. 186).

This in broad outline is Argyle's 'social skill model'. The part in the diagram labelled 'changes in outside world' refers, presumably, *inter alia* to the motions of other people, their motions not being in any fundamental way different from the motions of objects. To be fair to Argyle, we must point out that he does say, 'The model is of course only a starting point' (p. 186). But he does not go on to suggest that it might be wrong in principle, only that it will need elaborating to take more complex situations into account. It has already been useful, he says, in showing the various points at which social skill training may be needed, and in providing a classification of the ways in which social competence (in Chomsky's sense of 'competence') may fail.

The first thing to be said about Argyle's approach is that, as in Weiskrantz's, behaviour is viewed from the standpoint of an external observer; both are behaviourists. People's behaviour is viewed as a mere sequence of events, no different in quality to the motions of inanimate objects. So although the distinction between intentional and unintentional activity is one of Argyle's central concerns, it is for him a difference that can be identified in the *form* of people's behaviour. Thus people do not *act* in his social world, they 'perform like machines according to plans'. Now we have criticized this view extensively and we will not go over the ground again. However inadequate it is as an account of individual behaviour, it is even more inadequate as an account of social exchanges. To show this let us begin by listing the differences between our approach and Argyle's. For him people are not agents in their own actions, 'translation processes' in their brains prescribe what they do. Because for him people do not act in the attempt to realize intentions, but are driven, like cybernetic central-heating systems, to attain results of a pre-established form, there can be no assessments of the intention in their performances; as to whether it is sincere or cynical, meant or a 'matter of going through the motions'. But people *can* tell whether we mean what we say or do by seeing whether we act as we have implied we would, for meanings are to be explored in terms of their implications, how one act 'commits' us to another.

In Argyle's social world, people do not themselves make anything happen, they *construct* nothing essentially new or unique between themselves, they simply use one another in satisfaction of their needs. It is thus a social world with no real culture, no real morality and no real history; dialogue leading to the creation of new orders of meaning is impossible; and people certainly do not influence in any way the formation and development of their own selves. It is a social psychology in which people neither make nor are made by the system, they are simply idealized as existing to work the system to their own advantage.

Argyle's social world does not owe its basic structure to the efforts of men working in the face of physical, moral and political uncertainties, it owes its basic structure to the drives to which human beings fall victim. Besides basic biological drives, there are also 'cultural' drives – although because they have no instinctual basis and cannot be satiated like biological drives, Argyle asks, 'Is it correct to speak of these as "drives" at all?' (p. 42). He does not, as far as we can tell, answer the question directly, but he clearly assumes they are drives since under the heading of 'cultural drives' (p. 54) he discusses McClelland *et al.*'s (1953) idea of people being motivated by a 'need for achievements'. A people's culture thus enters this world in two ways, as a set of goals in addition to or linked with the basic biological goals to be achieved by use of social interaction, and centrally, as part of a store of 'translation' processes in the brain representing past collective solutions to problems of interaction. As to what *culture* is, Argyle says this (p. 78):

> Human infants are born with basic biological needs, but much remains to be acquired by learning. . . . As a result of the evolution of the power of language, human beings can communicate their solutions of problems to one another, and to the next generation, and can add continuously to this heritage of skills and knowledge. Different societies, over long periods of time, develop different ways of completing

instinctive equipment and satisfying biological drives. These alternative solutions are called cultures.

But a child who is assimilated into culture does not, on the one hand, face problems and find solutions to them and, on the other hand, learn a language in which problems and solutions can be represented and communicated to others. Part of what it is for a child to learn the language of his culture is to learn *what counts* for those in the culture as a problem and as a solution to it. Learning a culture's language is not just learning a symbolic means of communicating what one already knows, it is a matter of learning how to make judgments; it is a matter of learning how to act in ways which make sense to others. It is not only a matter of learning how to interpret or evaluate situations one encounters in the same way as other members of the culture, it is also a mattter of learning how to use things in what counts as the same way. When people in a culture talk about reality, they are talking about what they mean by the expression 'reality' in their language. And it is within this reality that their problems and the solutions to them appear. A child must construct his 'social reality' in the course of his exchanges with those who take care of him. While these exchanges may be motivated by an instinctual need for communion, they are not structured by that need; if they were the child would learn nothing but, presumably, more and more effective means of contact with his mother. They are structured, as we shall later argue in detail, by mothers acting as double-agents, structuring the exchanges between themselves and their children in accordance with their beliefs as to what one should be trying to do in one's actions in that culture. For Argyle, one's reality can only be that which relates in some way to one's drives. But a child who acquires a culture has not merely acquired 'solutions', developed over long periods of time, to the problems involved in satisfying his biological drives, he has acquired a whole framework of thought, feeling, perception and action, a reality he shares with others. And from within this reality he may begin to construct problems of the most interesting kind; not only may he question the nature of the trees and the stars, but also raise the question of his own nature. It is difficult to see how a form of social interaction aimed merely at manipulating others to satisfy one's needs can account for such constructive activity.

Argyle likewise fails to give a realistic account of morality. Again, as life is basically structured in terms of individuals' needs to satisfy their drives, they have no sense of right and wrong. Moral values are merely values 'embodied in social norms which enforce conformity by threat of rejection or punishment' (p. 87), a necessary expedient if the culture is to be maintained as a 'solution to life's problems' (pp. 88–9). But when people act, quite irrespective of whether their act conforms to social norms or not, we are able to judge whether it is morally right or wrong. Time and again it is right to resist social norms; morality is not a statistical and emotional matter but inherent in the very concept of culture.

When people act they must do this and not that; whether people deliberate before they act or not, their action, as the actualization of one from a number of possibilities, involves selection or choice. And, presumably, as agents they attempt in their acts to choose appropriate and reject inappropriate action. Part of what it is to be able to act is to distinguish correct from incorrect action, i.e. act in relation to a standard. Now in a culture, people face the task of acting in terms of what they understand the values of their culture to mean; if they are to be rational, having acted in one way in one situation, they must commit themselves to acting in certain other ways in certain other situations. A set of such commitments would constitute the standards for morally right action in that culture. In practice, of course, there are difficulties of interpretation, but they are not insurmountable. These difficulties do not mean that we must give up and take a vote on it; as each difficulty arises we have to discuss our interpretations until we arrive at one upon which we can all agree. Actions are then judged as right or wrong according to it. Morality is not a matter of conformity at the risk of rejection, it is a matter of rational judgment.

Not only are people unable to apply any rational standards to their conduct in Argyle's social world, they are unable to contribute in any significant way to the development of their culture. We have already said that Argyle's is a social psychology of those who merely work the system, rather than a social psychology of those who by their efforts construct the social system. Now we must point out that it is one thing to 'work the system' and quite another to keep it working. Modern cultures face the task of continually reconstructing themselves as a result of new conditions which they themselves, usually, have created! Now, clearly, cultures cannot construct or reconstruct themselves from scratch. Like organic structures they grow and develop. Cultures must therefore reconstruct themselves in a rational manner; that is, they must link their new structure to their old in an intelligible manner. People who act as Argyle describes, doing merely what is expedient for the satisfaction of their needs, can have no access to the type of knowledge needed to reconstruct cultures. Only those who know a culture's history and can compare what used to happen with what happens now can evaluate the efficacy of the behaviour it currently prescribes. Argyle's 'performers' may nose out new modes of conduct by trial and error methods as circumstances change, but only those with a clear idea of what a culture prescribes, and the historical reasons why, are in a position to judge what aspects of a culture's way of life still serve their purposes and what aspects need changing, and why they need changing. It is difficult to see how a process of feedback merely to do with sensing deviations from pre-established goals can provide the type of knowledge needed in the rational reconstruction of modern culture.

One could continue: a social psychology which characterizes other people as 'changes in the outside world', might run into the problem of accounting for how it is that we come to credit the existence of other people at all. One's suspicions would be increased to find that the task is indeed so difficult that 'At first infants treat others as physical objects' (p. 59), and it is suggested that it is only by the end of the first year that they treat them as people – an assertion that is just not true (M. P. M. Richards, 1974). No doubt Argyle would suggest that one could decide upon the basis of *observations*, that there were indeed patterns of activity in one's outside world very like the patterns in one's own activity, and that one could thus infer, analogically, that there were indeed beings like oneself producing them. But how could one justify the move to the belief that indeed there were minds and selves like, *but other than* our own? We will later offer our own account (chapter 10). We shall not now continue further. We feel, however, we have said enough to show that, (1) to the extent that people appear as merely changes in an external world, Argyle's approach is not truly 'social', and (2) to the extent that, like Weiskrantz's, it seeks to understand not what people do but merely to describe how their behaviour appears in a chain of circumstances, it is not 'psychology' either. It is a 'new look' that still fails to see anything of significance.

6

The Shape of an
Hermeneutical Psychology

At this point it will be useful if we recapitulate the argument so far. We began by distinguishing two broad traditions of thought with regard to the explanation of human action, viz. the mechanistic and the hermeneutical. The mechanistic tradition, which accords so well with the practices and presuppositions of modern science, has been generally predominant, and never more so than in the decades since the Second World War. We argued, however, that despite optimistic proposals that mechanistic and hermeneutical explanation function at separate and non-conflicting 'levels of discourse', the two sorts of explanations are incompatible, and that furthermore in the event of conflict between them mechanistic explanation is bound to give way to hermeneutical.

This does not mean to say that when we come to analyse the operation of our nerves and muscles, brains and other organs we shall not find them operating in an orderly and consistent manner. Indeed, it is necessary that they do so, for if they did not, we would be unable to express our intentions in our actions without being continually surprised by the difficulty we found in controlling our bodies. It is, rather, that if we try to extend the kind of account which we might give of the operations of our nerves and muscles to cover also the intentions, choices, actions, etc., of a rational human agent, the enlarged account will inevitably conflict with any hermeneutical account of the same phenomena. And we claimed that in the event of such conflict the only hope for mechanistic explanation is for its proponents to give us mechanistic 'translations' of the key concepts of hermeneutical psychology; for them to show, in other words, that it is in principle possible for us to design mechanistic systems whose states and operations could properly be described in such terms as 'intending', 'acting', 'believing', 'following rules', etc.

In order to discuss this possibility, we made use of the fact that the modern mathematical theory of automata makes it possible to give a definition of 'mechanistic system' which is at once very general and very precise. A 'mechanistic system' is one whose operations and state-transitions can in principle be represented by a machine-table and formally paralleled on a GM. It is widely agreed that the functioning of all systems falling within the purview of classical physics, and of all systems whose overall properties are determined by the properties and interactions of their elements, can be thus represented and formally paralleled. We then argued in some detail that possession of concepts, rules, intentions, etc., cannot be analysed in terms which admit of translation into a machine-table of finite length. We concluded that the principal notions of hermeneutical explanation cannot be translated into the terms of mechanistic explanation, and added that these notions are interrelated in a way which ensures that if one or more of the central hermeneutical terms are not susceptible of a mechanistic interpretation, none is. We accordingly claimed that, at least in most cases, hermeneutical explanations of human actions are ineradicable and irreducible, and we commented briefly upon the shortcomings of two alternative approaches developed within the general tradition of mechanism. Our overall conclusion is that the conceptual framework within which the psychological study of human action must, at least in the first instance, be carried on is that appropriate to hermeneutical explanation. And since the 'meaning' of actions for the agents who execute them are given by those agents' intentions, hopes, fears, beliefs, anticipations, desires, plots, plans, reasonings, schemes and immediate perceptions, it is these everyday, yet systematically related, psychological concepts that must constitute our initial, though not necessarily our final, framework of thought.

We propose, then, that explanations of human action must for the most part be hermeneutical, and that the conceptual framework of the psychology of human action must, therefore, be that of the everyday notions – action, agent, intention, purpose, desire, belief, hope, fear, reason, plan and so on and so on – within which such explanation has its being (Berlin, 1976). It is accordingly incumbent on us to give some account of what a psychology conducted in these terms will be like, of the problems it will tackle and the methods by which it will tackle them. Our account will necessarily be of the most general and tentative kind. We shall, however, in a sense be supplementing what we shall say here in part II of this book; for in part II we shall try, albeit sketchily, to exemplify some of the theoretical and analytic activities, and to describe some of the practical activities, which might figure in an hermeneutical psychology.

An activity which is little practised by contemporary psychologists, but which must, we feel, play a larger role in the psychology of the future, is that of *conceptual analysis*, and in particular analysis of the 'framework' concepts of hermeneutical psychology. We have claimed that no general approach to the explanation of human actions which does not incorporate hermeneutical explanations can even get off the ground. There are no other terms in which our initial study and explanation of human actions can be conducted.[1] It is no use supposing that one can investigate a certain range of natural phenomena, vaguely labelled 'intentions', 'desires', etc., and as a result of one's investigations work out a 'scientific' concept of intention or desire which will perform its functions even better than the old one. The only upshot will be concepts of 'intention', 'desire', etc., which have no relevance to the phenomena which we ordinarily classify as intentions, desires or expressions of such, and hence no part to play in the psychological understanding of thought and action. Something of this kind has happened in connection with modern 'theories of learning' (cf. S. C. Brown, 1972; C. Taylor, 1964, chapters 6–11). The ordinary concepts of intention, desire, etc., are therefore, so to speak, the psychologist's working tools. It is only prudent for him to get to know them thoroughly and to ensure that when he engages in discussion with his colleagues the field of play has been marked out in at least a preliminary way.

The following objection to our remarks might be raised. We have suggested that 'ordinary people' have a 'concept' of intention, 'a concept' of desire, etc. But why should one suppose that ordinary people have *any* concept of intention, etc., let alone one which they all (more or less) share? Most 'ordinary people' would be quite stumped if asked to define 'intention'. To this objection three lines of reply might be proffered: (1) We have already discussed (pp. 29–31) the undeniable fact that people may be 'versed in' a concept of a set of rules, i.e. act successfully in terms of it, without being able to produce any explicit verbal definition. (2) Most people are without doubt thoroughly 'versed in' the concepts which constitute the framework of hermeneutical explanation. They conduct their lives in the clear if implicit appreciation that other people have intentions which they will endeavour to fulfil, that if one is fortunate someone else will grasp one's intention and help one to fulfil it, that the fulfilment of some of one's intentions may be incompatible with the fulfilment of other intentions, one's own or other people's. Anyone who did *not* have this kind of appreciation would not be able to comport himself as an adult member of our society. (3) Ordinary people can be brought to formulate a coherent if not articulate account of intention by suitable questions stimulating them to 'thought experiments'.

It is perhaps worth noting *en passant* that the process of analysing the framework concepts of hermeneutical psychology is very likely to bear a strong resemblance to the practice of old-fashioned 'introspectionist' psychology. This is because the concepts concerned are b-concepts as defined above (p. 45), i.e. ones of which it is an essential feature that they may correctly be applied in making judgments regardless of whether or not any given publicly observable state of affairs obtains. In attempting to analyse such concepts one has continually to ask oneself questions about the states of affairs in relation to which they *may* correctly be applied, and these states of affairs are *not*, or not *all*, publicly observable. They are in short 'mental' states or events. We should wish to add that such states or events are not *privately* observable either (cf. chapter 10), but this does not mean that we regard a systematic study of the phenomenology of mental processes as impossible or illegitimate. (In much 'introspectionist' psychology the borderline between conceptual analysis and empirical enquiry is extremely hard to make out.)

We must next consider what sort of empirical problems might be investigated within the confines of an hermeneutical psychology. An immediate answer might be that the principal task of the hermeneutical psychologist will obviously be to supply hermeneutical explanation of actions. However, a little reflection shows that this answer is over-simple. Just as in hermeneutics it is only obscure texts that require elucidation, so in hermeneutical psychology it is only the relatively small number of individual actions whose 'meaning' is not clear that requires examination. We do not need a psychologist to tell us why a mother stops her child from running into a busy road or why the child tugs her mother to the toyshop window. Our understanding of these actions is, in a real though limited sense, complete, and it is not founded upon generalizations drawn up after the observation of numerous comparable incidents. No amount of psychological study could enable us to clarify the 'meaning' of such actions better than the agent's nextdoor neighbour who well knows his concerns and interests. Nor is it in general the task of the hermeneutical psychologist to frame statistical generalizations about the actions that people will commonly carry out when confronted with a certain set of circumstances, and then to explain what 'meaning' those actions had for those agents in those circumstances. In many cases at least the answers will be obvious to all and sundry.

Is hermeneutical psychology, then, to be primarily a matter of conceptual analysis? By no means. To begin with there are always *some* actions whose 'meanings' are obscure even to the agents, and some reliable generalizations about how people act in particular circumstances of which the explanation is not at once apparent. In the former class come many psychopathological symptoms, and perhaps also actions or action sequences done in accordance with rules which the agent cannot himself formulate. In the latter come such findings as that the threat of mild punishment may be more effective in producing conformist behaviour than the threat of severe punishment (Aronson and Carlsmith, 1963; Freedman, 1965), and that a person in trouble or difficulty is less likely to receive help if a group of persons is present than if a single person is (Latané and Rodin, 1969). It is a task of the hermeneutical psychologist to seek out or deliberately attempt to bring into being such anomalous findings; for they will tend to have both theoretical and social importance. And it is also his task to explain the findings, to elucidate by any method that he can the 'meanings' which the actions had for the agents. This task is completed when after psychotherapy the patient comes to understand that his strange action was a symbolic piece of aggression against his father; or when an agent comes, through 'thought experiment', to be able to formulate more clearly the rules which have all the time guided his behaviour; or when, through further experimentation, or through questioning of the subjects, it becomes apparent that self-restraint occasioned by a mild threat has a different 'meaning' from self-restraint occasioned by a severe threat (in the latter case the self-restraint is carried out in the context of simple fear, whereas in the former case the agent tends to *justify* his self-restraint by seeing his action in the context of moral rules); or when it similarly becomes apparent that to someone in a group part of the 'meaning' of the action of helping the distressed person would have been the infringement of the group's collective inactivity, or that to someone in a group the inactivity of the group might alter the perceived situation in such a way as to minimize the supposed need for intervention and hence to change the 'meaning' of intervention from that of an act of duty to that of an act of supererogation. Once the formerly 'obscure' meanings of these various actions have been made clear, so that the actions are now as well understood as the commonplace actions which everyone can comprehend, this stage of the hermeneutical psychologist's task is over.

However, it may in some circumstances prove impossible to interpret a particular action without first assigning an interpretation to the action-sequence of which it is a member; impossible, as it were, to interpret a word or a phrase except in the context of an interpretation perhaps tentatively assigned to a paragraph. This will be especially the case if the views of certain psychopathologists are valid. For instance, according to Laing and others some sorts of psychopathological symptoms are to be regarded as attempts by a sufferer who is somehow 'cut off' from his fellows to communicate with them. They can be interpreted in the light of the sufferer's history. Similarly, according to psychoanalytic doctrines, neurotic symptoms are to be interpreted as symbolic expressions of unconscious and repressed desires and purposes. The key to the interpretation of any symptom lies in the complex of symptoms of which it is a part taken in the context of the history of the sufferer and his response to various suggested interpretations. Another realm in which interpretation of 'words' or 'phrases' can be undertaken only in conjunction with the interpretation of 'paragraphs' might be, for example, that of the religious and other ceremonies of an alien culture. One could hardly assign a 'meaning' to some individual action within a ceremony without hazarding some kind of interpretation of the ceremony as a whole.

Once the interpretation of an action has been agreed upon a whole range of further empirical problems suggest themselves. Were the actions typical of their agents? Of the members of that society? If so, how did they come to be thus typical? How did each agent acquire the concepts and rule-systems and goals and beliefs and attitudes which gave his action its 'meaning'? Are they characteristic of his society, or of all societies? Did he work them out for himself? Were they imposed upon him by some influential and persuasive person, or by a group of which he is a member? How did he come to regard that action as a step on the road to that goal? Did he reason it out? If so, how did he come to reason as he did? Do all members of his society reason like that? Did his reasonings reflect universal features of all processes of reasoning? How did he come to choose that action out of those open to him as the best way of promoting his goal? Was it through balancing the probability of a successful outcome against the amount of effort needed? Or was it mere superstition? How did he come to be pursuing that goal at that moment instead of some other one of the goals which he has? Such questions branch out in all directions. There is no apparent end to them and they do not seem to fall into any clear order or system.

They do, however, for the most part have this in common. They are questions about how the factors involved in instances of the hermeneutical explanations of actions – such factors as the agent's intentions, attitudes, desires, concepts, beliefs, emotions, hopes, expectations, plans, schemes, appreciation of the rational connection between relevant propositions, and views as to what is expected of him in his society – came to be as they were at the time when the agent carried out the action concerned. One might say that, in a sense broader than that commonly adopted, they are nearly all 'developmental' questions. And the provision of answers to such questions may have at least the following function. Whereas in the absence of answers to such questions the 'meanings' of different actions could be related to each other only through some arbitrary method of classification and listing (so that all cases in which, for example, an agent did what he did in order to catch a train are flung together), given coherent and empirically verified answers it becomes possible to exhibit the different 'meanings' of different actions as having arisen through the operation of similar processes, and hence as systematically related in a non-arbitrary manner.

Now, of course, substantial parts of current social and developmental psychology are of relevance to these 'developmental' questions. There have been extensive investigations of such matters as: the development and change of beliefs and attitudes through persuasion, rationalization, propaganda, group pressures, etc., the aetiology and progress of social deviance; the acquisition of values and goals; the relationship between values and choices; the principles of rational choice between different possible routes to the same goal and between the pursuit of different goals; induction into and the playing of roles guided by rules prevalent in a society; social pressures towards conformity and consistency in role-playing; the development of prejudices and of hostility to outgroups; the effect of educational practices upon reasoning ability; the processes of socialization and of induction into a culture with all that that involves; the question of whether aggressive or affiliative tendencies are genetically determined and of the extent to which their expressions may be culturally shaped. Plenty of materials for the construction of this part of an hermeneutical psychology already exist. But, of course, one cannot evade one very obvious yet very important problem. Most of the findings are the result of work carried out only within Anglo-American cultures. Is there any reason to suppose that findings obtained from these cultures will hold true cross-culturally? It is difficult to give any firm answer, but many writers have doubted it, and it is in many instances far from easy to see how the relevant comparisons could be made. Different cultures may have developed so differently that the same categories of potential influences upon development may not exist in all of them. That being so, the natural pressure of this part of hermeneutical psychology is probably towards the study of development in early infancy. For the factors influencing neonates throughout the world are more simple and more similar than the factors influencing adults, so that one might reasonably hope for greater clarity in the findings. Indeed, it seems likely that some of these primeval factors operative in infancy may have important effects upon the whole of an individual's subsequent development, including his development in adulthood. Furthermore what one can study in infants is not just the genesis of this or that concept, intention or belief or attitude or rule-system, but, as it were, the genesis of intending, the genesis of acting, the genesis of believing, the genesis of the comprehension and following of rules. One can study, in short, not just how the factors which determined the 'meaning' of such and such an action came to be as they were at the time of the action, but the genesis and development of the general factors which make meaningful action possible. Here, if anywhere, one will find it possible to make cross-cultural generalizations.

At this point we must insert two warnings. The first is that in studying and attempting to understand these developmental processes it is important to resist the obvious temptation to try to derive action from non-action, the conceptual from the non-conceptual, the intentional from the non-intentional and so forth; in other words, to make it appear that the infant's coming to act, to have concepts, frame goals and intentions and so on, is the upshot of some synthesis or compounding of behavioural (or, for that matter, mental) elements each individually non-conceptual and non-intentional. This has been a perennial temptation in psychology, but the argument of a good part of this book has been that it is fatal to give way to it. The development of the conceptual and the intentional can only be thought of as a process of the differentiation and unfolding of capacities in an organism which is not non-conceptual and non-intentional, but rather inchoately proto-conceptual and proto-intentional, or latently conceptual or latently intentional. We must use the framework notions of hermeneutical psychology, in other words, everyday psychological notions, even when discussing and investigating the behaviour of the neonate. We shall later on (chapter 13) cite empirical studies which suggest how a child's mother in interaction with him brings out and directs these latent capacities.

The second warning is as follows. We have talked as though an hermeneutical psychology will have two distinct aspects, interpretative and developmental; but it is readily apparent that any attempt to study processes of development will from time to time involve further interpretations of action, indeed of 'paragraphs'. For one cannot chart processes of development, long-term or short-term, without asking oneself how certain of the agent's past actions are to be interpreted, indeed without asking oneself whether or not he had some overarching purpose or plan for self-development which would limit the possible interpretations of whole 'paragraphs' of his actions. Further, one can hardly gain an understanding of developmental processes in general, or in particular cases, without asking oneself how at the time other people interpreted the actions of the agent or the agents concerned. For how other people respond to one may profoundly influence the development of one's desires, beliefs, intentions, principles, etc.

We have now briefly indicated some of the sorts of empirical problems which might be investigated within the framework of an hermeneutical psychology. We shall next consider the form which the results of those investigations will be likely to take.

It would, of course, be rash to assert at this stage that an hermeneutical science of human action will necessarily have such and such a shape or form. It does, however, seem probable that the shape of such a science will differ importantly from that commonly attributed to the conventional physical sciences. For an interpretation of the 'meaning' of an action, an interpretation which enables us to see why the agent did what he did can, as it were, stand on its own feet. Its explanatory power requires no support from statistical generalizations to the effect that other agents in that society, when similarly placed, do the same things, indeed do the same thing for the same reasons. Such generalizations may be of interest or value to us in posing a problem or revealing a fact about the behaviour of a certain group of people. But we cannot by relating a particular instance to such a generalization (as we might in physical science relate an individual event to the 'causal law' or 'covering law' which it exemplifies) explain why the agent did what he did. We understand why an agent did what he did when we grasp the intentions, desires, etc., from which he acted, and the belief or rule-systems which constrained or affected his choice of means to his goal or his reasoning about means to his goal. Whether anyone has ever had those beliefs or those intentions or gone through those processes of reasoning before is irrelevant to our understanding of the present case. Thus in an hermeneutical psychology the interpretation and explanation of individual action can be carried on to a large extent independently of any generalizations about how most people act in such sets of circumstances.

It might be replied here that although it is true that we could certainly in some cases, at least, fully understand the actions of an agent whose intentions, beliefs and reasonings were all quite novel to us, indeed without parallel in the history of the globe, still this would not show that our 'understanding' was not at root the subsumption of the present instance under some generalization or law based on past observation or experience. For have we not based upon past experience generalizations like, 'Anyone who has an intention will do whatever in the light of his beliefs and reasonings, and of other relevant conceptual systems which he may possess, may seem to him most propitious for the furtherance of that intention.' Under such generalizations we can subsume as instances the actions of agents whose particular intentions, beliefs, reasonings, conceptual systems, etc., are completely unprecedented; just as we can, say, subsume under observationally established laws of celestial mechanics the motions around each other of the members of a binary star system whose particular masses are unique in our experience.

However, this analogy breaks down for a variety of reasons. In the first place, our understanding of human actions seems, generally speaking, not to involve explicit or implicit reference to any 'generalization' or 'covering law'. We understand actions directly, in so far as they are the rational outcomes of intentions and belief-systems of which the implications are clear to us. In the second place, as we shall argue in chapter 8, the sequences of events involved in ratiocination and discursive thinking (and the proper interpretation of an action commonly requires reference to the agent's processes of ratiocination) do not readily lend themselves to analysis in terms of 'causal laws'. And in the third place, the state-ment, 'Anyone who has an intention will do whatever in the light of his beliefs and reasonings, and of other relevant conceptual systems which he may possess, may seem to him most propitious for the furtherance of that intention', seems clearly to express not an induc-tive generalization about what as a matter of fact is true of those who have intentions, but part of what is meant by the term 'inten-tion'. The statement, 'Anyone who has an intention will do what-ever may seem to him least propitious for the furtherance of that intention', is a self-contradiction rather than an erroneous inductive generalization. And it is self-contradictory not because of a *post hoc* decision or convention to the effect that we shall henceforth call 'intentions' only those intentions which are, as a matter of fact, followed by the agent's doing that which seems to him most propiti-ous for their furtherance. It is self-contradictory because it is intrin-sic to the state of intending that the agent regards as to be done by him, and *a fortiori* tries to do, whatever actions strike him as conducive to the fulfilment of his intention.[2]

It thus appears that the results obtained by an hermeneutical psychology will differ in an important respect from the results which it has often been thought the task of science to produce. Scienti-fic endeavour, it has commonly been supposed, results in the for-mulation of inductive generalizations about regularly recurrent sequences of events ('causal laws', 'covering laws'), and scientific explanation involves the subsuming of individual cases under the generalizations. But in hermeneutical psychology there is very often a divorce between explaining a particular action (i.e. 'interpreting' it as arising from the intentions, etc., of the agent in a manner understandable to more or less rational human beings), and any generalizations, however suggestive or practically valuable, which we may be able to lay down about how human agents in our society will usually act in that kind of situation. We do not need to refer to the generalizations in order to understand the actions, nor does it seem that in most cases reference to the generalization adds anything to our understanding of the actions. We 'understand' why people who have intentions do what they believe most likely to fulfil those intentions because we know 'from the inside' that this is part of what is involved in having an intention. And there is no other way of knowing what is involved in having an intention. To intend is, as we shall argue in chapters 9 and 10, in part to conceive in a characteristic way, to exercise a certain sort of conceptual capacity, and a person devoid of this form of conceptual capacity could neither intend nor acquire knowledge about intentions. Thus one's understanding of intentions depends upon one's capacity to intend and not upon the observation of numerous examples of intending.

We suggested a little while ago that the actual interpretation of actions will probably play only a modest part in the actual practice of hermeneutical psychology, a good deal of which is likely to be concerned with the 'developmental' side of things, with explaining how the factors which must be referred to in interpreting the actions of an individual or of a number of individuals in a certain situation came to be as they were at the relevant time. However, it seems likely that even in the results of these 'developmental' studies there will not infrequently be a comparable divorce between our 'understanding' of the developmental processes and the descriptive or statistical generalizations which we may be able to formulate concerning them. For in order to explain why the factors referred to in an instance of hermeneutical explanation came to be as they were at the relevant time one might well have to consider such matters as: the development of a certain intention or strategy as a rational means to the fulfilment of a certain antecedent or longstanding desire; development of and change in belief-systems as a result of rational reflection; why someone's prior reasoned reflections took one course rather than another; the diversification of an established purpose or strategy as the result of reflection and increased information; whether a person's current 'attitudes' have been rationally arrived at as a result of, or despite, the persuasions and propaganda to which he has been subjected; an agent's having deliberately, and as a matter of conscious policy, paid attention to certain aspects of his environment; and so and so on. Where, as in these instances, we have, in arriving at an account of how the factors referred to in an hermeneutical explanation came to be as they were, to invoke intentions, desires, beliefs, processes of reasoning, etc., we are again utilizing explanations which rely upon the 'understanding' which we, as human agents capable of intending, desiring, believing, reasoning, etc., have of intentions, desires, beliefs, reasonings, and their likely upshots. We are not utilizing explanations which relate particular instances to inductively established 'causal laws'.

The divorce between explanation and inductive generalization which becomes evident in hermeneutical psychology reinforces the suggestion which we made earlier that conceptual analysis must figure prominently in such a psychology. For since most action-explanations will depend upon the non-inductive understanding which we all have of desires, intentions, actions, etc., and their interrelations, the principal way open to us to amplify such explanations will be to sharpen this non-inductive understanding and to make explicit what is latent or implicit in it. And to sharpen such a non-inductive understanding of, for example, intention simply *is* to investigate one's concept of 'intention'.

So much by way of brief commentary upon the form which the results of empirical investigations conducted within the framework of an hermeneutical psychology will be likely to take. What of the closely related question of the methods which such a psychology will use in its empirical investigations? We certainly cannot dogmatize here. No rational method of inquiry that has prima facie relevance to a particular problem need be rejected out of hand. We shall therefore confine ourselves to making one central point, viz. that we must not suppose that the classical methods of science, as many psychologists have conceived or misconceived them, will have frequent applicability. We must not, that is, expect often to proceed by detachedly observing regularly repeated event-sequences, varying the possible variables until we are sure that events of class A 'cause' events of class B, and embodying our findings in descriptive generalizations or 'causal laws'. And this will hold true even when we are engaged not in the activity of 'interpreting' actions, but are trying to arrive at statistical generalizations about the actions which people in a certain culture are likely to carry out in certain circumstances, or about the processes of development which have led to those agents acting in that way in those circumstances.

A primary reason for this is, of course, simply that in very many cases the sort of class A events and the sort of class B events we will be interested in are not susceptible of a culture-neutral definition, of a definition which would be comprehensible to any detached observer of the flux of events. For example, an act of deliberate aggression, one whose 'meaning' to both aggressor and target is 'deliberate aggression for such and such an end', would (unless of the crudest kind) in most cases be recognizable as such only by persons thoroughly versed in the language, rules and customs of the relevant culture. A certain act or gesture, for example, may constitute an insult in one culture and not in another. Thus ladies of the Foulah tribe of Africa show respect to someone by bowing with head away from him and posterior towards him; ladies of the Kikuyu tribe and in the East End of London perform a very similar action as a gesture of insult and derision. Now you cannot come to grasp the language, rules and customs of a society by the sort of detached observation and classification of events that a scientist trained in the orthodox physical sciences is supposed to practise. The important classes of events cannot (as we have just pointed out) be defined in these terms. A physical scientist who attempted to describe a football match by setting forth statistical generalizations about the movements of the players in the red shirts and the movements of the players in the green shirts would have totally failed to grasp what was going on (cf. Searle, 1969, p. 52). The rules, concepts and rule-regulated activities which constitute a culture are far more complex than the rules, concepts and rule-regulated activities involved in playing a game, and understanding of them cannot be achieved by noting physical regularities in the behaviour of the participants. Hence the 'classical methods' can, even in apparently favourable cases, often be applied only after procedures have been gone through which are quite alien to them. (What the procedures are by which an adult may come to comprehend an alien culture is a question indeed. We shall discuss in chapter 13 some of the ways in which a child is inducted into his culture.)

When it comes to actual interpretation of individual actions classical methods will have practically no part to play. To understand the 'meaning' of someone's actions, why he did what he did, one may need to ascertain his current beliefs about the world and his situation in it, and the moral and social rules by which he regulates his conduct. How, for example, does one come to understand the scarcity of good Samaritans when people in a crowd see someone in distress, and their relative frequency when the same people encounter the victim on their own? Essentially by finding out what the people concerned thought it was appropriate to do in group and non-group situations, what they thought their duty was, and by finding out in what way the presence of others altered their view of the gravity of the victim's condition ('if nobody's taking any notice he can't be very bad . . .'). And finding out these things is best achieved not by further controlled experimentation but by discussion with the experimental subjects, question and answer, in a sort of conceptual analysis of the concepts particular to those subjects in that situation. Only by such analysis can the subjects' actions be interpreted and understood.

The problem gets even more complicated with investigations (which we shall touch upon later) of mother-child interactions during the early processes of socialization. For here the mother is, as it were, conducting her own analysis of the child's nascent concepts, working out what behaviour will be implied by his possession and what by his non-possession of such and such a concept, while at the same time the investigator is trying to keep track of the mother's concepts, the child's concepts, and the mother's concepts of the child's concepts.

It is, however, possible to conceive of what are in effect conceptual analyses relevant to the 'interpretation' of action being conducted by what could certainly be called experimental methods. If one has reasons for supposing that a particular group of people hold, and regulate their conduct in a certain area by reference to, certain fairly circumscribed concepts or rule-sets, one can proceed to manipulate their current situation in such a way that one can say on the basis of one's own understanding of the concepts or rule-set, 'If they hold concept-set $\{C1C2C3\}$ and rule-set $\{R1R2R3\}$, then they ought to do so and so in this situation; for in terms of these concepts or those rules this situation will be a such and such, and these concepts or rules imply or prescribe doing so and so in a situation of that sort.' Recent experiments utilizing the notion of 'distributive justice' (Homans, 1961) are somewhat of this character (Stephenson and White, 1968; 1970), and we shall discuss the 'conceptual' component in such investigations in chapter 12.

An important point here is that one must not regard the vindication of such an hypothesis as directly yielding a descriptive generalization about the behaviour or mental processes of the persons involved. The fact that the members of a certain group regulate their thought or behaviour in terms of a certain concept- or rule-system (perhaps one to which they cannot give an adequate verbal formulation) does not mean that we can elevate that concept- or rule-system into a law-like description or set of descriptions of their thought or behaviour, standing to that thought or behaviour as do, for example, the laws of Newtonian mechanics to the motions of heavenly bodies. Psychologists have in the past been somewhat prone to make this error, the most notorious example being nineteenth-century attempts to treat the rules of logic as law-like descriptions of thought-process.[3] No doubt some have of late been similarly tempted by the formal rule-systems of transformational grammar. But such a procedure would be quite misconceived. It is impossible to turn a set of rules or prescriptions or regulative concepts into a set of descriptions of the behaviour of people following the rules or prescriptions. For in the first place it is essential to the activity of the people concerned that they are *following rules*, and this fact is entirely by-passed by a set of simple descriptions of their behaviour. In the second place the thought or behaviour which is regulated by the rules cannot be identified with the behaviour which is prescribed by the rules. For example one's behaviour of correcting an error, of bringing one's activity back into line with the rules, is not prescribed by the rules, yet it is certainly regulated by the rules. And in the third place one's thought and behaviour can be regulated by rules which, if 'translated' into description, do not describe one's thought or behaviour or anyone's thought and behaviour. For example the rules of chess are stated in terms of the 'powers' of the pieces. The definitions, axioms and rules of the propositional calculus do not prescribe manipulations which are to be made by people using the propositional calculus. They define the conceptual framework within which the manipulations are possible. 'Translated' into a 'description' of the thought and behaviour of students of logic working examples, they would be vacuous, inapplicable.

When one proposes that a certain group of people are guiding their behaviour in terms of a certain concept- or rule-system, and that their actions must be interpreted in that light, one is not propounding, in terms of those rules or concepts, a descriptive generalization about their thought or behaviour and then testing the truth of this generalization. What one is doing is, working out for oneself the moves one thinks they would make in certain circumstances if one's hypothesis about the rules they have accepted is true. One is working the rules oneself and noting their implications. One is, as it were, running with the people whose thought and behaviour one is studying, and not standing back and looking at them in the manner of the (putative) detached scientist. This is an important method in hermeneutical psychology, and what one gains is an understanding through participation, even if only imaginary participation, not an understanding derived from generalizations about the regular recurrences of events. This sort of understanding can be committed to paper in a systematic form; but, of course, one will need as many pieces of paper as there are people following different sets of rules. Here we return to the problem touched on above, of whether any of the findings of hermeneutical psychology are likely to hold true across cultures.

A final issue upon which we must make some brief comments is this. The quantity of reported findings from the world of orthodox psychology has now grown almost unbelievably large. The writers of ten substantial psychology textbooks could cut ten different swathes through the available material and never intersect, the more so since the number of agreed generalizations to emerge from this material is vanishingly small. In what way, if at all, do these findings bear upon an hermeneutical psychology? Which of them must be incorporated and which rejected? Let us consider the different branches of psychology in turn.

We have already dwelt upon some of the findings of social and developmental psychology and related fields, and made it clear that, though social psychology must surely hold the leaden trophy for sesquipedalian verbiage, we think many of its results are of potential relevance to hermeneutical psychology. We have also said a little about physiological psychology, dwelling mostly on its short-comings so far as advancing our understanding of rational human agents is concerned. This is not to say that a background of physiological information is not necessary for the proper understanding of human behaviour. Furthermore we have neither denied (nor affirmed) the ultimate possibility of a physiological account of agency, action and mental phenomena in general.

Our major difficulties arise over the multitudes of findings hatched under the broad but drab wings of 'experimental psychology'. Its whole tradition has been a mechanistic one entirely opposed to the views presented in this book. A central procedure within this tradition has been to take some everyday term descriptive of psychological function or of a class of psychological phenomena (such terms as 'memory', 'learning', 'attention', 'thinking'), redefine it by fiat so that it can be brought within a simple mechanistic framework,[4] and then carry out experiments and report findings which are supposed to throw light on memory, learning, attention, thinking, etc., as they are ordinarily conceived. But, of course, since memory, learning, attention, thinking, etc., as they are ordinarily conceived are first and foremost conceptual phenomena, phenomena in which the exercise of conceptual capacities is essentially involved, and since after tailoring and redefinition they are no longer conceptual phenomena, or conceptual only in some Pickwickian sense, this experimental work on 'memory', 'learning', 'attention', 'thinking' and so forth, however ingenious and successful, is unlikely to tell us any of the things we should like to know about memory, learning, attention and thinking.

The current state of experimental psychology is certainly not a happy one. A prodigious multiplication of findings has not been clarified and simplified either by a growing number of agreed generalizations, or even by any great unanimity as to which findings are 'genuine' and which are not. In fact quite the reverse. One recent critic (Allport, 1975, p. 142) has remarked:

> Hick's Law, split-span recall, refractoriness, high-speed memory scanning . . . everyone will have his own favourite examples, in which what once appeared clear becomes increasingly confused. But are there actually exceptions? Provoked by Newell's sweeping critique to find some counter-example, I personally drew a blank. In the areas of psychology I happen to be acquainted with, I cannot point to one laboratory phenomenon whose interpretation is secure enough for one to build confidently upon it. Of course, in fields one knows at second or third hand it is different. . . . Well, it may be so.

However, fortunately for us, the problems of experimental psychology are not our problems (a more extensive account and diagnosis of them will be found in Joynson, 1974). We have only to consider the question of whether any of the findings of experimental psychology are likely to be of use to an hermeneutical psychologist, and not the larger question of whether they are likely to be of use to anyone at all. The answer to the former question will, as we have already indicated, very probably be 'not much'. In fact almost the only positive proposal we can make here is this. Experimental psychologists have very commonly so arranged their experiments that their subjects are working at or near the limit of their capacities for that task. This has not been true just in such areas as the study of sensory thresholds or of the resolving power of the eye. As Herriot (1974, p. 4) remarks:

> It has been assumed that the limitations of the system are more important than its potential. Experimental psychologists have asked why we forget more often than they have asked how we remember. They have made tasks difficult by presenting unrelated meaningless items at a fast rate, instead of giving the subject the opportunity to use the immense resources at his disposal in the leisured perusal of a meaningful whole.

Part of the explanation for the popularity of this approach is no doubt that it makes for greater uniformity of results and ready quantifiability of variables. However, be that as it may, in so far as experimental psychology provides us with reliable information about the limits of human capacity, its findings may be of relevance to hermeneutical psychology. Whether or not a person performs a certain action in a certain situation will obviously depend upon whether he can discriminate relevant features of his environment, react sufficiently quickly, take in or memorize so much in the time available. It will obviously also depend not just on what his capacities are, but (a related but also quite different thing) on what he believes them to be. The study of these limitations has perhaps little claim to be called 'psychology': a not dissimilar study of the limits of athletic performances under varying conditions could easily be developed. Still, such as it is, we can hardly deny that its results, *if consistent and reliable*, may be marginally relevant to hermeneutical psychology.

This completes our brief sketch of some of the leading features which an hermeneutical psychology might possess. We have made various proposals about the concepts, problems, methods and results which we think likely to characterize such a psychology. It is, however, important to be clear what we are *not* proposing. We are not proposing at least the following things:

(1) We are *not* proposing that precisely the same framework concepts – action, agency, intention, hope, fear, belief, desire, etc. –

which figure in hermeneutical explanations in our society, will figure in precisely the same form and manner in such explanations the world over. Indeed one might well anticipate that even within our own culture there will be considerable local variations. For instance to understand the actions of persons who believe themselves the special recipients of divine inspiration one might need to introduce some such concept as 'promptings, ostensibly divine', while in the explanation of the behaviour of quietists notions like intention, purpose and desire would be much less prominent than is normally the case. It is alleged that certain Eskimo tribes have a concept of action somewhat different to our own – an agent is someone who reveals what is already latent in nature rather than someone who creates a new object or situation (Carpenter, 1966). According to Needham (1972), the members of some societies possess no words for or concept of 'belief', from which he concludes that belief is not a fundamental psychological category. (One might object, however, that similar linguistic studies could show that Arabs have no concept of camel and Eskimos no concept of snow.) Examples might be multiplied indefinitely of variation in the conceptual settings of hermeneutical explanation, but we do suggest that however numerous the possible variations, each variation represents only a relatively slight departure from, or change of emphasis within, a common central core. For, as we have already pointed out, the concepts concerned are so interrelated that if we are properly to apply one of them to someone's actions or psychological state, we must generally speaking be able to apply all or most of the others. Thus there *could not be* a person in describing whose actions or psychological states the term 'intention' alone, out of the range of everyday psychological concepts, could correctly be used. And a human-like being, to whose behaviour and psychological states no concept from this range, or none of the major concepts (and it is these which hang together most closely), could properly be applied, would be absolutely incomprehensible to us; the being would be an alien one and a wholly incomprehensible form of life, one which we should end by classifying as not human.

(2) We are *not* proposing that the conceptual repertoire of ordinary hermeneutical explanation cannot be enlarged, developed, built upon. For example, many commonplace words describing or evaluating people's personality characteristics refer to the sorts of intentions, desires, goals, hopes, beliefs, fears, etc., that they characteristically cherish, and hence to the sorts of 'meanings' their

actions have for them. Consider such words as 'vindictive', 'sociable', 'patriotic', 'intellectual', 'domineering', 'lecherous', 'benevolent', 'practical', 'religious'. These words are, as it were, superordinate terms which can be used to tell us the nature of large numbers of a given person's actions, intentions, desires, beliefs, etc. The psychologists of personality also have developed a specialist vocabulary of terms which are in part superordinate to these terms, and which therefore in part derive their meaning from them. In Cattell's terminology, for instance (Howarth and Cattell, 1973, pp. 802–5), we find such 'personality factors' as *Autia* ('Unconventional, eccentric, aesthetically fastidious, sensitively imaginative, "a law unto himself", occasional hysterical upsets, intellectual, cultural interests'), *Parmia* ('Adventurous, likes meeting people, shows strong interest in opposite sex, gregarious, genial, responsive, kindly, friendly, frank, impulsive ... self-confident') and *Radicalism vs Conservatism* in a much wider than political sense. We certainly cannot say a priori that such terminological innovations are illegitimate or without point.

(3) We are *not* proposing that in all cases an agent is himself the supreme authority as to the 'meaning' of what he does, that he is always fully aware of his desire or his intentions or of the rules and beliefs by which he shapes his actions. The literature of psychopathology is full of cases in which this has apparently not been so. This is a vast and difficult subject, and one which we cannot consider in detail here. There is also another sense in which one's actions may have a wider 'meaning' than one is aware of. An action may have a meaning in the context of a concept or rule-system which the agent but dimly understands, and which perhaps only a few persons fully comprehend. A simple example would perhaps be the casting of a vote at a general election by a voter who has only a minimal grasp of the complex electoral and parliamentary institutions in which he is an almost unknowing participant. But here we cross into the realm of sociology.

(4) Although we have argued that the everyday framework of psychological concepts, comprising the concepts of intention, belief, desire and the rest, is ineradicable from the explanation of human action, we are *not* proposing any special status for 'common-sense' psychological generalizations couched in those terms, for pieces of proverbial wisdom and old wives' tales.

(5) We are *not* proposing that physiological explanation of human action is *impossible*, or that the mind is (or is not) something

over and above the functioning of the brain. We do, however, make the following two claims. (a) No physiological (or other) account of human action which does not *incorporate* hermeneutical explanation can get off the ground. For, as we argued in chapter 1, hermeneutical concepts such as 'intention' are ineradicable from the explanation of human action. (b) No account of human actions cast, as all extant speculations in physiological psychology are cast, in terms which permit of formal paralleling on GM, could incorporate hermeneutical explanations. If physiological psychology is to advance in this area it must look, presumably along the frontiers of physics, for physical concepts and theories which are not of this 'mechanistic' kind. Further, its most fruitful area of research might be to investigate the influence which an agent's beliefs about the functioning of his nervous system may have upon its actual functioning.

(6) We are *not* proposing that it is *never* appropriate to offer causal explanations of human actions and of aspects of human actions, still less are we claiming that it is never appropriate to offer causal explanations of the processes which we have called 'developmental'. We would, however, claim with regard to the explanation of actions (a) that as a rough approximation the more deliberate and carefully thought out an action is (and, hence, often the more significant it is in the life of the agent), the less likely it is to be subsumable under any 'causal law' or statistical generalization, and (b) that even in those cases where an action seems most readily susceptible of causal explanation, the causal law or statistical generalization concerned is likely to have its being only within a context which requires description in hermeneutical terms. For example, one might explain a certain action, say saluting a person wearing a peaked cap, as the effect of alcohol, hypnotic suggestions, hardening of the arteries, or long and robotizing years in the army. And it may be perfectly true that one can lay down as an empirical generalization, based on experience of comparable cases, that had the agent not been drunk, hypnotized, arteriosclerotic or subjected to military training, he would not have saluted as and when he did. None the less, it is equally the case that had the action of saluting not in the past acquired a certain 'meaning' for the agent, as a symbolic gesture that it is appropriate or imperative under pain of sanctions to make before an officer, he would not have saluted as and when he did. And very similar problems may well arise with regard to the sorts of causal explanations which are offered of developmental

processes (it is to be noted that many of them are explanations of abnormalities of development). For instance, it might be laid down as a causal law, or at any rate a statistical generalization, that a child which is systematically rewarded for socially acceptable behaviour and punished for socially unacceptable behaviour will come in the course of time in general to act in a socially acceptable manner. And then one could say of some instance of a child's behaving acceptably, 'He would not have done that had he not been systematically rewarded and punished, etc.' Still, the question must arise of *what* the child has thus learned. Has he learned simply to make certain movements in response to certain stimulus situations, or has he learned to carry out actions with a certain 'meaning', a 'meaning' which derives in part from the 'meanings' which the social situations he finds himself in have acquired for him? These possibilities could in principle be empirically separated, and the argument of this book has been that only one answer is conceivable. Even though we may lay down what looks like causal law, relating the training which children undergo to their development of socially acceptable (or unacceptable) behaviour, the 'law' concerned has its being only within the conceptual framework of an hermeneutical psychology. And this framework, as we have seen, is incompatible with the mechanistic-causal framework of physical science as that has not uncommonly been conceived.

One might compare the regions of human behaviour to which hermeneutical explanations are applicable to the tip of an iceberg. They are supported by, and depend for their eminence upon, much larger areas within which hermeneutical explanation does not hold sway. The relationships between the respective spheres of applicability of the two sorts of explanation, and hence between the explanations themselves, are extraordinarily complex and difficult to elucidate. We do not profess to have any special clues for unravelling these relationships, and the problem is made even harder by the existence of areas in which, as we noted above, ostensibly causal explanations have applicability, but only in an hermeneutical setting.

(7) We are *not* proposing that the adoption of an hermeneutical framework for the psychology of human action will lead to any immediate and drastic revolution in the kinds of work which psychologists undertake. We should rather expect certain changes of emphasis. Conceptual analysis will, as we have already indicated, play a larger role than heretofore. This will not just be because the

framework concepts of hermeneutical psychology for various reasons stand in need of analysis (cf. p. 78 above); it will be because to understand the 'meaning' which an action has for the agent at the moment of acting we will frequently need to discover how he conceived his action, the situation he was in, and the bearing of his action upon his situation. Practical investigations, both interpretative and developmental, will often be conducted, and their results set down and explained, in terms of the everyday psychological concepts which constitute, or dwell within, the framework of hermeneutical psychology (cf. chapter 13); and past studies, conducted in other and more pretentious terms, will be correspondingly reconsidered and reinterpreted (cf. chapter 12). The chief benefit to psychology (apart from bringing its concepts into line with the problems it has to tackle) will be the easing of an intolerable pressure – the pressure to build up a 'science' like the 'hard' sciences in which particular phenomena are to be explained by relating them to universally applicable systems of causal laws. Once we admit that this ideal is impossible of attainment, and admit further that we often have an understanding of why people acted as they did, and of why they developed as they did, which is in no way based upon induction from observed series of past similar instances, we shall no longer find ourselves tempted, in the desperate search for scientific respectability, to elevate into 'laws' the concept or rule-systems which constrain the actions of a certain class of people in a certain sort of situation (cf. pp. 90–1 above), or such trivially or definitionally true statements as 'high-status communicators are more persuasive' and 'restrictions on communication result in lower satisfaction for the isolated' (these and other examples are discussed in Joynson, 1974, pp. 1–17). Correspondingly we may anticipate that a higher percentage of psychological endeavour than heretofore will be devoted to problems of immediate practical or social importance. For since the framework of hermeneutical psychology cannot be displaced by, and is unlikely to contain, large-scale 'hypothetical-deductive' theoretical systems of the kind which are prominent in the physical sciences, no one need waste time and energy in attempting to prove or disprove them by empirical investigation. The prime determinant of which empirical investigations are undertaken will be relevance to some practical issue.

Part II

7

Intensionality

In part I of this book we described and contrasted two approaches to the psychological investigation of human action. We called them the 'natural scientific' and the 'hermeneutical', and indicated our reasons for preferring the latter to the former. We then gave a sketchy account of the leading features which an hermeneutical psychology of human action might possess. Our aim in part II will be to illustrate the conceptual and empirical inquiries which might figure in such a psychology. We first (chapters 7–11) attempt to give some examples of the sorts of conceptual analyses which, we argue, will figure prominently in an hermeneutical psychology. In chapter 12 we discuss some current experimental work in social psychology and argue that the findings require reinterpretaion within an hermeneutical framework. In chapter 13 we describe and comment upon examples of the sorts of empirical investigations to which an hermeneutical psychology would naturally lead.

In this chapter we begin on the first of our illustrative conceptual issues. We shall consider each of these issues separately, but we hope to show that they are, in fact, closely interconnected.

During the last couple of decades there has been a good deal of philosophical debate on questions concerning 'intentionality' and the 'mental'. (In this book we shall use the alternative spelling 'intensionality' to make it clear that 'intentions' are only one among the classes of phenomena to which 'intensionality' may be attributed.) This debate springs from a renewed interest in proposals made by Brentano (1874) for distinguishing those phenomena which are the proper subject-matter of psychology from those which are the proper subject-matter of the physical sciences. Chisholm (1960, p. 4) interprets Brentano's proposals as follows:

> Our psychological activities – thinking, believing, desiring, loving, hating, and the like – are 'directed upon' objects, Brentano said, in a way that distinguishes them from anything that is merely physical. Whenever we think, we think *about* some object; whenever we believe, there is *something* we believe. But the objects of these activities need not exist in order to be such objects; the things upon which these activities are directed, or to which they refer, need not exist in order thus to be directed upon or referred to. No physical phenomenon, according to Brentano, has this type of freedom. . . . We can desire or think about horses that don't exist, but we can ride on only those that do.

Intensionality is here represented as a property of mental *phenomena*, and thinking of it in this way has tempted some writers to postulate a realm of immaterial entities to serve as the 'non-existent' objects of intentional activities. Partly, no doubt, because of this development recent writers on the subject have tried instead to devise criteria of 'intensionality' which will distinguish *sentences* which describe or express psychological states of affairs from sentences which do not. A set of criteria propounded by Chisholm (1957, chapter 11) has been especially influential. A sentence is intensional if it fulfils at least one of the following criteria:

(1) A simple sentence is intensional if it uses a substantival expression – a name or a description – so that neither the sentence nor its contradictory implies that there is or is not anything to which the substantival expression truly applies. Thus the truth of 'Diogenes looked for an honest man' does not imply that an honest man existed, whereas the truth of 'Diogenes sat in his tub' does imply that a tub existed.

(2) A sentence which contains a propositional clause is intensional if neither the sentence nor its contradictory implies either that the propositional clause is true or that it is false. Thus the truth of 'Rupert Gould believed that there was a monster in Loch Ness' does not imply either that there was a monster in Loch Ness or that there was not.

(3) Chisholm (1957, p. 171) expresses his third mark of intensionality as follows:

Suppose there are two names or descriptions which designate the same things and that E is a sentence obtained merely by separating these two names or descriptions by means of 'is identical with' (or 'are identical with' if the first word is plural). Suppose also that A is a sentence using one of these names or descriptions and that B is like A except that, where A uses the one, B uses the other. Let us say that A is intentional if the conjunction of A and E does not imply B.

From the statement 'Holmes knows that Jack the Ripper is an English barrister', together with the statement 'Druitt is identical with Jack the Ripper', one cannot infer that Holmes knows that Druitt is an English barrister.

We are not at present concerned with Chisholm's attempt to mark out the domain of psychology. What is of concern is the fact that the verbs which commonly figure in hermeneutical explanations of actions – verbs like 'intend', 'believe', 'desire' and indeed 'act' itself – are obviously ones which, when used as the main verbs of sentences, make those sentences 'intensional', together with the suggestion that phenomena describable only in intensional terms must necessarily elude explanation in non-intensional (including physical) terms. This suggestion is of obvious importance. An argument which might be used to support it runs as follows.

Let us consider any intensional sentence, for example, 'Holmes believes that Jack the Ripper is an English barrister.' The embedded sentence 'Jack the Ripper is an English barrister' must be assumed to have its ordinary meaning. For Holmes's belief will be true or false dependent on whether the embedded sentence taken in its ordinary meaning is true or false. But the truth or falsity of the whole sentence is quite independent of the truth or falsity of the embedded sentence. Now it has been widely supposed that declarative sentences such as 'Jack the Ripper is an English barrister' can be exhibited as truth-functions of sets of simpler sentences, which are truth-functions of statements simpler still, and so on, until some basic descriptive level (for example that of sense-data or of some kind of physical event language) is reached. In the case of the sentence we are considering the process might begin by translating it into: '(For some x) (x is Jack the Ripper and x is a barrister).' But such analyses are manifestly impossible for intensional sentences. Thus 'Holmes believes . . .' cannot on its own be either true or false. 'Holmes believes that Jack the Ripper is an English barrister' can be, but its truth or falsity is independent of the truth or falsity of the sentences upon which the truth or falsity of 'Jack the Ripper is an English barrister' allegedly depends. It appears therefore that an intensional sentence cannot be equivalent in meaning to any concatenation of non-intensional sentences. For the only component sentence which can be teased out of 'Holmes believes that Jack the Ripper is an English barrister' to form the start of a truth-functional analysis is 'Jack the Ripper is an English barrister'. We have already seen that the truth or falsity of the sentences of which this last sentence is a truth-function has no bearing upon the truth or falsity of the original intensional sentence. The meaning of the latter therefore cannot be equivalent to the summed meanings of a concatenation of non-intensional sentences.

Even if this line of argument were valid, it would not show that intensional *phenomena* are not identical with certain sorts of physical *phenomena*. It would, however, force those who believe in their identity to admit that there is a way of describing intensional events or states of affairs which is not reducible to the ways in which physical states of affairs are ordinarily described. This leads directly to the 'different levels of discourse' view of the relationship between psychological explanations of the bodily movements involved in actions and orthodox or mechanistic explanations of the same bodily movements. We argued above (chapter 1) that this position cannot be sustained, and if we are right the 'intensionality' of psychological phenomena is likely to create a disturbing problem for the upholders of mechanism.

However, Chisholm's opponents have confronted him with numerous examples of sentences which, though 'intensional' are obviously not 'psychological', and in many cases are obviously 'physical' (for example Clark, 1965; O'Connor, 1967). Thus Chisholm's first criterion is fulfilled by such sentences as 'This fire needs coal', 'His lungs need oxygen', 'She resembles a mermaid', 'This rabbit will bite anyone who touches it', 'The law forbids drinking and driving', 'He merits a reward'. His second criterion is fulfilled by sentences like 'It is possible that the hypothesis is correct', 'It is obligatory that one pays the entrance fee', 'The law requires that all motorists drive at less than forty miles an hour'. The third criterion is fulfilled by 'It is necessarily true that Caesar's assassin killed Caesar', for from that sentence, together with 'Brutus was Caesar's assassin', it does not follow that it is necessarily true that Brutus killed Caesar. One can of course easily translate

many of these sentences into 'non-intensional' form, for example
'This rabbit will bite anyone who touches it' can be turned into 'If
anyone touches this rabbit it will bite him'. But the same is true of
many psychological statements, for example 'Holmes is firmly convinced that Druitt is Jack the Ripper' could be turned into 'That
Druitt is Jack the Ripper is one of Holmes's firm convictions'.

Chisholm and other writers have attempted to find more satisfactory criteria of intensionality; see especially Lycan (1969). We do
not think that any of them have completely succeeded. However,
their efforts are not our immediate concern.

Some writers of mechanistic convictions (for example Armstrong,
1968; Boden, 1970, 1972) have taken a more positive line than that
of merely collecting counter-examples to Chisholm's position. They
have attempted to show that it is in principle possible to design
mechanical systems whose behaviour has to be described in intensional terms. We shall consider the views of Boden, for her arguments also bear upon other issues which have been our concern.

Boden introduces the notion of a 'model'. Mechanical systems
can contain 'models' of their environments which will adjust the
system's behaviour to those environments. 'Insofar', she goes on to
assert (1972, p. 128), 'as a machine's performance is guided by its
internal, perhaps idiosyncratic model of the environment, the overall performance is describable in intensional terms.' For example,
suppose that a machine had been programmed to move around and
locate potatoes. Then statements describing its behaviour might
fulfil Chisholm's third criterion of intensionality. For from the truth
of 'The machine is trying to find a potato' and 'Potatoes are members of the family *Solonaceae*' it would not follow that 'The machine
is trying to find a vegetable of the family *Solonaceae*'. 'If the
machine's cognitive structure does not include the information that
potatoes are of the family *Solonaceae*, any such statement about its
performance must be false' (1972, p. 128). One might add that the
machine's searching behaviour could be guided by the potato model
even when there were no potatoes, so that it could be said to be
'trying to find' non-existent potatoes. And so on.

There is no doubt that *if* we are prepared to describe a machine's
activities by using, in a humourless and non-Pickwickian way, such
intensional phrases as 'trying to find a potato' our statements will
fulfil one or another of the standard criteria of intensionality. If they
did not they would not be intensional sentences. So the question

which has to be tackled is obviously this. Why does the fact that a machine's behaviour is guided by an internal 'model' of its environment justify, necessitate or make compellingly apposite, the use of intensional sentences in describing its behaviour? We can hardly deal with this question until we have asked ourselves what 'models' are.

Boden quotes two definitions of the term 'model'. The first (1972, p. 125) is from Minsky (1965). 'We use the term "model" in the following sense: To an observer B, an object A* is a model of an object A to the extent that B can use A* to answer questions that interest him about A.' On this definition possession of a 'model' cannot possibly be that which makes apposite the use of intensional sentences in describing a machine's behaviour. For only a system whose activities *already* called for description in intensional terms could, as it were, take readings from the model and refer them to the external world. However Boden also quotes (1972, p. 299) another definition of 'model', this time by K. J. W. Craik (1943, pp. 51, 99; cf. Arbib, 1972):

> By a model we thus mean any physical or chemical system which has a similar relation-structure to that of the process it imitates. By 'relation-structure' I do not mean some obscure non-physical entity which attends the model, but the fact that it is a physical working model which works in the same way as the process it parallels in the aspects under consideration at any moment . . . On our model theory neural or other mechanisms can imitate or parallel the behaviour and interaction of physical objects and so supply us with information on physical processes which are not directly observable to us. Our thought, then, has objective validity because it is not fundamentally different from objective reality but is specially suited for imitating it – that is our suggested answer.

These are famous passages by a famous psychologist, but their meaning is excessively unclear. A phrase like 'works in the same way as the process it parallels in the aspects under consideration at any moment' seems rather to suggest that 'models' are used by some second system which takes readings from them and refers the readings to some feature of external reality. This lands us in the regress previously noted. Even odder is the talk of models supplying us with 'information on physical processes which are not directly observable to us'. This seems to imply that the models in our brains *are* in some sense 'directly observed' by us. However Craik's actual thesis seems to be something like this. The environment in some way stamps its patterns or causal sequences on the brain so that the operations of subsystems within the brain come in some sense to 'parallel' those patterns or causal sequences. The subsystems in the brain are then 'models' of the patterns and causal sequences in the environment in that they are capable of adjusting the behaviour of the organism to the patterns and causal sequences. And obviously it is the adjustment of behaviour to the environment which is of crucial importance. For if models were simply marked out as models because their structure and operations 'paralleled' certain happenings in the outer world, they would be 'models' of events in the Andromeda galaxy if they paralleled them more closely than they paralleled events in the organism's neighbourhood. No doubt it is for this reason that Boden (1972, p. 308) says: 'Appropriate response to the environment . . . is a criterion of having a "model" in the required sense. That is, appropriate response is a sufficient condition of having a model.'

We can now assess the view that the guidance of a machine's behaviour by a Craikian 'model' would make it appropriate to describe that machine's activities in intensional sentences. A good place to begin is with the fact that Boden has, as we noted a moment ago, little option but to work into her definition of 'model' the notion of behaviour 'appropriate' to an organism's environment. 'Models' in the brain have, according to Craik, a similar 'relation-structure' to that which they model. Now let us consider a brain 'model' of, for example, the ebb and flow of the tides (it was Kelvin's tidal predictor that so impressed Craik). Some process or subsystem in the brain functions so as to exhibit a 'similar relation-structure' to that of the cyclic recurrence of the tides. But it will also, of course, have in greater or lesser degree a 'similar relation-structure' to innumerable other cyclically recurrent processes in the universe. Accordingly it is necessary to make 'appropriate response to the environment' a criterion of a 'model'. However all Boden tells us about the notion of 'appropriate response' is that 'In general, an "appropriate" response is one that enables the organism to pursue its various purposes with some success' (1972, p. 308). And she adopts from McDougall criteria of the purposiveness of behaviour (goal-directedness, plasticity, persistence, etc.) in terms of which the 'goal-seeking' behaviour of quite simple organisms can be called purposive. She can thus hardly avoid saying that the tidally linked colour changes of littoral crabs, the tidally linked gaping of oysters, and so on, indicate the operation of 'models'. They fulfil the 'goals' of the organism (baffling predators, obtaining nourishment). The time sequences will change to fit different tidal rhythms. The behaviour is extremely persistent, in fact the colour-changes of crabs and the gaping of oysters will persist for considerable periods in non-tidal aquaria, thus being at a superficial glance 'directed upon' absent phenomena. There is no doubt that in *some* sense such creatures *do* have an inner model of tidal rhythms. And since their responses are undoubtedly 'appropriate' to their environments, they appear by definition to possess 'models' which make the overall performance describable in intensional terms.

No zoologist would dream of saying 'that oyster believes the tide is on the turn' and so forth. What is going on here is fully described by non-intensional sentences, such as 'that oyster is gaping, as oysters always do, with the incoming tide'. Thus the mere fact that a piece of behaviour is guided by a 'model' does not of itself make it apposite to describe that behaviour in intensional sentences. If Boden wishes to convince us that guidance of an organism's behaviour by a model makes apposite the use of intensional sentences in describing that behaviour she must present a more restricted definition of 'model'. Now Boden could sharpen her notion of 'model' in one of two ways. She could tighten her definition of 'appropriateness', or else try to make some particular *kind* of similarity of 'relation-structure' between model and world crucial in rendering the organism's behaviour susceptible of intensional description. We shall try to show that neither of these two courses is open. Let us begin with the first.

Boden links the notion of 'appropriate' behaviour to that of responses enabling an organism to pursue its purposes successfully. She adopts McDougall's criteria of purposive behaviour. These criteria allow one to say that both gaping oysters and rational agents have goals or purposes. Now we might say that an oyster's behaviour was 'appropriate' given its 'purpose' if that behaviour tended to exemplify certain patterns characteristic of oysters, ones tending to promote the nutrition and so forth of the individual and the survival of the species. We could call this sort of appropriateness 'functional appropriateness'. But the behaviour of a rational human agent can be 'appropriate' or not given his purpose in quite another sense. In this sense we cannot possibly know whether someone's behaviour is appropriate or not unless we know his 'purposes' in the strong sense in which purposes are conceived goals, and his beliefs about his environment, i.e. how he currently conceives it. For example a man on the beach moves his chair towards the advancing tide. By the standards of 'functional appropriateness' this behaviour is quite inappropriate. But we may discover that the man is a keen fisherman or that he is King Canute and then we know that *in the light of what he has in mind* his behaviour is perfectly appropriate. Again, if we know that the man's purpose is simply to enjoy a peaceful sleep, we might say that his behaviour is 'functionally inappropriate' given the state of the tide but perfectly 'appropriate' given his beliefs about the state of the tide. We might call this kind of appropriateness 'rational appropriateness'.

Now since behaviour that is 'rationally appropriate' may be 'functionally inappropriate' and vice versa, Boden can only link one or the other to her definition of 'model'. And manifestly it has to be rational appropriateness. For there would be little point in her developing a notion of 'model' in terms of which the non-intensionally describable behaviour of oysters could be called 'model-guided', and the intensionally describable activities of rational human agents could not. But only the behaviour of entities some of whose activities (desiring, intending, believing, etc.) *already require* description on intensional terms could exhibit 'rational appropriateness'. Since Boden has to define 'model' in terms of 'rationally appropriate' behaviour, possession of a 'model' presupposes that an organism's activities are intensionally describable, and cannot explain it. Thus Boden must find some way of excluding the notion of 'appropriateness' from the notion of 'model'.

Could Boden sharpen the notion of 'model' by picking out some particular *kind* of similarity of relation-structure between a 'model' and that which it models? We shall argue that no 'model' could, simply in virtue of having some particular form of Craikian 'similarity of relation-structure' to an environmental event, process or pattern, guide behaviour in such a way that it could properly be described in intensional terms. Suppose that in some mechanistic system a 'model' of tidal processes has been switched into operation and now controls or influences behaviour. To make us attribute intensionality to the system, the model would have to cause the system to behave in such a way as to convince us that it possessed an intelligent understanding of tidal phenomena or at any rate an intelligent misunderstanding of them. The system would have to exhibit some grasp of the defining characteristics of tides, for without that it could not be said to direct its activities in an intensional way upon tides at all. If you do not know what tides are you cannot think about them, act in relation to them and so on. The system would have, at least in a primitive way, to be able to reason about tides, predict future tides, extrapolate to past tides and so forth. For if you do not appreciate the cyclically recurrent nature of tides, you do not know what tides are, cannot think of tides as tides. And *a fortiori* the system would have to be able to recognize tidal phenomena when it met with them. Now clearly the mere controlling of a system's behaviour by a subsystem whose 'relation-structure' paralleled those of tidal phenomena, would never give rise to behaviour exhibiting intelligent understanding of tidal phenomena. For the neural basis of our understanding of tidal phenomena cannot wholly consist of some part of the brain *behaving like a tide*. Tides do not themselves comprehend or understand or act rationally, and accordingly 'models' which parallel them in some respect cannot *ipso facto* be capable of so guiding behaviour as to justify the attribution to those systems of an intelligent understanding of tidal phenomena. It is abundantly clear that in order to show that there may be mechanistic systems to the behaviour of which intensional sentences may properly be applied, Boden cannot lean upon that broken reed, the 'model'. What she has to do is give, in mechanical terms, some account of the (intensionally describable) processes by which models are *utilized*, and, one must add, intelligently utilized. It is to her account of this process of utilization, when she shall give it, that we must look to find arguments demonstrating that mechanical systems may require description in intensional terms.

Chisholm's original criteria of the intensionality of sentences appear to be in effect criteria – not completely successful ones – for picking out sentences which describe conceptual phenomena, i.e. phenomena which involve the exercise of conceptual capacities by some rational agent. We argued in chapter 3 that among the marks of a person's possessing simple object-concepts is the capacity to make judgments, formulate propositions and so forth, about classes of objects, and about individuals considered as exemplars of those classes, both in the presence, but also in the absence (and perhaps despite the non-existence) of a specimen. It does not seem a large step to shift focus from persons to phenomena and say that when the exercise of conceptual capacities is involved in some phenomenon that phenomenon may in effect involve or incorporate making a judgment about or formulating a proposition concerning a state of affairs which may in fact not obtain. We could look at the matter as follows. As we argued in chapter 3, someone who 'possesses concepts' at least has a set of principles of grouping in terms of which he divides up and handles the thus simplified world in which he lives. Facts like the fact that John believes his car is in the garage, or that he desires his lunchtime beer, are, in part, facts about John's present use and application of his ways of dividing up and handling the world. From such facts nothing follows as to whether John is deploying his principles of division in a realistic or viable manner, i.e. nothing follows as to whether his car *is* in the garage or beer *is* on tap.

If we are correct in supposing that the 'criteria of intensionality' amount to criteria for picking out sentences which describe phenomena involving the exercise of conceptual capacities by some rational agent, it becomes quite comprehensible why writers such as Boden assume that if they can make what are in effect mechanical theories of concept-possession seem plausible they have shown that mechanical systems can act in an 'intensional' manner. Such systems may 'search' for non-existent objects of certain specifications and so forth.

It is of course true that the activities of any system which possesses and exercises conceptual capacities will require description in 'intensional' terms. None the less it seems to us that 'intensionality' is a prerequisite of conceptual activity rather than something which can be elucidated by reference to such activity, and that it is better looked upon as a characteristic of active selves or agents than as a characteristic of sentences or of psychological phenomena considered without reference to agents. We may note to begin with that Brentano's original remarks about intensionality or 'intensional inexistence' are moderately obscure, and have not always been paraphrased quite as Chisholm paraphrases them (cf. Macalister, 1974). Thus G. F. Stout (1896), who was much influenced by Brentano, represents him as primarily interested in classifying mental phenomena by means of irreducible differences in the mode in which consciousness refers to an object. According to Stout, Brentano's 'object' is 'an appearance in consciousness', and Stout is concerned to uphold, against Brentano, a view something like

Chisholm's paraphrase of Brentano (I, p. 45): 'If the object exists at all in the sense in which the thinker refers to it, i.e., means or intends it, it exists independently of this consciousness, and the same is true, *mutatis mutandis*, of its non-existence.' According to Stout the function of 'appearances in consciousness' is to define and determine the direction of thought to this or that special object. As to the nature of this thought-reference he says (I, p. 51):

> Objective reference supervening on purely anoetic (i.e. presentational) experience would be a completely new psychical fact. It is the more necessary to note this, as attempts have been made to explain the emergence of the distinction between subject and object out of 'mere feeling,' by supposing special constituents of the total sentience to acquire salience and prominence. This can only mean that special sensations are intensified out of proportion to the rest. But an intensified sensation is merely a sensation intensified, and not, *eo ipso*, the perception of an object.

With these latter remarks we cannot but agree, but they leave us with a problem. For if discriminative thought-processes, i.e. thought which refers to this or that *kind* of object, which divides the furniture of the world into categories and thus involves the exercise of what we called conceptual capacities, cannot be derived from the phenomena of mere sentience, it can, so far as we can see, only be derived from less discriminative thought-processes. Thought must from the very beginning have some tendency to 'point beyond itself' to a 'something' however vague which is other than itself (cf. pp. 83–4 above). Without such a pointing, the process of conceptually dividing the world could not get a toehold from which to begin. You cannot divide up the world in thought unless you have an inkling that there is a world. Without that inkling (which contains within itself the possibility of error) one's experiences could not lead one to the belief in a world of objects. Any process of inference from present data presupposes, and could not arrive at, some apprehension of a reality beyond and outside the immediate thought.

Thus it is in the 'pointing beyond itself' which pervades and characterizes all thought (we are here, with Stout, using the term 'thought' in a very wide sense) that we may find the roots of intensionality; and without this generic 'pointing beyond', the specific conceptual capacities round which Chisholm in effect builds his 'criteria of intensionality' could never have arisen.

It may be remarked in passing that even where the object of thought is one of one's own immediate experiences, thought still 'points beyond' the immediate experience of the moment. As Stout observes (I, p. 44):

> it will be found on examination that whenever we try to think of an immediate experience of our own, we can do so only by investing it with attributes and relations which are not themselves immediately experienced at the moment. For example, I may think of a momentary appearance in consciousness as an occurrence in my mental history, an incident in my experience. But neither my experience as a whole, nor the position and relations of any part within that whole, can be given as the content of momentary consciousness. . . . Again, I may think of the content present in consciousness, abstracted from the fact of its presentation. In this case also I am obviously not thinking of the momentary experience as such at the moment at which it is experienced. The presented content is regarded as something which remains identical through the fleeting moments of its appearance.

We have talked hitherto of thought 'pointing beyond' itself and 'referring to an object', but this is a somewhat misleading way of putting it. It would perhaps be better to say that in thinking the thinker points beyond his momentary self, his self as engaged in thinking *that* thought. For to talk of thoughts 'pointing beyond' themselves is to make them sound like momentary agents in their own right. Furthermore, the object of a thought is not thought of as set over against that thought; it is thought of as set over against the thinker as he now is.

It might well be alleged that expressions like 'pointing beyond' are purely metaphorical, and have no place in serious scientific or philosophical discussion. Our reply would be that we are here discussing a fundamental and irreducible feature, or rather presupposition, of all thought, all conceptual activity and all action, and that our aim is simply to bring it to people's notice, to try to help them to grasp what we are talking about. It can only be noticed or grasped, or not; it cannot be further described or defined. Under these circumstances metaphor is our only recourse.

We are now in a position to understand the failure of Boden's attempt to demonstrate that mechanical systems can be designed whose behaviour could properly be described in intensional terms, and to see why any other similar attempt must also fail. For Boden's procedure was in effect to attempt first to show that a mechanical system might possess 'concepts' in the shape of Craikian 'models' of the external world, and then to show that such 'concept-possession' would make its behaviour describable in intensional terms. Whereas, as we have argued, a system which did not already exhibit intensionality could not develop conceptual capacities. Intensionality is a prior condition of conceptual development.

8

Discursive Thought

We have several times pointed out that the ability to frame and implement long-term intentions is reciprocally involved with the capacity for rational thought. A man who could not think out strategies for compassing his ends could live only from moment to moment, or at best from day to day. Most of us do not live like that. Anyone who wants to understand why one did what one did must find out why one reasoned as one did, and what place one's action had in one's overall rational scheme. Hence among the framework concepts of hermeneutical explanation, the concepts of rationality and of discursive thought have an important place, and we must do our best to clarify them. And it must be said at once that work in this area by psychologists (lucidly reviewed by Bolton, 1972), has been for the most part so vitiated by theoretical presuppositions that illumination is not to be sought from that quarter.

Some philosophers have suggested that there is no problem of defining discursive thought, because the concept of thinking is 'polymorphous' rather than 'monomorphous' (Mouton, 1969). As Ryle (1951, p. 68) puts it: 'There need be nothing going on in one instance of thinking, such that something else of the same species or genus must be going on in another of them.' 'Thinking' is thus like 'working' – any activity of any kind may under some conditions qualify as an instance. The terms 'thought' and 'thinking' are indeed often loosely used to cover almost any way in which a person can make use of his conceptual capacities (cf. Ginnane, 1960). But it would be most extraordinary to propose that different instances of discursive thought may be instances of quite different kinds of activities. Someone who set out to justify such a view by discursive thought would be in a very peculiar position. For anyone who engages in discursive thought is engaging in an activity the aim of which is not just to reach 'conclusions' but to reach them by processes of rational and valid inference rather than by, say, intuition, association or auto-hypnosis. In other words his aim is to exclude from his operations activities which do not fall under the heading of discursive thought. We shall, however, not argue the matter further. Mouton (loc. cit.) criticizes the 'polymorphous' view in detail. We shall assume that the problem of defining discursive thought remains.

It will be convenient to begin by examining the views of A. I. Goldman, whose *A Theory of Human Action* (1970) is a sustained attempt to demonstrate that actions may be brought within the net of orthodox scientific explanation. As part of this programme, Goldman offers a causal account of discursive thinking. It is to be noted that his account is *not* as such an analysis of the concept of thinking. However, we hope that a discussion of it will help to indicate what some of the features of that analysis must be. Goldman distinguishes between *cognitive inferences*, inferences 'in which a person comes to believe one proposition on the basis of his believing one or more other propositions', and *practical inferences*, 'where a person comes to have a certain want on the basis of some combination of other wants and beliefs' (p. 100). As an example of a set of propositions which might figure in a cognitive inference he cites the following:

(*p*):　All men are mortal.
(*q*):　Socrates is a man.
(*r*):　Socrates is mortal.

As an example of a set of 'propositions' which might figure in a practical inference he gives this:

(*k*):　Let it be the case that I eat some pizza.
(*l*):　If I call Domino's and order a pizza, I will be able to eat some pizza.
(*m*):　Let it be the case that I call Domino's and order some pizza.

Philosophers who deny that inference is a causal process have considered only the logical 'because' of '(*r*) is true because (*p*) and (*q*) are true' and of '(*m*) is acceptable because of (*k*) and (*l*)'. Naturally they have concluded that inference is not a causal process.

But this is to confuse the propositions believed with the believings of them, and the expression of what is wanted with the wanting of it.

> There is no causal relation between Socrates being a man, all men being mortal, and Socrates being mortal. But there is a causal relationship between *S's believing (p) and (q)* and *S's believing (r)*. The process in which *S* sees that (*p*) and (*q*) are a good reason for accepting (*r*), and thereupon accepts (*r*), is a causal process. . . . When a person is engaged in practical inference. . . . He is not thinking *about* his own mental states. Now since the successive objects of his thought – viz., (*k*), (*l*), and (*m*) – are not causally related, one would be apt to conclude that the inference process is not a causal one. But while (*k*) and (*l*) do not cause (*m*) – indeed, such an idea would be utter nonsense – *S's* accepting (*k*) and *S's accepting (l)* do cause *S's accepting (m)*. The process in which *S* finds good reason for accepting (*m*), and thereupon accepts it, is a causal process (pp. 100–1, 103).

It is to be noted (1) that Goldman uses the term 'want' in a very extended sense, so that all 'intentions' qualify as 'wants', (2) that by 'want' and 'belief' he means 'occurrent' wants and beliefs rather than 'dispositional' ones and (3) that inferences may take place in a split second, without one's uttering, even to oneself, the relevant sentences.

Three aspects of Goldman's views call for comment. The first is his claim that cognitive inferences and practical inferences are to be regarded as sequences of events causally related. The second is his suggestion that 'practical inference' is a form of discursive reasoning. The third is the idea, not mentioned above, that the relation between the concluding 'want' in a practical inference, and the ensuing action, is an ordinary causal one. The first and second of these proposals will be discussed now. The third will be discussed in the next chapter.

In Goldman's view, then, the 'thoughts' which make up a piece of discursive reasoning constitute a causal chain (cf. Armstrong, 1968, chapter 9; Richards, 1971, p. 56; Nagel, 1961, pp. 398–546). To this position we may advance the following objections:

(1) It leads almost inevitably to 'logical psychologism', the view that logical 'laws' and the normative statements made by logicians are in effect generalizations about the mental processes of thinkers. For if valid and invalid inferences are alike determined by the

antecedent beliefs of the reasoner, it is difficult to see how the two are to be distinguished except either (a) in terms of the causal laws which they exemplify, or (b) in terms of whether or not they conform to patterns of events in the outside world. Since the causal laws are bound to reflect external events, these positions inevitably coalesce. Logical 'laws' are the mental correlates of environmental regularities. If this were so we should expect certain physical truths to have the same sort of compelling necessity as do logical or mathematical ones. Yet we have no difficulty in conceiving the reversal of these physical laws; whereas we cannot conceive its being false that if p implies q, and p is true, then q is true, or that the angles of a plane figure bounded by three straight lines add up to 180 degrees. Again we should expect the mental events involved in reasoning to exhibit regularities of sequence which they do not in fact exhibit (cf. (2) below). However, these issues are very complex, and we cannot pursue them here (cf. Mansel, 1860; Husserl, 1970). We shall instead note

(2) that Goldman's account of the processes of reasoning is psychologically quite unrealistic. Goldman presents inference as an event which supervenes upon two or more occurrent beliefs, or beliefs and wants, and results in the formation of a further belief or want. And something like this sometimes happens. We create a new occurrent and thereafter dispositional belief or want to fit the vacant slot engendered by the logical relations of two propositions previously entertained or states of affairs wanted. But it is no less likely that given three occurrent beliefs successively or simultaneously held we suddenly grasp a hitherto unrealized logical relation between their contents; or that given an occurrent belief which we feel in our bones to be true we search painfully around until we find two other credible propositions which we recognize as 'justifying' it. Here the sequence of events is not Bp, Bq, grasping of relations, Br, but Bp, Bq, Br, grasping of relations, or Br, Bp, Bq, grasping of relations. Causal relations as usually conceived are not thus reversible. They are exemplifications of observed sequential regularities. A world in which events occurred in all sorts of orders would be a world *without causal laws*, and hence without causal relationships.

(3) In the case of cognitive and practical inferences there *could be no such causal laws*. Beliefs and wants can be characterized only by their 'objects', by the states of affairs conceived as obtaining or as desirable. Now the number of such 'objects' is indefinitely large. Hence the number of possible classes of beliefs and of wants is

indefinitely large. If we wish to frame causal laws concerning sequences of beliefs and wants, we must therefore find some way of grouping those beliefs and wants into a manageably small number of categories. For this purpose, there would be no point in attempting to group them in terms of the nature of their 'objects', for example in grouping into one class all beliefs about pigs and into another all beliefs about quadratic equations, for laws (if any) relating sequences of beliefs thus categorized would not yield sequences or beliefs amounting to inferences. It is clear that in the case of beliefs the categorizations would have to be in terms of the 'logical forms' of the propositions believed, and that some equivalent for this would have to be worked out for the case of wants. But at once difficulties spring to mind. If one frames a 'causal law' about the inference-sequences of beliefs in terms of the logical forms of the propositions believed, for example

> If John believes that (All A's are B),
> And that (Some C is A),
> He will come to believe that (Some C is B),

this law will cover not only inferences which anyone might make, but inferences which it is quite impossible that anyone should make, for example, All elephants are crocodiles, some square root is an elephant, some square root is a crocodile. I.e. we have here a 'causal law' which states that if someone has beliefs which it is logically impossible for him to hold, he will draw a conclusion which it is logically impossible for him to maintain. (No one who understood the meanings of the terms 'crocodile', 'elephant' and 'square root' could make these inferences because he would understand that elephants *are not* crocodiles, etc.; he might of course use these terms as dummies to illustrate inference forms but that is another matter.) The equivalent in terms of ordinary causal laws would be (say) a law which implies both that if you pour acid on zinc the latter will dissolve, and that if you pour scorn on gravity the latter will give birth to triplets. This is at best an untidy and absurd situation, and it can only be rectified by reintroducing some reference to the non-logical aspects of the 'objects' of belief. But of course to the extent to which this is done, the original problem will reappear.

(4) Even if causal laws of the kinds in question, i.e. ones specifying regular sequences of beliefs, wants, inferrings, etc., could be established, they would be irrelevant to our understanding of processes of inference and discursive thought. For one could observe

10,000 persons go through precisely similar belief, want and inference sequences and fail to understand why they inferred as they did, or why they stopped when they did, i.e. regarded the inferences as completed. The observed regularities in their belief and inference sequences and in their stopping points would cry out for explanation, and one would only regard them as explained when one had come to understand why those inferences and those stopping points seemed appropriate to the thinkers concerned. Contrariwise, one would have no difficulty in explaining to one's satisfaction some inference unique in the history of mankind, i.e. one which could not possibly relate to some established 'causal law' describing regularly observable belief sequences, and inference sequences, provided that one could grasp the reasoner's premises, line of argument, and the relation between these and his conclusions. That someone reasons correctly requires, generally speaking, no further explanation than that his reasoning is correct.

The idea that there is a species of inference characteristic of thought concerned with the fulfilment of wants, and in which 'wants' are reached on the basis of combinations of other wants and beliefs, is certainly very convenient for writers of Goldman's persuasion, for it enables them to present actions as caused by wants, and wants as the final events in causal chains of 'reasoning' which may begin with other and perhaps longer-term or more fundamental wants. Thus a want, the working out of a means to its fulfilment, and the implementation of that means, can all be made to seem part of the same causal chain. However, the whole notion of 'practical inference' has recently been criticized by Norris (1975). Norris's main points are as follows:

(1) It is not generally true that the sequence of our thoughts in reasoning is isomorphic to the patterns of proofs which may be found, for example, in logic textbooks.

(2) The idea that *wants* might be premises and conclusions in processes of inference owes its plausibility in part to a common, but loose, way of talking about *beliefs*. We use the term 'beliefs' both to refer to mental states or events, and to talk of *what is believed*, and here the term 'proposition' could in effect be substituted. We talk of *his* or *her* present belief that Aristotle is dead, and we also talk of *the* belief that Aristotle is dead. Only in the latter case, that of beliefs as propositions, can we speak of a belief as having been inferred from another belief, as being a premiss or a conclusion.

... in that use of 'belief' in which a belief is a state of some particular person's mind, it is wrong to speak of a belief as if it literally were a premiss or a conclusion; because it is wrong in general to speak of mental states or processes as if they literally were premisses or conclusions (p. 79).

Once this distinction is appreciated it will not seem so plausible to regard wants as premisses or conclusions of arguments. For whereas *what is believed* is always a state of affairs expressible by a proposition, what is wanted may be a physical thing. 'One would be hard pressed to justify insisting on the use of the expressions "he *concluded* (or inferred) a pistol from a watch," or "he believed that a pistol was *a logical consequence* of a watch".' (p. 80)

(3) A position which might be adopted in reply to these arguments is that wanting and believing both involve propositions in much the same way; both consist in pro attitudes to different sorts of propositions (which Goldman calls 'declarative' and 'optative' propositions respectively), or for that matter in different attitudes to the same sort of proposition. Then even though wants are not literally premisses or conclusions, wants and beliefs alike have propositional 'parts', and there is 'no more difficulty in the idea that coming to want something might constitute a case of inferring than there is in the idea that coming to believe something might constitute a case of inferring' (p. 80).

However, to this suggestion Norris replies that one can give an account of the role of wants in rational action in a more conventional way. 'One would propose instead that a want affects an agent's calculations insofar as *some* proposition describing conditions which the agent would recognize as satisfying that want is entertained in the calculation.' (p. 81) Wants are clearly very closely related to such propositions, perhaps even 'logically' related.

(4) The remaining problem about so-called 'practical inference' is simply whether, when we reason in the service of our wants or intentions, the inference patterns which constrain us are essentially different from those which constrain us in any other kind of thinking. Norris holds that the answer is, 'No!' Most of those who believe there is a special form of 'practical reasoning' have conceptualized it as involving

(a) as premiss an expression of a want or intention,
(b) as premiss an expression of a belief about how to fulfil that want,

(c)   as conclusion, an expression of a want or intention to do that
which is specified in (b). For example

> Premiss: 1 Oh would that I could get William's watch.
>
> Premiss: 2 If I acquire a pistol in good working order, then
> I get William's watch.
>
> Conclusion: 3 Oh would that I could acquire a pistol in work-
> ing order.

Norris suggests that the thinking which occurs here is simply
constrained by the commonplace principle of *modus ponens* (if *p*
implies *q*, and *p*, then *q*). One begins by wanting a watch, and one
realizes that one must do something to get it. One has, as it were,
burdened oneself 'with a degenerate case of an enthymeme: an
argument with *all* of its premisses missing' (p. 82). The conclusion
is, 'I get William's watch.' One then engages in a process which
might be called 'premiss hunting', and as soon as one realizes that
there is some set of conditions such that *if* one could satisfy them,
then one would get William's watch, one has accepted the constraint
which *modus ponens* places upon the sort of premisses one will
accept.

One passes from

> Premiss: 1 ?
>
> Premiss: 2 *If* ? *then* I get William's watch.
>
> Conclusion: 3 I get William's watch.

to

> Premiss: 1 I acquire a pistol in good working order.
>
> Premiss: 2 If I acquire a pistol in good working order then I
> get William's watch.
>
> Conclusion: 3 I get William's watch.

Here the first premiss is temporally the *last* proposition which one
entertains or assents to, and, given one's desire to make the conclusion true, one naturally endeavours to make the antecedent true.

(5) Norris believes that supporters of 'practical inference' have
failed fully to grasp two important distinctions. The first is between
psychological descriptions of the order of events in reasoning, and
the patterns of logical proof which constrain those inferences.
'. . . those who would have us suppose that there is a kind of inference, practical inference, peculiar to such cases of reasoning, have
become so entranced by the [putative] temporal order of thoughts
that they get the logic of the situation backwards' (p. 83) and end up
with Premiss 1 as the formal 'conclusion'.

The second is the distinction between a reason and a premiss.

One's 'reasons' for acting as one did are the wants and beliefs which constrained one's rational action. Given one's wants and beliefs what one did was 'reasonable'. But it does not from this follow that one's wants and beliefs found direct expression in the premisses of one's argument. For example in the above example one's wanting a watch was a reason why one did any calculating at all, and it was also a constraint upon the hypothetical propositions which one was prepared to entertain (they had to be ones whose consequent was 'I get William's watch'). One might even say that one of the reasons why one reasoned as one did was one's belief in the validity of *modus ponens* arguments – one accepted *modus ponens* as a constraint in one's 'premiss-hunting'. But *modus ponens*, or the validity thereof, was not *itself* a premiss in one's reasoning, and nor was one's wanting the watch. For (p. 84)

> To say that my wanting the watch, or a proposition associated with my want, was a *premiss* in my reasoning, does not explain anything beyond what we already would have explained by taking note of the facts that my wanting the watch was the reason why I calculated at all, and that my wanting the watch was one of the reasons why the hypothetical which occurred to me had the content it had.

It is now time for us to give some sort of account of the concept of discursive thought. It will be useful if we first list some points that have emerged from the preceding discussion:

(1) The order of events in reasoning is hardly ever isomorphic with the order of steps in a logical 'proof'. The sequence of steps in a logical 'proof' cannot be regarded as giving the form of a 'causal law' describing processes of reasoning.

(2) An essential feature of any process of reasoning is that the reasoner grasps the logical relations between the propositions, and is able through so doing to 'infer' one proposition from another, and to recognize the natural 'stopping point' of his reasonings.

(3) Beliefs or thoughts, *regarded as datable mental events*, cannot be *premisses* or *conclusions* in arguments; for the conclusions of a valid piece of reasoning have a 'timeless' quality, and if valid at time *t*, are valid at any other time.

(4) Reasoning may often plausibly be regarded as a process of 'premiss-hunting', or of finding propositions to fill in gaps in a logical schema.

(5) A logical schema, for example that of *modus ponens*, may determine which propositions will be entertained and which rejected, but neither itself constitutes a premiss in reasoning nor yields a description of the reasoning process. It is a standard to which processes of reasoning may be compared.

Consideration of these points suggests certain things which any successful analysis of the concept of discursive thinking must emphasize. If we can make a few of them clear it will be a start. The list of 'points to be borne in mind' makes it very tempting to argue as follows. The crucial feature of discursive thinking appears to be *not* that the thinker should entertain propositions of certain forms in a certain order, but that he should recognize certain patterns of relationships obtaining between sets of propositions entertained simultaneously or successively by him. Recognition of a 'completed' pattern of such relationships constitutes recognition (and occasionally misrecognition) of a valid logical argument or set of entailments. Any procedure whatsoever by which the thinker endeavours to find propositions which will 'complete' a pattern, or to order propositions so as to facilitate recognition of a pattern, could legitimately be termed 'discursive thinking'. Such procedures might involve sequences of events determined by 'causal laws', for example one could perhaps 'hunt premisses' by letting associations run freely. At other times, of course, the procedures concerned will not be describable in terms of causal laws. There is, for example, no doubt that not all 'premiss-hunting' and 'conclusion-hunting' is carried out by trial and error, by simply searching until the missing piece of the pattern is hit upon. One can, very often, without trial and error straightaway construct a proposition which will fill a gap in a logical pattern. Given premisses, one can 'see' a conclusion, or given conclusion and a premiss, one can 'see' the missing premiss, etc. This may be called 'reasoning' proper, and for reasons given earlier, no account of it can be given in terms of causal laws.

We are thus proposing a teleological definition of thinking. 'Discursive thinking' is, very roughly, any form of mental activity, or indeed overt action, directed towards finding propositions to complete certain kinds of patterns of relationships which may obtain between propositions, or towards grasping a complete pattern which is presumed already to exist among propositions currently before one. We must next mention some of the many shortcomings of this formulation.

The two most obvious ones are these. (1) We have talked of

discursive thinking as being directed towards the recognition or completion of patterns of relationships obtaining between propositions. But we have said nothing as to the nature of the relationships and of the patterns. (2) We have talked of the thinker recognizing patterns of relationships between propositions as though propositions were a bit like pieces of a jigsaw, existing independently of the person contemplating them. Some writers have indeed apparently supposed that propositions, as the 'objects of thought', are quasi-objective and 'subsist' in some special realm of being. But such a position is exceedingly difficult to maintain, and appears to reduce the thinker to the role of spectator of his own thoughts. Yet if we say instead that propositions have no being outside the thoughts in which they are entertained, we meet the difficulty noted by Norris, namely that *a* thought or *a* belief, considered as a datable mental event, cannot be regarded as the premiss or conclusion of an argument.

As a preliminary move here we will attempt to restate our proposal without making use of that notoriously troublesome term 'proposition'. In so doing we will adopt the term 'thought'. We shall use this term to refer to what would once have been called 'judgments', and would now probably be spoken of as the entertaining or affirmation of a proposition. According to Blanshard (1939, I, p. 51) 'judgement is thought at its simplest because nothing simpler could yield either truth or falsity'. A thought in this sense is always a thought that something is the case or a supposal that something is the case.

Now when one has such a thought it could always truly be said that one's thought has a specificatory aspect or function, or perhaps more truly that when one thinks one specifies; one exercises various of one's conceptual capacities so as to specify, as it were upon a grid of intersecting co-ordinates, some state of affairs beyond the thought itself. The specifying function does not exhaust the thought – there is, prima facie, a difference between thoughts in which the specified state of affairs is affirmed, and those in which it is merely supposed – but it is a *sine qua non* of there being any thought at all.

One might say that its specificatory function is a characteristic of a thought, is that which stamps it as the thought *of* so and so, and, in the cases presently to hand, the thought *that* so and so (we shall suggest shortly that there is no hard and fast division to be made here); and that it also yields or constitutes *a characterization or specification of* the state of affairs which the thought would be said to be of or about. (Somewhat similar views are attributed by Willard (1972) to Husserl.) In so far as the specificatory aspects or functions of temporally distinct thoughts may be the same, in so far as the same conceptual capacities are exercised in the same way on different occasions, the same state of affairs may be thought of, specified, affirmed, supposed, doubted, called to mind, in numerically different thoughts. It is because its specificatory function characterizes a thought that we may say that the 'same' thought can be thought on numerically different occasions; and it is because the specificatory function may remain constant from thought to thought that the 'same' state of affairs can be 'thought of' or postulated on different occasions. There appears, therefore (to return for a moment to our original 'proposition' terminology), to be a *via media* between supposing that propositions 'subsist' independently of the thoughts in which they are affirmed, and supposing that a thought, regarded as a temporal event, can be the premiss or the conclusion of an argument. We can say that propositions are in effect characterizations of states of affairs, which characterizations *also* exist as, and only as, *a characteristic of* an indefinitely, indeed infinitely, large number of actual or possible thoughts. Each such 'characteristic' can recur again and again, and whenever it recurs it will be capable of standing in certain relations to other such characteristics (rather as the characteristic 'red', which characterizes many different objects, will, *whenever it recurs*, resemble the characteristic 'yellow' more than it resembles the characteristic 'green'). In other words, such a characteristic may serve as the 'premiss' of an argument, even the 'same' argument, now or a thousand million years from now.

And this brings us to the other shortcoming which we mentioned, viz. that we had not clarified the 'relations' that we envisaged holding between propositions, and the patterns into which the related propositions may fall. It may perhaps help if we again avoid the slippery 'proposition' terminology. We might say something like this. What we called the 'specificatory function' of a thought consists in the thinker's exercising his conceptual capacities so as to specify, pinpoint, a putative state of affairs 'beyond' or 'outside' the thought itself. Among the conceptual capacities exercised are ones which may be called 'logical' – capacities for example to specify 'all x's', 'some y's', 'no z's', 'two w's', to conjoin or disjoin envisaged states of affairs, to postulate relations ('greater than', 'above') holding within the state of affairs specified, and so on and so forth.

In so far as such conceptual capacities are exercised in 'specifying' states of affairs beyond the immediate thought of the thinker, certain relations may obtain between the specifications or characterizations concerned. The relations are such that, if the thinker apprehends or grasps them, he will understand, for example that a certain two specifications cannot both be simultaneously applicable to the world; that of a set of three specifications, if two are applicable to the world, the third must be; that if two are applicable to the world, a third of a certain form may be constructed which will also be applicable; and so on. What we are saying here is, translated into 'proposition' terminology, that the propositions which a given person entertains may be related in terms of the logical concepts which figure in them, and that sometimes these relationships fall into patterns such that if the thinker grasps them he will realize that the truth or falsity of certain of the propositions he entertains is bound up with the truth or falsity of certain others.

If anyone feels that our brief remarks have left these issues as obscure as before we can only reply as follows. The 'patterns' we have been discussing are *sui generis*, in the last resort unanalysable. How, indeed, could any reductive analysis of them be possible? For either such an analysis would not be rational, logical, in which case it would be of no avail; or it would be rational, logical, in which case we should have applied logic in order to analyse logic into something non-logical.

One might say that what we are dealing with is an irreducible 'form of order' obtaining among certain members of a class of events ('thoughts') itself not susceptible of reductive definition. By 'form of order' we mean any dimension along which objects, events, phenomena or qualities or aspects thereof may be related; for example colour, weight, temporal succession. Some of these dimensions must be ultimate, i.e. not analysable in terms of some combination of other dimensions, and others will be derivative. For instance some writers (for example R. Taylor, 1966) have held that the causal form of order is *sui generis* and not further analysable, while others (like Hume) have claimed that causal relationships are analysable as combinations of spatio-temporal with qualitative and quantitative orderings.

That a thinker can grasp, recognize, the 'patterns' we have been discussing, or endeavour to bring them into being, are facts which, in the last resort, appear susceptible of no further explanation than that he has, or has developed, the capacity to do these things. One can trace the development of the capacity, but one cannot exhibit it as derived from capacities to do other things. The logical cannot be derived from the non-logical, only from the primitively logical. The point here is quite general, and is reflected in the concern of an hermeneutical psychology with the development rather than with the origins of man's capacities.

Of the many further problems which arise we can only touch upon three. The first concerns what it is to possess 'logical' concepts; the second concerns the distinction between beliefs and mere supposals; the third concerns how we can give 'body' to our definition of a 'thought', how we can relate it to experience and action in everyday life.

(1) In chapter 3 we touched very briefly on logical and related concepts, which we characterized as 'stimulus-independent'. We must now amplify what we said. We shall concentrate upon 'not', 'or', 'and' and 'if . . . then' (the 'logical constants' of the propositional calculus) and especially upon the concept of negation, perhaps the most central of them all. Some writers have suggested that exercise of the concept of negation is involved in the formation of every other concept. One cannot so divide the world in thought that some parts of it are classed together as A's without at the same time creating a class of Not-A's; for he who accepts some things as being A's must also reject, say 'no' to, other things. If he did not thus reject some things the distinction between A's and Not-A's would be obliterated and the 'class' of A's would collapse. If this argument is correct, we are faced with a difficult problem over how the concept of negation can be formed, for its formation appears to presuppose its existence.

As a preliminary move we may point out that logical concepts can exist on a number of different levels. People who possess no 'concepts' of negation, disjunction, conjunction, etc., in the sense of being able to think about negation, disjunction, etc., can none the less exercise the capacities to negate, disjoin, etc. They can divide objects into classes marked out by the conjunction or disjunction of characteristics, they can develop negative concepts, they can affirm or deny negative, conjunctive and disjunctive propositions, and so on and so forth. These capacities are not 'conceptual' ones in terms of the definition which we offered in chapter 3. They do not involve the ability to group objects, events, or phenomena together on the basis of some implicitly understood set of defining characteristics.

But since the exercise of the capacities to negate, disjoin, conjoin, etc., results in the formation of new conceptual divisions, and makes a difference to what state of affairs is conceived on any occasion, we can properly describe these capacities as conceptual. They are, however, syncategorematic, in that their exercise depends upon the conjoint exercise of other and more full-blooded conceptual capacities, and yet they are not parasitic upon these other capacities, for those other capacities are reciprocally dependent upon them. The capacity to negate might thus be admitted without self-contradiction to be involved in the formation of the logical concept of negation; for this would not be tantamount to saying that the concept of negation is involved in the setting up of the concept of negation.

How, then, is the transition from possession of the capacities to negate, to disjoin, etc., to possession of the concepts of negation, disjunction, etc., brought about? We are not rash enough to claim to know, but one thing at least is clear, viz. that these concepts are not acquired by any process of abstraction, of noting and registering common features present in all simple examples of negating, disjoining, etc. There are no such common features. The only remaining possibility appears to be that the concepts of negation, conjunction, disjunction and implication arise from progressively more refined exercises of those same capacities. One passes, by steps which we cannot trace or account for, from being able to exercise these concepts only in conjunction with concepts of observable states of affairs, to being able to exercise them in conjunction with such bodiless concepts as those of 's' (any subject of any predicate), 'p' (any predicate), $\forall x$ (all x's), p (any proposition), and so on. Somewhere along this route it becomes apparent to one that a distinction can be made between the *form* of a proposition ('specification of what is or may be the case') and its content. In other words it becomes apparent to one that what the specificatory aspects of thought specify is in part determined by recurrent factors which are independent of what *kind* of thing or *kind* of state of affairs is specified. These recurrent factors – the capacities to negate, disjoin, etc. – are conceptualized in terms of their roles in determining that which the specificatory aspects of thoughts specify to be the case, and *not* in terms of their psychological substrate or embodiment. These roles could be understood only by somebody who possessed the capacities to negate, disjoin, etc., but prior possession of the concepts of the roles, i.e. of the concepts of negation, disjunction, etc., would not be required. The capacities themselves, in their primal or unrefined form, appear to be *sui generis*, and not derivable from any other kind of capacity, certainly not from the 'internalized motor sequences' of Piagetian mythology. (Either the motor sequences concerned are 'actions', in which case conceptual capacities, including the capacities to negate, disjoin, etc., are presupposed, or they are not actions, in which case the position reduces to abstractionism of the crudest kind.) We are not asserting that babies are born with these capacities, still less that they have the 'structure' of the predicate calculus built into their nervous systems. But we do suggest that babies are born with the potentiality of developing and exercising these capacities, and that this potentiality is, in ways that we do not understand, stirred into life and thereafter expanded and differentiated.

(2) We have used the term 'a thought' to cover both acts or events in which a proposition is 'affirmed' or 'assented to', and ones in which it is merely 'entertained': to cover, in short, both instances of occurrent beliefs and instances of mere supposals. What is the extra ingredient that converts a mere supposal into a belief? One answer has been to postulate in addition to the specifying or conceiving or supposing of such and such a state of affairs, further acts or processes, for example of affirmation that the conceived state of affairs obtains. There seem to be good reasons for regarding this account as implausible. Generally speaking one does not first conceive some state of affairs and then affirm it. And it seems most unlikely that in the early stages of conceptual thought one first acquires the ability to conceive or suppose a state of affairs and only then can acquire or exhibit the capacity to affirm or believe it.

Another way of looking at the matter might be this. We have suggested that the intensionality of our thoughts is not a consequence of our conceptual activity, but a presupposition of it. For conceptual divisions could only be imposed in thought upon the 'world beyond' thoughts if the existence of such a world is assumed or posited by thought. Now this 'pointing beyond' cannot consist of a relationship between the thought, or rather the thinker, and the world. The 'pointing beyond' is a feature of the thought itself, and there *may or may not be anything in its 'direction'*. Thus we have present at the very outset of any actual process of concept formation and exercise a feature of thought in virtue of which it can be called true or false.

The conceptual divisions imposed in thought upon the world may be looked upon as diversifications of this primitive pointing to or positing of 'something beyond' the immediate thought. All such processes of division presuppose, have latent within them, an assumption of 'something beyond' the present experience. Indeed it is not easy to see how the notion of a 'something beyond' could have arisen from any possible sequence of experiences which did not somewhere along the line assume it. Thus from the outset the dividing in thought of the world and the subsequent use of these divisions in handling the world are 'for real', not imaginative exercises or speculations as to what might be the case. To think of a spotted cow is to think that there is such a cow; to think of a spotted cow in the garden is to think that there is a spotted cow in the garden; to think of cows as creatures which chew the cud is to think that all cows, or some group of cows, do in fact chew the cud. This is the tendency which was called by Bain and James 'primitive credulity'. H. H. Price describes it as follows (1969, p. 214):

> the human mind has a spontaneous (unacquired) tendency to accept without question any proposition which is presented to it; and this tendency operates as a matter of course, unless there is something else to hold it in check. The power of suspending judgment, of asking questions and weighing evidence, the power on which reasonable assent depends, is not something we possess from the beginning. It is an achievement, which has to be learned, often painfully.

What we have to explain, then, is not how belief supervenes on processes of supposal, on specifications merely dreamed up, but how primitive credulity is harnessed and restrained. This in itself is a considerable problem and we certainly cannot go into it here. It is obvious that through painful experience one must come to realize that one's beliefs may be erroneous and so to envisage alternative possibilities.

We have talked here and elsewhere of conceptual capacities being capacities to divide 'the world' in thought, and have suggested that an inkling of 'the world's' existence is a presupposition of the development and exercise of these capacities. It might be more nearly correct, and would harmonize better with the analysis of concept-possession offered in chapter 3, to talk of an inkling that there exist 'things-with-attributes'. For just as it is difficult to see how the idea of a world 'out there' can be derived from the flux of experience except by some process which tacitly assumes it, so it is difficult to account for our tendency to divide the world into 'things' except on the supposition that we cannot but think that way. The world is not as it were pre-cut into thing-sized lumps. What count as 'things' in our dealings with the world change as our immediate interests and purposes vary. It is we who impose thing-divisions on the world. Thinking of things is logically prior to thinking of attributes, for one cannot conceive of unattached attributes. Attributes of things are not to be equated with parts of things (cf. Stout, 1938, pp. 416–20). And assigning attributes to things is in turn logically prior to marking out classes of things and placing individual things in those classes, for it is on the basis of attributes that things are assigned to classes. One cannot offer class-membership propositions – for example 'this is a red object' – as grounds for attribute-propositions – for example 'this is red' – but one can do the reverse (cf. Mitchell, 1962, p. 88). Thus upon logical grounds we reach conclusions about the lines along which 'intensionality' must diversify, if diversify it does. Whether this logical order is paralleled by a temporal order of development is a question for empirical research.

The above remarks might be countered with the following objection (cf. chapter 3, pp. 24–5). We have proposed that classes are set up in thought (i.e. conceptual divisions are marked out) on the basis of attributes. Thus the class of red objects appears to be the class of all objects which possess the attribute 'redness'. But then to acquire the concept of red object would not one already have to possess the concept of redness? We might get round this difficulty by proposing that there is as it were a preconceptual felt affinity between red objects based on their attribute of redness, an affinity which makes them as it were 'belong together' (cf. Wertheimer's 'laws of grouping' of objects). Marking out the class of 'red objects' is then something like an act of definition (cf. Barrett, 1963), or act of 'synthesis' as it would once have been called (Dawes Hicks, 1938, pp. 124–30). It amounts to thinking 'those' of all the objects sharing in the affinity, and also 'and not those' of all objects not sharing in it. Thinking of 'redness' in the abstract would then be thinking of that in virtue of which the objects concerned belong together or have an affinity, and would be posterior to the classing of them together.

(3) We have made liberal use in this chapter of the notion of 'a thought', which we defined in formal and abstract terms. Our discussion has therefore been somewhat bodiless, and will remain so unless we can anchor the notion of 'a thought' to common experience. What is it *like* to have 'a thought'? It might seem that anyone

who is capable of sufficient discursive thought to pose the question should already know the answer. But that intelligent and reflective people do not already know the answer is sufficiently shown by the number of them who have been, and indeed are, prone to lend credence to the view that 'a thought' is to be identified with visual or verbal images, or some concatenation thereof, and that discursive thinking consists in the occurrence of a train of associated images. The objections to this view are numerous and decisive (see for example Blanshard, 1939, chapter 7). As Hartnack (1972, p. 544) remarks,

> The criterion of two persons thinking of the same thing must
> be the answer they give to the question what they are
> thinking of and such an answer will belong to another logical
> category than the answer to the question what mental images
> they have.

None the less few of those who think 'in images' would be happy to admit that the images are mere bubbles on the stream of thought. Surely images are sometimes, and for some people, the core of a 'thought', even if at other times thoughts are 'imageless'? A possible approach to this difficulty is suggested by the notion of 'pregnance' developed by Cassirer. Cassirer develops this notion initially when discussing perception. The idea seems to be that when, for example, one 'recognizes' some aspect of an object, for example the back of a clock, as being what it is, one is in effect placing it within a 'family' of such aspects (the sides, the face, etc.), the members of which are related together in terms of a definite rule of progression which in its turn derives from a systematic grasp of how they all so to speak fit together in a spatio-temporal unity. In the moment of recognition one's consciousness is characterized not just by the perceived attributes of the observed aspect, but by an awareness (not fully unpacked or unpackable into images) of the relations of the presently perceived aspect to the other aspects and of the rule by which they are related. We recognize a thing in terms not only of what it is but in terms of what it might become; our perception is pregnant with this knowledge. Of course the knowledge of the rule would not, even if made explicit, be susceptible of formal expression; rather it consists in a *being versed* in the way the different aspects are related, and of how it would be appropriate to act towards any given aspect or towards the whole to which the different aspects systematically relate. A grasp of all these factors is somehow latent in one's conscious state, and it could not be otherwise if the aspect is to be recognized *as* an aspect of, for example, a clock. Even if a series of associated images of successive aspects of a clock passed before the mind, they would no more 'fit together' to yield the idea of a three-dimensional clock than would a series of comparable images from a strip of cine-film. As Cassirer (1953, I, p. 100) says:

> We intuit spatial *configurations* only by combining into *one* idea complete groups of sensory perceptions which mutually displace one another in immediate sensory experience, and on the other hand by diffusing this unity through the diversity of its particular components.

Something similar holds true in the rather more complex case of object-perception (McDougall, 1923, pp. 250–8). The traditional sensationist account of object-perception, of seeing a horse *as* a horse, an orange *as* an orange, or *that* something is a horse or an orange, and so forth, was in terms of a sensation coming to arouse associated images. The inadequacy of the sensation-image analysis can be brought out by noting how much is involved in perceiving an orange as an orange. A vast amount of past experience is utilized, involved or mobilized even in this simple act. Consider how many different discoveries would falsify the claim that what is now before one is an orange. Suppose it floated in the air, or was as heavy as lead, or made of wax, or was hollow, or poisonous, or resistant to a knife, or . . . there are countless ways in which our first impression may be disconfirmed. This 'meaning' is far richer than any imagery which is to be found when one perceives an orange as an orange. In perceiving an orange as an orange, a whole organized system of knowledge, cognitive and practical, is deployed. An act of perception is, so to speak, a synthetic activity of the mind which brings all this underlying complexity into play in one unitary thought.

Now let us turn to 'thoughts'. The 'pregnancy' of propositional thought has been aptly characterized by H. H. Price (1969, p. 201; cf. Findlay, 1972, pp. 16–17) in a discussion of 'entertaining' a proposition. Even when we do *not* spell out to ourselves or picture what it would be like for a proposition to be true, we have none the less a 'readiness' to begin such spellings out or picturings.

> It is not just that we are capable of considering or realising what it would be like for the sentence (or other symbol) to be true, though we do of course have to possess this capacity if

we are to entertain the proposition. The readiness I speak of
is rather like being poised to run in a certain direction, if need
arises; this is something more than just having the capacity to
run – and also something less than actually running. This
readiness to consider or realise is something actually felt or
experienced. It is a feature – and an important one – of the
actual experience of entertaining . . . I find it difficult to give
any further account of what this felt or experienced readiness
is (though I think we are all perfectly familiar with it).

Price here puts his finger on an important general feature of 'pregnant' experiences, whether perceptual or propositional, namely
that what is latent in them is capable of being unfolded, drawn
out, according to circumstances. When, for instance, a thought
'specifies' (cf. pp. 127–8 above) a certain object or state of affairs, the
object is usually not in the first instance thought of as possessing in
detail the characteristics of that sort of object, nor are all the
minutiae of what is involved in the obtaining of that state of affairs
either apprehended in the momentary thought or subsequently
spelled out. But a readiness to formulate or picture or act upon
those details or minutiae, and a being versed in their systematic
relations, must in an indescribable manner be latent in the thought,
must inform or charge it, and must be capable of being made
manifest as the developing situation requires. Otherwise the thinker
would at best have simply a dim intuition that there is more to the
state of affairs specified in his thought than he can adequately grasp.

 We can now offer some account of the role which images and also
overt symbols may play in thinking. Just as, for certain purposes, a
substitute object may be, as it were, assigned the systematic place of
a real object (as in *Kriegspiel*), so that latent in the act of perceiving
it will be some of the pregnance of the original, so we can *create for
ourselves* the semblances of objects or of states of affairs to play a
similar role in certain kinds of thinking, including certain kinds of
propositional thinking. And in thinking about concrete objects,
images have to be at any rate compatible in 'appearance' with what
they represent. For if latent in the experience of an image is to be the
pregnance usually found in the experience of some perceptible
physical object, the *image itself* must not purvey pregnance incompatible with that of the object it represents. In so far as propositional
thought is thought *that* such and such a concrete state of affairs
obtains – for example that the Australians are batting at Lord's – the

summoning of an appropriate image may create a state of mind with some of the pregnance which the act of perceiving the scene itself would have carried. However in more developed propositional thought, thought which is about very general or very abstract matters, veridical imagery, which would tend to introduce the wrong pregnance, would in most cases be somewhat disadvantageous. The introspective studies of the Würzburg school (see Humphrey, 1951, chapters 1–3) strongly suggest that there can be not merely 'imageless' transitions from one thought to another, but imageless entertaining of abstract propositions, entertaining in which the multitudinous pregnance of the thought is all, and quasi-sensory content is entirely lacking. But these are topics for other books than this.

9

Wants, Intentions and Beliefs

We have tried to make it clear that the concept of intention is a central, perhaps the central, concept of hermeneutical explanation. It is correspondingly important to give some account of it. We must, however, begin by noting that the explanatory force of citing an intention is derivative. If one explains an action x as arising from the intention to do x one has explained nothing, for one has in effect only stated that x was a premeditated action. The question of why the agent formed the intention to do x remains. If one explains an action x as arising from the intention to do or bring about y then x is explained, at least if we set aside the question of how intentions give rise to overt actions; but the problem of why the agent should have formed the intention to y remains. One can explain the intention to y as being the outcome of, or a subintention within, the superintention to do or bring about z; but sooner or later the buck must stop. Generally it stops when an intention is reached which is not to promote the fulfilment of a further intention, but to promote some state of affairs which the agent reckons worth procuring for its own sake. There is something that the agent wants or desires in the strong sense of 'wants' in which the agent believes that the occurrence or obtaining of what is wanted will give him pleasure, happiness, relaxation, uplifting of spirits, etc., or else the ending or relief of displeasure; or else there is something the agent deems it morally right or obligatory to bring about, some state of affairs that is-to-be-brought-about for its own sake and regardless of whether or not it brings him pleasure. Some writers would say that it is intrinsic to the state of 'wanting' something, and perhaps also to the state of deeming something morally obligatory, that it should gel into a firm intention to act; for a 'want' which never passed into intentional action or into intention would at best be an idle daydream. The relation between want and intention would thus be non-contingent much as is, allegedly, the relation between intention and action (cf. pp. 151–3 below). Thus the fact that the explanatory force of citing an intention is derivative does not make intention any less central a notion in explaining actions.

Our own position is that the notion of intention can neither be eliminated from action-explanations nor yet reduced to other notions. We argued previously (pp. 12–13) that the notion of intention cannot be eliminated, and we also argued (pp. 53–8) that intentions cannot be represented within the mechanistic paradigm of the generalized machine. There have been, however, a good many attempts to analyse the notion of intention in terms of other (and often no better understood) notions (cf. Meiland, 1970, chapters 8–10). 'Belief' and 'want' or 'desire' have been the chief candidates. It is impossible here to consider all these attempts, so we will tackle a representative recent one, that by Audi (1973a, 1973b), with which may be compared Churchland (1970) and Goldman (1970, chapters 3 and 4). Audi analyses 'intention' in terms of 'want' and 'belief'. He further provides us with an explication of 'wanting' and we shall begin by outlining and commenting upon this.

Audi holds that the notion of wanting is 'analogous' to such theoretical concepts as that of an electron or a magnetic field. Like all such theoretical concepts it derives its meaning from the set of 'law-like' propositions in which it figures. These propositions are 'such that whoever employs – as opposed to only understanding or merely mentioning – the concept of wanting must believe them' (1973a p. 3). Audi proposes the following set (pp. 4–5):

W_1 If x does or would find daydreaming about p pleasant, and x believes that there is at least some considerable probability of p's occurring, then, under favourable conditions, xWp.

W_2 If (a) it would be (or is) unpleasant to x to entertain the thought that p is not (or probably is not) the case, or the thought that p will not be (or probably will not be) the case, and (b) x believes that there is at least some considerable probability of p's occurring, then, under favourable conditions, xWp.

W_3 If xWp, then (a) x tends to think (reflect, muse, or the like) or daydream about p at least occasionally, and especially in idle moments; and (b) in free conversation x tends to talk at least occasionally about p and subjects he believes to be connected with p.

W_4 xWp if and only if: for any action or activity A which x has the ability and the opportunity to perform, if x believes either (a) that his doing A is necessary to p, or (b) that his doing A would have at least some considerable probability of leading to p, or (c) that his doing A would have at least some considerable probability of constituting attainment of p, then x has a tendency to do A.

W_5 xWp if and only if: given that x has not been expecting p, if x now suddenly judged (or suddenly discovered, realised, or the like) that p is (is becoming, will become) the case, then x would immediately tend to be pleased, joyful or relieved about this.

W_6 xWp if and only if: given that x has been expecting p, if x now suddenly judged (or suddenly discovered, realised, or the like) that p would not be the case, then x would immediately tend to be disappointed about this.

W_7 xWp if and only if: under favourable conditions, x has a tendency to avow that he wants p.

A great deal might be said about this analysis of wanting. Audi's claim that 'wanting' is a 'theoretical construct' deriving its meaning from the 'law-like' propositions W_1–W_7 is a quite extraordinary one. For the essence of such 'constructs' as electrons and magnetic fields is that electrons and magnetic fields are assigned properties from which the truth of certain law-like propositions can be seen to follow. W_1–W_7 cannot be derived from any unitary set of properties assigned to 'wants': they are a (far from satisfactory) list of the ways in which someone who already knows about wanting (whatever it is) might say that it commonly manifests itself. Furthermore, this person's notion of wanting cannot possibly have been acquired in the way in which scientists acquire theoretical concepts such as 'electron' or 'magnetic field'. The give-away here is Audi's W_7–x wants p if and only if he has a tendency to avow that he wants it. How does x know that he wants p? Does he observe his own behaviour, note features of his own mental activities and *infer* that he has a certain want? This would be an extraordinary supposition. For in the first place if the concept of wanting is like the concept of a magnetic field, x's tendency to avow that he wants p must be based on his observation that W_1–W_7 hold in his own case; but this implies that before x can develop this tendency he must have observed that he has developed it ('W_7 xWp if and only if . . .'). And in the second place one does not (in general) need to observe anything in order to know that one wants something (cf. chapter 11).

W_1–W_6 are no more satisfactory than W_7. If they are to be taken as giving the meaning of the term 'wanting' then transient wants, sudden yearnings would not be wants, and looking forward to something would be equivalent to wanting it. However, the 'law-like proposition' of most interest for present purposes is W_4. Audi notes, as a possible objection to W_4, that it seems to make feeling an obligation to do something a form of wanting to do it. He appears, however, quite happy to accept this implication (1973a, p. 7).

> though we sometimes contrast wanting to do something with feeling obligated to do it, often we treat feeling obligated as involving wanting. We often say, regarding some task which we do not enjoy but feel obligated to perform, things like 'I'm working late; I want to study these applications'.

But this will not do. 'I want to study these applications' has, psychologically speaking, to be read as 'I want to get through the tedious task of studying these applications and back to more pleasant pastimes'. 'What one wants' here is different from what one feels obligated to do. Furthermore one's 'feeling obligated' to study the applications does not involve W_1–W_3 and W_5–W_7 holding true of one. Several of these are regarded by Audi as necessary and sufficient conditions of wanting, and 'feeling obligated' thus fails to measure up to his own specifications for 'wanting'. And these specifications, though they fail to pin down the notion of 'wanting', do reflect important features of it. There surely is a strong sense of 'wanting' in which wanting something involves regarding it as a likely source of satisfaction, enjoyment, pleasure, etc., or of the end of dissatisfaction, etc., and in which it is self-contradictory to talk of 'wanting' a state of affairs which one actively dislikes. It is possible to 'want' in this way to fulfil one's obligations: but it is also possible to feel constrained to fulfil one's obligations without in the least 'wanting' to fulfil them. The righteous headmaster of yesteryear thrashed his peccant pupils not (one trusts) because he wanted to, or even principally because he desired to reform them, but because the retribution was *just*, and justice *had* to be done however melancholy the doing of it.

We are now in a position to consider Audi's account of intention (1973b, p. 395):

> *x* intends to bring about *φ* by doing *A* if and only if
> (1) *x* believes that he will (or that he probably will) bring about *φ* by doing *A*; &
> (2) *x* wants, and has not temporarily forgotten that he wants, to bring about *φ* by doing *A*; &
> (3) either *x* has no equally strong or stronger incompatible want (or set of incompatible wants whose combined strength is at least as great), or, if *x* does have such a want or set of wants, he has temporarily forgotten that he wants the object(s) in question, or does not believe he wants the object(s), or has temporarily forgotten his belief that he cannot both realize the object(s) and bring about *φ* by doing *A*.

Audi proffers a parallel analysis of 'simple' intentions, i.e. ones in which *x* simply intends to do *A*.

Audi's (1) is ambiguous. It could be read either as '*x* believes that he will bring about *φ* and that he will bring it about by doing *A*', or as '*x* believes that if he does *A* he will bring about *φ*'. Audi's other arguments suggest that the former of these interpretations is the right one, and so we will begin with it. At first sight the view that intention contains such a component is very plausible; for if *x* does not believe that he will bring about *φ* and that he will bring it about by doing *A*, then surely he cannot intend to bring about *φ* by doing *A*? And yet he can. For in ordinary circumstances the question of whether or not one will do what one intends to do simply does not arise for one. One does not believe that one will or that one will not. One does not consider the matter at all. One just gets on with the job. Only if doubts are raised as to the feasibility of one's plan does one develop beliefs as to whether or not one will manage to implement it.

Even if we set aside this objection, others remain. For it is not difficult to think of cases in which (1) and (2) and (3) all hold but which would not amount to the having of an intention. Thus it is not impossible that *x* might believe that he will bring about *φ* and that he will bring it about by doing A and believe it because he is pretty sure that whether he likes it or not Svengali the evil hypnotist will work upon him to that effect; and at the same time he may want to bring about φ by doing A more than he wants anything that would conflict with it. None the less there would be no question of x's intending at the time of entertaining this belief and this want to bring about φ by doing A.

An obvious move for Audi at this point would be to insert '(2a) x believes that his want to bring about φ by doing A will cause him to do A' (cf. Grice, 1971). This (though psychologically most implausible) would dispose of the above counter-example, but unfortunately not of all possible counter-examples. Consider the case of someone who wants to bring about φ by doing A, heartily disapproves on moral grounds of this want, and yet has a strong suspicion that when presented, as he inevitably will be, with the chance to bring about φ by doing A, he will be weak enough to succumb to this want. He has not framed the intention to bring about φ by doing A, and yet he fulfils (1), (2), (2a) and (3).

The second interpretation of Audi's (1) – 'x believes that if he does A he will bring about φ' – has somewhat more to recommend it. It is at any rate true that if x intends to bring about φ by doing A he must believe that A will promote φ. However, even if (1) be interpreted in this way, it still does not when joined to (2) and (3) yield a satisfactory analysis of intending. To show this we must begin by examining (2) – 'x wants to bring about φ by doing A'. It is surely somewhat unusual for a want to have as its 'object' bringing about φ by doing A rather than just bringing about φ. Wants are not all or even often of the form 'I want to climb the mountain by ascending the (hitherto unclimbed) north col'. They are much more commonly of the form 'I want to get to the top. Now – what is my best route?' Anscombe's remark, 'The primitive sign of wanting is *trying to get*' (1958, p. 68), is somewhat misleading. The chief mark of wanting is trying to think of a way to get. Wants are pregnant with possible lines of action, possible intentions. Someone who wants something is very commonly (to adopt Price's simile) like a person poised to run in any direction that circumstances may require. He is prepared to adopt a policy for the fulfilment of his want, he feels a certain action-oriented restlessness, but he has not yet decided which policy is most propitious. Wants which were not thus pregnant with actions or with intentions would not be wants at all but mere plays of fancy.

From this two points emerge. The first is that so far from intentions being analysable into wants and beliefs, the (inseparable) notions of intention and of action are required for the analysis of wanting. The second is that if (2) is to have any generality of application it must be shortened to read simply 'x wants to bring about φ'. The 'by doing A' must be omitted. But in this case the combination of (1) (second interpretation), (2) (second interpretation) and (3) does not yield the blueprint of an intention. For it can be, and often is, the case that someone wants to bring about φ, believes that if he does A, φ will probably result, knows of no impediment to his doing A, and has not yet decided to do A. He may feel that the chance of φ's resulting is not good enough, yet know of no action more hopeful than A; he may be in no hurry and bide his time to see if a strategy still better than doing A turns up; and so on (cf. Meiland, 1970, pp. 115–17).

But in any case Audi's (2) (second interpretation) has no place in elucidating the concept of intention. We suggested above that wanting to bring about φ is not an essential component of intending to bring about φ. One sometimes does implement things out of a 'sense of duty' without even 'wanting' to do one's duty. And there are in everyone's life a large number of what may be called 'habitual' intentions – the intention to get up when the alarm rings, the intention to do one's daily dozen, the intention to fetch the children from school, the intention to mow the lawn. Intentions like these are in a sense just facts of one's daily life, affectively quite neutral. They relate to matters that are to be got on with whether or not one especially likes it. And in fact one usually does not stop to ask whether one likes it or not, or whether the actions concerned fulfil longer-term ends of which one approves or disapproves. That 'wanting', in any non-trivial sense of the word, figures in such intentions is perfectly incredible.

We must now give our own account of the concept of intention; we shall begin with some general remarks about the task ahead. We suggested above (chapter 4) that a characteristic of psychological phenomena is that they are 'intrinsically interdependent'. Without certain beliefs, intentions would disintegrate, without intentions or action-tendencies wants would collapse into idle wishes, without the exercise of a conceptual capacity to think of the future intentions and expectancies could not be sustained, and so forth. From this it follows that someone who does not have the notion of belief cannot grasp that of intention, that someone who lacks an idea of intention cannot know what wants are, etc. But it does not follow that if you have the notions of want and belief (or whatever it may be) you are fully equipped to grasp the notion of intention. Intentions may be intrinsically dependent on beliefs and so on, but intention as a phenomenon is not resolvable into beliefs and what have you. It cannot be fully characterized in other than its own terms. Any attempt to elucidate what intentions are, like any attempt to eluci-date what thinking is, or what visual perception is, can only be a process of bringing explicitly to people's notice features of their experience which they will then recognize to have been there all the time. It is a bit like writing an appreciation of a novel or a play. The aim is to highlight facets of what everyone has already read.

This analogy, however, over-simplifies things, for it does not allow for the enormous variety of possible intentions. The task is more like that of writing an appreciation of the greatly diversified works of an extraordinarily prolific author (Balzac's *Comédie Humaine* might be an appropriate example). For one can intend to do or bring about almost anything one can think of so long as one does not regard it as quite impossible of achievement. One can intend to get a cup of coffee or to become President of the United States; one can intend to jump over a fence or to spend the after-noon working mathematical problems; one can intend conditionally ('if he moves his knight I will move my bishop, but if he moves his queen, I will castle') or without qualification; one can intend to bring about a change, or to continue the *status quo*; one can intend to carry out a simple action, like waving the hand, or to bring about a state of affairs for which many actions are necessary, like making the room look nice; one's intention can map out a detailed sequence of actions, and thus contain within itself a set of definite subinten-tions, or it can merely lay down a general goal, leaving the means to be worked out *ad hoc* as circumstances change and develop; one can have transient intentions, mad impulses, or one can formulate what may be called 'standing' intentions, as when making New Year resolutions; one can frame a standing intention to be free, emanci-pated, untrammelled, or a standing intention to abide by the smal-lest detail of some intricate code of conduct, like a monastic rule. How, it might well be asked, can one hope, when intentions are thus indefinitely various,[1] to present any unitary account of what it is to possess an intention? It is, for example, often asserted that there is no kind of experience, no kind of activity, that characterizes all examples of intending (cf. Gustafson, 1974, p. 327). During a period of time, however long or short, when one intends to bring about φ, whether or not by doing A, there may be moments when one yearns for φ, moments when one grits one's teeth and says 'I will!', moments when one pictures φ in minutest detail, moments when one reminds oneself of one's aim; but none of these events *is* the intending or an example of intending. Furthermore there may be considerable periods during which neither *what* one intends nor the fact that one *is intending* is overtly present to one's consciousness, and this despite the fact that one may all the time be acting in pursuit of one's intention. The intention may appear to be, in the terminology of the Würzburg school, an unconscious 'determining tendency'. Wittgenstein (1958, p. 20) makes a very similar point with regard to expecting.

We will set aside the 'phenomenology' of intention until we have explored some further avenues. The problem before us is to give an account of intending which presents it neither as the having before the mind's eye of some distinctive image or introspectible process, nor as a tendency to exhibit certain kinds of behaviour when confronted with certain kinds of stimuli, nor yet as a mere concatenation of want and belief.

Perhaps a useful place to start may be with the affinity, often pointed out, between avowals of intention and the making of promises. The avowal of an intention may in some circumstances have the force of a promise. 'If it's on the market I'll buy it,' says Holmes, 'if it means another penny on the income tax.' Is this a promise or the avowal of an intention? It is both, or rather the two are one and the same. And it has sometimes been hinted that just as 'I promise that I will x . . .' is not a sentence which describes the mental state of the promiser but one which, uttered in certain circumstances, binds or commits him to a course of action, so 'I intend to x' does not describe the speaker's mental state but expresses his committal of himself to a line of action. Now we must not let the obvious if partial truth in these suggestions lull us into supposing that statements of intention are not psychological statements at all. Even promise-statements have fairly strong psychological implications. A man who says 'I promise that I will x' and is not merely mouthing the words must conceive himself as under a moral obligation to fulfil his promise, and there will be a period of his life during which, bound by his promise, he must from time to time give serious thought to the problem of implementing it. A man who says 'I intend to x' may be promising too, he may be stiffening his resolve by exposing himself to ridicule if he fails to try, but he is also indicating that he has made up his mind what to do and that he will if necessary direct further thoughts and endeavours to accomplishing it.

Is not talk of being 'committed' in this rather weak sense simply another way of talking about intending? The answer to this is, yes! However our aim is, as we remarked a moment ago, not to embark upon the hopeless task of producing a reductive definition of 'intention', but to try to make clearer what we mean when we use the term 'intention'. If the notions of intending and of being committed are synonymous or closely related, then examining the latter may help to highlight features of the former.[2]

For instance if we think of intending in terms of being committed we can readily see why so many philosophers have commented on the apparently definitional relationship between intention and belief. You cannot commit yourself to doing something you believe to be impossible, and you cannot commit yourself to achieving a goal by an action which you know perfectly well will not promote that goal. Such 'committal' would only be a kind of play-acting, like that of an army commander who 'commits' his troops to 'battle' knowing full well that the enemy is nowhere to hand.

Again, we can understand why some writers have talked of intentions in terms of commands and prescriptions addressed by the agent to himself,[3] an idea which might be thought to receive support from the developmental studies of Vygotsky (1962, 1966) and others. When one commits oneself to something one comes to regard the relevant actions as having a gerundive or imperative quality for one. And this is surely the central feature of intending. One comes to conceive an action, or a series of actions, as without qualification to-be-done-by-oneself, or a state of affairs as to-be-brought-about-by-oneself. We say 'without qualification' because our suggestion is that just as in the development of believing there is a stage of 'primitive credulity' (cf. pp. 132–4 above) in which whatever is conceived of the world is *ipso facto* believed to be the case, so there is in the development of intending a stage of 'primitive committal' in which whatever action is conceived of as to-be-done-by-oneself is without question accepted as *to-be-done-by-oneself* so that one deploys one's resources towards carrying it out. Only at a later stage does hypothetical thought about what is and is not to be done become possible.

Can one say any more about this special mode of conceiving an action? The answer must surely be, no! There is no more hope of reducing thought about what is-to-be-done-by-one to any other sort of thought than there is of reducing concepts of how things ought to be to concepts of how things are. But we may perhaps be able to bring out certain features of this mode of conceiving. One aspect of it is perhaps a switch in the kind of logic which the agent brings to bear on the situation, in the kinds of inference patterns which constrain his thinking. For when an agent comes to conceive some end as to-be-pursued-by-him, he will also come to conceive those actions which he believes steps on his envisaged road as to-be-done-by-him. And if he did not do this we should either have to say that he did not really have the long-term intention, or that he had not worked out the implications of being committed to his goal. Now in the last two decades, a number of logicians have studied what, following C. D. Broad, has been termed 'deontic logic', the logic of obligation and duty. Deontic logic is a development of modal logic, the logic of possibility and necessity. It deals in such statements as 'it is obligatory that p', 'it is forbidden that q', 'it is permissible that r', and in such principles as that whatever we are committed to in doing what is obligatory is itself obligatory, and that whatever is obligatory is permissible. Now on the face of it, it should be possible to develop a logic of intention-statements somewhat similar to deontic logic. This whole issue is, however, too complicated and difficult to be treated here.

Someone who has come to conceive a state of affars as to-be-brought-about-by-him does not merely apply a different sort of logic in his thinking about his projected actions. He becomes more ready to utilize certain of his conceptual capacities. He becomes more likely to notice objects and events of possible relevance to the fulfilment of his intentions; he actively searches for such objects and events; he tries to think of new strategies; and so on. In short he begins to view the world and his activities in it through conceptual spectacles of a new colour, and if he did not do so, doubt might be cast upon the sincerity of his intention, the genuineness of his committal.

Another aspect of the switch in mode of conceiving is this. When one conceives an action as to-be-done-by-oneself one is personally involved in a way which one is not when one simply believes or accepts that something is the case. One does not conceive one's limbs as going through movements which one can watch in a detached way. The action is to-be-done-by-oneself not just in that one's limbs are to perform it, but in that the movements of one's limbs are to-be-brought-about-by-oneself as source, initiator, guide. This 'self' is not identified with the moving body but rather as that which controls the moving body. If movements simulating the action conceived by one as to-be-done-by-oneself were carried out by one's limbs without one's intervention or control one would not regard oneself as having fulfilled one's intention or as having done anything at all. Essential to intending is that the action to-be-done is regarded as to be done by one's 'self', by the persisting source of thoughts and actions which *now* intends and *then* shall bring about the fulfilment of the intention (cf. chapter 11). It is one's *self* that is committed to bringing about the action.

We are now in a position to reconsider the issue which we earlier raised and left unresolved, the issue, namely, of whether or not there is an 'experience of intending'. It appeared at first sight that there is not. There seems to be no special kind of image or feeling characteristic of all instances of intending, and even if there were how could its presence make the difference between one's intending and one's not intending? Furthermore it has often been pointed out that one can go through whole stretches of thinking and acting which might truly be described as manifesting a certain intention, for example the intention to board one's morning train, without any such thought as 'the morning train is to be caught by me' being continuously, or even frequently, before one's mind. But in the light of what we have said about the switch from the ordinary or 'indicative' way of thinking to the 'imperative' mode of thought all this can be seen to be beside the point. For surely conceiving something as to-be-done-by-oneself yields a very different kind of experience from conceiving something as simply being the case. As James says (1890, II, p. 569),

> To the word 'is' and to the words 'let it be' there correspond peculiar attitudes of consciousness which it is vain to seek to explain. The indicative and the imperative moods are as much ultimate categories of thinking as they are of grammar.

And the working out of any intention is in a general way pervaded by this background awareness of something-to-be-done. Furthermore, is it not true that when one is doing something because doing it is a step on the road to the fulfilment of an intention, one's experience when doing it somehow embraces, is pregnant with, a grasp of the source of its to-be-doneness, of the place of this action in the overall plan of action? One is aware that the action has further point, and one's awareness of this can unfold or develop into an awareness of what the point is. If one loses the sense that there is a further point one is brought up sharply, puzzled and annoyed; then indeed one needs to remind oneself overtly what one's intention was. One has switched back to an 'indicative' frame of thinking.

A question which has been much, though not always profitably, debated is that of how intentions to act, whether simple ones or ones which involve or result from processes of discursive thought, or the consideration of moral principles, are translated into actions. An obvious answer is that intentions 'cause' the actions which fulfil them, but this answer meets certain difficulties. In particular, it has been argued that the link between an intention and the action which fulfils it is non-contingent and therefore non-causal (see especially C. Taylor, 1964). Part of what we mean, it is alleged, when we ascribe an intention to someone is that if nothing hinders or prevents him, if there are no 'countervailing factors', he will carry out the relevant action. For if he did not, when given the opportunity, carry it out his claim to have intended to carry it out could not be sustained.

These proposals have been highly controversial. Let us, however, assume that there exists a conceptual truth of the form 'A's intending to bring about φ will, *ceteris paribus*, be followed by his bringing it about'. Would it really follow from this that no causal relationship obtains between A's intending to bring about φ and his bringing it about? It would not. It is, for example, a conceptual rather than a logical truth that poisons cause sickness and death; but this does not preclude our explaining the connection in causal terms (Goldman, 1970, p. 112; Locke, 1974b, p. 175). For the substances which we call 'poisons' are susceptible of a fresh characterization in terms which do not mention their effects, and we can in these revised terms mark out a class co-terminous with the class of poisons, between ingestion of whose members and subsequent death an empirically establishable relation holds. Again, to take a somewhat more appropriate analogy, we might say that the intending agent is the acting agent in embryo – the intending agent has, as it were, transformed himself into a φ-pursuing system, and the acting agent is a φ-pursuing system too, one reaching its terminus. It would be very strange to say that the embryo was the cause of the adult form, the egg of the chicken, the leptocephalus of the eel. Part of what is meant by calling something an embryo is that, *ceteris paribus*, it will eventually develop into the adult form. Failure to develop could lead to the rescinding of the term 'embryo', as when it was found to be untrue that

> . . . Barnacles turn *Soland* Geese
> In th' Islands of the *Orcades*.

But from this non-contingent link it would not follow that the normal development of an embryo cannot be accounted for causally. For an 'embryo' might in principle be defined in terms purely of its present physical characteristics, i.e. ones in virtue of which it will *as a matter of fact* develop into an adult. The class of embryos thus redefined will be co-terminous with the class of embryos as traditionally defined.

May we then conclude that a causal account of the metamorphoses of intentions into actions can in principle be given? Unfortunately the answer is, no. For it does not seem possible to mark out in any way a class of events co-terminous with the members of the class of intentions. At the level of states we 'experience' or 'live through' any attempt to rebuild the notion of 'intention' without a definitional link to that of 'action' would inevitably land us with a class, for example that of 'idle dreams', whose boundaries were much larger than those of the class of 'intentions'. And then there would not be any special relationship, causal or other, between intentions and actions. Could we then identify 'intentions' with certain neurophysiological states? We have already given reasons (pp. 53–8) for supposing that intending, like any conceptual state or activity, cannot be represented within the paradigm of the 'generalized machine', whereas the linkages between nerve cells, and the activities of macromolecules within those cells, do lend themselves to such representation. Any neurophysiological account of intentions and their relations to actions will have to be couched in terms of which we have as yet scarcely an inkling.

An alternative approach might be to develop a revised notion of 'cause'. This is a task which most of us are happy to leave to someone else. And even if it were accomplished it is far from clear that the problem would not crop up again in a different guise. For instance, if we produced a definition of cause in which the idea of an empirically observable regularity of sequence ('A is always followed by B') no longer figured, we would still be faced with the fact that some kinds of causes exhibit such regularities while other kinds do not. And it would be the regularities which scientists would continue to pursue. Somewhere along the line we should have to confront the idea that the form of order exhibited in intentions and their fulfilment is prima facie different from that in which scientists have traditionally interested themselves. Indeed if proposals which we discussed in chapter 4 concerning the relations between volitions and actions have any weight, the problem might arise twice over – once in connection with the relation between intention and volition, and once in connection with the relation between volition and action. The non-contingent link, however, appears more plausible in the former case.

Some further relevant remarks will be found on pp. 171–2.

10

Knowledge of Intention and of Action

We have argued that no account of human behaviour, or at any rate of those aspects of it that are not totally trivial, can hope to succeed which does not rely heavily upon the everyday notions of intention and of action and upon the network of other notions to which they are inextricably related. We have also argued that these notions cannot be behaviourally reduced. It thus appears that empirical knowledge of intentions and actions, such as would figure in an hermeneutical science of human actions, cannot be knowledge of people's behaviour. Presumably, therefore, such knowledge must in part be knowledge of events or processes that are 'private' or 'mental', or it must at any rate be based on such knowledge. Now many psychologists would repudiate the idea that a science could ever be built up which was based on knowledge about purely private objects or happenings. And one must recognize that these psychologists have a point. Two investigators who set out to study their experiences are very much in the position of two persons each of whom is looking into his own private what-the-butler-saw machine. Suppose that each claims to observe scenes which to the other are singular and incredible, and that whenever one of them attempts to look into the other's machine the shutter at once falls. Neither can decide whether the other is telling the truth, lying or misinterpreting what he sees. It must accordingly remain quite impossible for them to reach any agreed generalizations about the contents of what-the-butler-saw machines.

In recent years a certain way of resolving this problem has been advocated by a number of philosophers influenced by Wittgenstein.

It is based on one of his more cryptic utterances, viz. 'an "inner process" stands in need of outer criteria' (1953, §580). This idea is developed with special reference to the concept of purpose by Boden (1972, pp. 263–81). Boden's view is that if purposeful behaviour were merely the contingent effect of some inner and completely private mental event we could never pass by any satisfactory process of inductive inference from the behaviour to the mental event. In the case of ordinary inductive inferences, the conclusion can be checked by observation; but when the inference is from behaviour to a mental event supposedly 'behind' that behaviour, further checking is logically rather than contingently impossible.

We must instead suppose that 'the meaning of psychological terms is at least largely behavioural'. Behaviour cannot be just a contingent symptom of some underlying mental state or process. It must provide us with 'logically adequate criteria' justifying the ascription of psychological predicates. Indeed, if it did not, Boden seems to think, we could never, in our interactions with our fellows, learn how to handle psychological language and communicate by means of it.

What exactly is the relationship between the behavioural criteria and that of which they are the criteria? Like other writers of similar views, Boden leaves this crucial matter obscure (on philosopher's uses of the term 'criterion' see Kenny, 1967; Mundle, 1970, pp. 118–19, 234–7, 241–2; Lycan, 1971). For the moment it will suffice if we bear in mind that the relationship is held to be a non-contingent one.

Boden claims a number of advantages for the 'criterion' way of looking at the problem of our knowledge of the purposes and mental states of others. First of all, it seems that we can eat our cake and have it too. We can ascribe psychological predicates to others on the basis of their behaviour without being forced to hold that the whole meaning of the psychological predicates is carried by the behavioural terms (p. 271).

> The point is that the introspective self-ascription of psychological terms is a secondary use, which is intelligible only because of its background of behavioural criteria, and which one learns only after being taught the primary use by means of such criteria.

Second, although some psychologists have wanted to extrude

teleological notions from psychology, we can now see that this is impossible. For McDougall has given behavioural criteria of purpose (spontaneity, persistence, plasticity, cessation with attainment of goal, etc.) which Boden apparently finds satisfactory, and which without doubt are in practice often fulfilled. But, third, this does not commit us to explaining the purposeful behaviour as caused by private conscious states. For the relationship between the mental or inner and the outer or behavioural aspects is non-contingent (cf. pp. 151–3 above), whereas it is essential to the notion of cause that the relationship between cause and effect be empirically discoverable. Fourth, Boden seems to think that the behavioural features which are criterial of purpose are also criterial of consciousness in general. Thus it would appear that no kind of conscious event can be assigned causal efficacy, which greatly simplifies the problems of explaining behaviour. Fifth, it might be that this weakens the argument that one never could assign consciousness and hence mental predicates to machines. For if the criteria for the application of such predicates are behavioural, these predicates could conceivably be applied to machines which showed the right kind of behaviour.

It would be possible to take issue with a number of these claims; but there is no disputing that the criterial approach to the problem of our knowledge of other people's purposes and intentions would simplify the issues on several fronts. We shall therefore have to consider this approach at some length.

An obvious place to begin is with some ordinary uses of the word 'criterion': by which we mean, roughly, the uses listed in the *OED* and in Webster's *Dictionary*. The central idea seems to be that a criterion is a convention or standard by reference to which something can be assigned to a category or to one category rather than another, or by reference to which we can decide whether or not it fulfils certain specifications or a certain norm or standard. Webster's mentions 'the criteria of a healthy diet' and the *OED* the 'criteria of beauty'. To *possess* a criterion is thus to possess a conceptual ability, which is brought to bear in making a particular categorial or other decision (cf. above, pp. 43–4). The word 'criterion' is also somewhat confusingly used for the properties by reference to which the category assignment is made. Such terms as 'criterial property' or 'criterial characteristic' might be better here. Wittgenstein's 'an "inner process" stands in need of outer criteria' could then be read as 'an "inner process" needs to have outer "criterial characteristics" '.

We shall suggest that the 'criterion' approach to the problem of our knowledge of other people's intentions and purposes (and of their mental states generally) misunderstands or misrepresents the logic of the selection and utilization of criteria (criterial characteristics), in these respects:

(1) Generally speaking, criteria are set up only in the context of some problem requiring resolution or some decision needing to be made. We do not set up criteria for deciding whether or not the feathered creatures in our henhouse are chickens, or whether the vicar beat the curate in the church croquet championship. In these cases there is no problem to be solved or decision to be made. The question of the creatures not being chickens, or of the vicar's not having won fairly and squarely, does not arise. We might, however, set up criteria when decisions do have to be made or problems resolved. We might need to set up criteria for differentiating the pale chanting goshawk from its European cousin, for deciding who most deserves a Nobel prize, for deciding whether or not Arthur Orton is Sir Roger Titchborne. Now for the most part there is no problem for us, no decision to be made, over whether other people's behaviour is the outcome of their intentions, purposes, feelings, etc. We do not need to set up criteria to help us reach conclusions in the matter. Just occasionally, perhaps, a mother may decide to assume that her son 'really' has a pain if he refuses breakfast and will not go out to play. But ordinarily we should, when confronted with an apparently normal human being, be more likely to set up criteria if it were suggested that he was *not* sentient or *not* purposeful, or was lying about his feelings and purposes, than if it were proposed that he was sentient or was telling the truth. For then a decision would be forced upon us.

(2) Criteria are always criteria *of* something whose nature is grasped independently of them. Setting up criteria of something, and certainly of the occurrence of an event or obtaining of a state of affairs, presupposes that you *already have* a general and more complex concept of the something concerned. In fact it is only in terms of this background concept that the different criterial characteristics can be seen to have any relationship to each other. For example the healthiness of a diet might be assessed in terms of (*inter alia*) muscle tone, blood chemistry, and the crinkliness of the finger nails. But considered on their own these things would appear a mere arbitrary assortment. Furthermore in order to be taken or accepted as properties or characteristics criterial of something, rather than as

a mere arbitrary assortment, the characteristics concerned must stand in an already agreed relationship to that of which they are supposed to be criterial properties. And in the case where criteria are supposed to be criteria of the occurrence or non-occurrence of events or of the obtaining or non-obtaining of states of affairs, the criteria concerned must either be agreed signs or symptoms of the event or state of affairs or else must be agreed to be parts or aspects of the event or state of affairs. For if, antecedently to being selected as criterial properties, the properties concerned had not had an agreed relationship to the events or states of affairs of whose occurrence they were to become criteria, a relationship such that had the events or states of affairs not been realized the criterial properties would not have come into being either, there would have been no grounds for selecting the criterial properties as *criteria* of the occurrence of *that* sort of event or the obtaining of *that* state of affairs. They would have been a mere arbitrary assortment of wholly disparate characteristics or happenings.

The application of what we have just said to the case currently under consideration is obvious. We have suggested that would-be criteria of the occurrence of events and states of affairs can only be advanced to the rank of fully-fledged criteria if their relationships to those events or states of affairs are antecedently agreed upon. If that is so, then we have to be able to communicate in a general way about purposes and their behavioural manifestations *before* we can take some among the latter as criteria of the occurrence of the former. But if behavioural criteria have to be proven signs of 'inner' happenings, or else proven aspects of wholes, parts of which are 'hidden', before we can accept them as criteria, the whole basis of the criterial view is removed. For we would have to solve the 'other minds' problem *before* we could set up criteria of the occurrence of events in or states of other people's minds; we could not solve it in terms of 'criteria'.

(3) Once criteria have been set up, the relationship between the criteria (criterial characteristics) and that of which they are the criteria is indeed analytic, definitional. It is of course understood by all that this relationship has been set up for a specific and localized purpose, and that if the criteria do not function adequately they can be abolished or changed. But if the criteria are fulfilled, then that of which they are the criteria *is deemed for present purposes* to be so or to be the case. Accordingly, and *within that context*, it does indeed become self-contradictory to affirm the criteria and deny that of which they are the criteria.

Now with regard to the problem of our knowledge of other minds the following further difficulty at once arises, namely that our ordinary concepts of intention, purpose, and other mental states, events or entities appear to be such that an analytic relationship does *not* obtain between on the one hand certain sorts of bodily behaviour and on the other hand purposes and other mental states. Prima facie, it is never self-contradictory, although it may be most implausible, to affirm the behaviour and deny the psychological predicate, or vice versa. At the very least one might claim that to reverse this estimate detailed analyses of these concepts would be required, and advocates of the criterial viewpoint singularly fail to provide them. In fact the whole force of their position seems to depend upon the claim that if there were no behavioural criteria, as distinct from behavioural signs, of psychological events or states, we should never have learned to communicate with each other about such events or states. This claim seems to rest upon the assumption that we 'decode' other people's behaviour not upon some long-term habits or principles which might be antecedently justified, but by means of a continuous series of inferences, each of which is to be looked on as justified or not in its own right. If the inferences were inductive, they would each be invalid, so we must in fact be using some other kind of inference. Straightforward deductive inference is ruled out, since we can here lay down no principles on which to base it. So we end up with peculiar and distorted ideas about 'criteria' and about their relationship to that of which they are criteria.

It might, of course, be said that our remarks so far are beside the point, because post-Wittgensteinian philosophers have developed their own, semi-technical, sense of the term 'criterion', whereas we have taken it in its ordinary or *OED* sense. It is certainly true that philosophers have of late years developed various idiosyncratic, mutually conflicting, and largely spurious uses of this word (see especially Mundle, 1970), some of which are very far from anything licensed by the dictionary. A common view is that the relationship between criteria and that of which they are the criteria is neither inductive nor yet simply deductive. Lyon (1974, p. 211) adapts the following from Lycan (1971, p. 110):

(1) the relationship between C (a criterion) and X (the state of affairs of which it is a criterion) is neither empirical

      nor such that the presence of C either entails or is
      entailed by the presence of X,

and

(2) ' "C is a criterion of X" means . . . it is *necessarily true*
    that C is evidence for X . . . it is necessarily true that
    instances of X accompany instances of C in *most* cases, or
    in all "normal" ones.'

Lyon suggests as an example the relationship between a lemon
and its defining properties.

(a) 'A lemon is a smallish ovate fruit, with a green or yellow
waxy skin, pips, and juice of a characteristically acidic taste'
. . . we will say that the characteristics or properties
mentioned in (a) are *criteria* for something's being a lemon:
although most (and perhaps all) of them are separately
neither logically necessary nor logically sufficient for
something's being a lemon, nevertheless they are related not
empirically but *a priori* with the characteristic of being a
lemon – they are the properties that would properly be
mentioned in explaining the meaning of the word 'lemon'.

Furthermore it is at any rate plausible to suppose that any one, or
any subset of these criteria, constitutes 'some *grounds* or *evidence*
for claiming' that one has before one a lemon.

Now there is no reason why philosophers should not for their own
purposes define 'criterion' as they wish. But redefining seems most
unlikely to help in any way with the problem of our knowledge of
other minds. The Lycan-Lyon formulation, for instance, could not
possibly do so, as Lyon shows in his article. For (1) simply equates
'criterion' with 'defining characteristic' and then points out that all
or most of the members of a set of defining characteristics have to be
satisfied before a category assignment is made. The occurrence of
one or a few of the defining characteristics does not entail the
occurrence of that which they define; and vice versa. But, as we
have noted, where the defining characteristics are pieces of bodily
behaviour, and that which they are supposed to define is a 'mental'
state or event, there is *no* set of defining characteristics which entails
the occurrence of the 'defined' state or event. Therefore the 'defining characteristics' are not defining characteristics at all. Are they
then 'criteria' in some sense *other than* the *OED* one? But it was

such a sense of 'criterion' that we were trying to arrive at when we introduced the term 'defining characteristic'.

(2) conflates 'criteria' and 'evidence' in a grossly misleading manner. This is perhaps most readily made apparent if, in accordance with what we have just said, we substitute 'defining characteristic' for 'criterion'. The occurrence of a 'defining characteristic' of something is not *per se* any evidence at all for the existence or occurrence of that something. For example a defining characteristic of a unicorn is that it possesses a horse's tail; but the appearance before one of a horse's tail is not in the minutest degree evidence that a unicorn is there. As Lyon remarks (1974, p. 223), whether the presence of certain defining characteristics from a set gives us good grounds for betting on the presence of the other defining characteristics from the set, i.e. of the thing itself, is something which only observation can tell us. Thus even if for the sake of argument we agree that mental states or events may have behavioural criteria, this does not mean that we can regard the fulfilment of the outer criteria as grounds for betting on the occurrence of the 'mental event', the thing itself, both inner and outer aspects. These grounds could prima facie only be provided by observation; but if we could have observation-knowledge of the 'inner' aspects of other people's mental states, we would not have needed to have adopted the 'criterion' approach to the problem of our knowledge of the minds of others.

We remain with the problem on our hands of how, or indeed whether, we can attain intersubjectively valid knowledge of each other's intentions and other mental states, and of the 'private' aspects of each other's actions. We may perhaps usefully begin by setting aside completely the model of our knowledge of psychological phenomena with which we began – the model, that is, which represented it as based on a kind of interior perception, or 'introspection', something like looking in on one's own private theatre performance. This traditional model has been many times attacked (see especially Shoemaker, 1963) but it is still implicitly accepted by many, and even finds explicit defenders (Armstrong, 1968, pp. 100–17, 323–38).

If we modelled our account of our knowledge of our minds straightforwardly on standard accounts of the nature of ordinary perceptual knowledge, we should have to suppose at least the following four things: (1) A sense organ or kind of nerve ending or special nervous apparatus by means of which the interior perception is carried out. (2) A kind of sensory or quasi-sensory experience characteristic of such perception. (3) A perceiver who at some level of analysis is set over against that which he perceives. (4) That the events perceived continue independently of the process of perceiving them. It does not appear that the alleged process of 'introspection' fulfils any of these specifications. If anything which would fall under (1) exists it has so far eluded the investigations of neurologists. As for (2), there is certainly no *special* kind of quasi-sensory experience characteristic of the supposed inner sense. In fact an obvious difficulty with the 'inner perception' view is that such vital aspects of one's mental life as intending, desiring, thinking, etc., clearly do not consist in a succession of sensations and images. When one has an image of a hoof and yet is thinking of a horse, there is not something observable over and above the hoof which one additionally perceives and which makes the difference between thinking of a hoof and thinking of a horse. One thinks of a horse, one means a horse. The thinking or meaning is a feature of one's mental life, and it cannot be analysed into the occurrence before the mind's eye of a cluster or sequence of quasi-perceptibles.

If we turn to (3), we find that, generally speaking, the perceiver in the alleged process of inner perception cannot in the relevant sense be set over against that which he perceives. Consider such states or episodes as intentions, desires, longings, ponderings, decisions. One could not simply watch an intention to *x* or a longing for *y* as it were pass through one, or a decision be arrived at within one. For intentions which one could watch detachedly would not be *one's* intentions, and decisions that one just noticed happening would not be *one's* decisions. In that case they could not be intentions, desires, decisions, etc., at all, one's own or anybody else's. This point could be elaborated.

(4) involves the supposition that one's intentions, desires, deliberations, decisions, etc., could progress normally without one's being aware of them. This suggestion is remotely plausible only in the case of sustained mental activities like longing for something, which, it might be assumed, one could hardly help noticing after a while if they were sufficiently intense. But try applying it to such 'mental acts' as one's deciding to do this, or its striking one that so and so, and the preposterousness is at once apparent. Suppose one was not watching oneself or was attending to trivial tickles when an important thought struck one. Then one might never know one had

thought it. One might look and to one's surprise find oneself exploring its consequences.

What other account can one give of one's knowledge of happenings 'in' one's own mind? It seems to us quite unlikely that there is any single type of account that will cover all the different kinds of case. Be that as it may, we shall have to confine ourselves to a brief consideration of the nature of our knowledge of our own intentions and the nature of our knowledge of our own actions. The literature on these questions is surprisingly small (see for example Anscombe, 1958, pp. 13–15, 29, 57; Donellan, 1963; Fleming, 1964; Broadie, 1967; Powell, 1967; Olsen, 1969).

We may usefully begin by distinguishing between knowledge of *what* we intend or intended or of *what* we are doing, and knowledge *that* we are now intending or then intended, or *that* we are now acting or then acted. In other words we must distinguish between our knowledge of the 'objects' of our intentions and actions, and our knowledge that certain past and present episodes in our histories are properly classified as intentions or actions. The former sort of knowledge is, in a way, much less difficult to deal with than the latter. For, as we have already pointed out (pp. 43–4), it is not merely a contingent fact that when a person acts he knows what he is trying to do, and it is not merely a contingent fact that when a person intends he knows what he intends. Such knowledge is intrinsic to intending and acting, and it cannot be observational knowledge, for if one could discover what one intended or was trying to do, either one did not know it until the moment of discovery and could not before then have been intending or acting, or one did know it, in which case one's 'discovery' was not a discovery. It is rather the case that one conceives a state of affairs and *makes it true* that bringing about that state of affairs is the goal of one's intention or action. Making it true that so and so is one's goal gives one a kind of 'knowledge' of, a kind of certainty as to, what one's goal is; and this kind of 'making true' can only be described as one of the 'powers' of an agent. Of course, whether or not one *actually achieves* one's goal is something one can only learn from observation.

At first sight one might suppose that our knowledge *that* we are now intending or acting or *that* we then intended or acted would require an analysis very different from that accorded to our knowledge of *what* we intend or intended and of *what* we are doing or did.

Take the case of intending. We have ruled out the possibility that our knowledge that our present or one of our past states is one of intending can be based on any kind of 'observation' of mental 'contents'. There is a temptation to suppose instead that since intentions are not observables, but, so to speak, phases of ourselves, episodes through which we live, our classing of them together, and consequent ability to think about them as a class, results from our recalling and reflecting upon certain past episodes, noting an affinity between them and realizing that *how we were* on each of those separate occasions was somehow, and indefinably, alike. However, if our tentative account of intention (chapter 9 above) is correct, there is no need for us to begin a despairing search for such recurrent quasi-observable features of intentions between which affinities can hold. Our account of intending was in terms of one's conceiving something as to-be-done-by-one, or a state of affairs as to-be-brought-about-by-one. This conceptual state – conceiving something as to-be-done-by-one – *characterizes* one. If one remembers oneself as one was, one's mental state as it was, on each of a number of occasions on which one intended something or another, one recollects oneself in the conceptual state 'something is-to-be-done-by-me'. Since that conceptual state characterized one on those occasions, one can only recollect oneself as one then was by deploying, as it were, *inter alia* the conceptual capacities which enable one to think of something as to-be-done-by-one. If one brought other conceptual capacities to bear on the question of how one was on those occasions one would not come up with the right answer. One would misremember. Analogously, if one spent an afternoon studying the anatomy of echinoderms, one could recall what one was doing only by exercising, *inter alia*, one's concept of echinoderm. If one forgot what echinoderms are, totally lost the concept, one would not be able to recall precisely what it was one was doing. Thus if one remembers those occasions one is bound to apply partially the same concepts in characterizing each of them; one is bound to class them together. The conceptual capacities which one exercises in intending are also the conceptual capacities which, *inter alia*, one has to exercise in recollecting examples of intending, in thinking about intending, and so on. The question of how one *comes* to class different occasions on which one intended together as examples of conceiving something as to-be-done-by-one cannot be raised; all one can ask (and it is a difficult enough problem) is how one comes to be able to articulate the categorization one is bound to make if one in fact recollects different past occasions on which one intended to do something.

The case of one's knowledge that one is acting is an extraordinarily difficult one, and we do not pretend to be able to give more than the most nebulous account of the matter. One is again tempted to suppose that there must be a characteristic experience of initiating, guiding, controlling one's movements. One notes that this experience commonly accompanies important segments of one's behaviour and so one abstracts or arrives at a notion of action under which future similar occurrences can be subsumed. But this will hardly do, for acting appears to have the characteristic that if one does not in some sense know that one is acting one cannot *be* acting (cf. Macmurray, 1957, pp. 90–1, 127–8). One might say that one invests oneself in one's actions. If they are blocked, *one* is blocked, if they go astray, *one* is going astray. This kind of investment can only be done by someone who knows, at least implicitly, in the moment of investing himself, *that* he is investing himself. It cannot be done by power of attorney and afterwards learned of by the investor. Thus a realization that what is happening emanates from oneself, that *one* is knowingly making it happen, appears to be intrinsic to action. If one did not in acting – in initiating, directing, guiding, controlling one's bodily movements – have this realization one could not *be* acting, *be* initiating, guiding, directing and controlling. One would be in a spectator relationship to one's own behaviour, and this relationship is incompatible with acting. To recollect one's past actions is to recollect events which were in part constituted by the way one categorized them at the time they happened, viz. as brought about by one, and to recollect them correctly one must recollect them as so categorized. There is no question of one's having to note features common to all of them in order to class them together.

Once again we are left with the exceedingly difficult problem of how this implicit knowledge becomes articulated; and also with the equally difficult developmental problems to which the supposition that the concept of action is essentially involved in acting gives rise. We do not feel sure how to resolve the problems, but it is better to be confronted with these issues than to have to attempt to make sense of the proposal that one learns to class one's 'intendings' together, or one's actings together, on the basis of a common quasi-observable aspect or feature possessed by all of them.

·   ·   ·

We now come to our central problem, namely that of whether, and how, our claims to have 'knowledge' of each other's actions and intentions may be justified. It would be idle to pretend that we are going to overcome or resolve the traditional perplexities which here arise. The most we can hope to do is make, in the light of conclusions we have already reached, some points which may be relevant to the resolution of these perplexities. We have two such points to make, and they are as follows:

(1) Once one is rid of the idea that one obtains one's knowledge of one's own intentions and actions from some kind of inner perception, one need no longer worry about the validity of the inductions by which one allegedly passes from what one observes in one's own case to what one presumes that other people must observe in themselves in comparable circumstances. No one 'perceives' or 'observes' their own intentions, or the 'inward' aspects of their own actions. The paradigms of observation-knowledge are not applicable to one's knowledge of one's own intentions and actions, nor is it appropriate to think of other people as having this kind of knowledge of their intentions and actions. To doubt the validity of one's knowledge of other people's intentions and actions on the grounds that one can neither perceive those intentions and actions oneself nor legitimately infer their existence from the statements of those who have perceived them is wholly to misconceive the situation.

(2) The position of those who believe we obtain knowledge of 'other minds' by an 'inference from analogy' is presumably this. One observes in one's own case that certain pieces of one's behaviour, or certain adventures of one's body, are generally accompanied by certain characteristic experiences. When one observes the bodies of others executing similar behaviour, or undergoing similar adventures, one infers 'by analogy', i.e. by a weak and complex kind of inductive inference, that these persons are undergoing experiences like those one commonly undergoes oneself in such circumstances. These hidden experiences provide an explanation, presumably a causal explanation, of the behaviour concerned. Now there is no doubt that we do from time to time speculate on the basis of other people's behaviour about their present states of mind and that we, for example, regard someone's being in pain as a sufficient explanation of his moaning and writhing. But it is simply untrue that our understanding of other people's intentions and actions is based upon an unceasing series of inferences from each item of their behaviour to the conscious pro-

cess supposedly accompanying and producing it. That other people's behaviour is to be understood and explained as action, as the
conscious product of more or less rational agents, is a background
assumption which we bring to all our dealings with our fellows.
People's behaviour makes sense to us if we regard it in this light; it
does not if we do not. It only occurs to us to doubt this assumption
on occasions when we are confronted with behaviour that is very
bizarre and irrational indeed. Otherwise we interpret behaviour as
action and look for its explanation to the intentions, desires and
reasonings of the agent. And to reconstruct an agent's intentions
and the reasonings he pursues in the hope of fulfilling them is not
necessarily to speculate about the sequence of his conscious states.
One can reconstruct a mathematician's solution of a certain problem by saying to oneself, 'Now, for so-and-so the problem was
to-be-solved; given the methods available to him, he would probably have taken this step and then this step', and so on. Similarly, one
can reconstruct the processes of reasoning gone through by someone who has framed a certain intention. One says to oneself, 'For
him, such and such was to-be-done or to-be-brought-about. In his
circumstances he would probably have reasoned thus and thus and
done this and this.' In neither of these cases is one in any direct way
speculating as to the moment by moment consciousness of the agent
involved. One is simply tackling a certain problem *as one thinks he
might have tackled it*. If one's results square with his observed
actions one feels one has understood what he did and why.

Of course behind all this is the overall assumption that the other
person is a conscious, purposeful and more or less rational agent
pretty much like oneself. But this is not an assumption that we make
(presumably at some point in our early development) as a result of
an inference or series of inferences which can be retrospectively
brought out and set up for critical assessment. A variety of empirical
and logical considerations (which we will discuss further in chapter
13) combine to suggest that from its very first days an infant is in
dialogue with what is for it a 'Personal Other' (usually its mother).
Its problem is not to learn that there is a Personal Other, but to learn
that some part of the 'Other' is not personal. The Personal Other is
in effect a participant with the developing infant in the formation
and implementation of joint intentions. The Personal Other will
take up and help the infant complete an unfulfilled intention which
the infant is unable to implement itself. The Personal Other will, so
to speak, direct the infant's nascent intentions into a mould of her

own making. Things are 'to-be-done-by-one' because the Personal Other makes them so; and often the things that are-to-be-done-by-one' are successfully done by one because of the assistance and intervention of the Personal Other. That the Personal Other, *though not directly under one's own control*, is *not* a bona fide participant in the game, or business, of conceiving things-as-to-be-done and then doing them, is a possibility which never arises for the developing infant. The assumption that the Personal Other *is* a participant is too basic even to be properly called an 'assumption' – it is part of the fabric of the infant's universe.

The 'justification' of this assumption, and of continuing it into adult life, can (if a justification is required or indeed conceivable) only be that upon no other hypothesis can we even begin to understand the actions of our fellow men or our interactions with them. We cannot dispense with the supposition that other people think, act, have intentions, and we cannot think of thinking, acting or intending except as we know them in our own case. Thoughts, actions, intentions, thought of in any other way would not *be* thoughts, actions or intentions. No mechanistic or any other reduction or elimination of them is possible – at least such has been a principal contention of this book.

11

Selfhood and Agency

At a number of places in this book we have explicitly or implicitly invoked the closely related terms 'self' and 'agent', and have proposed that several of the leading notions of hermeneutical explanation cannot be elucidated without introducing these concepts. For instance, we suggested that in the analysis of action an agent appears as that which brings a conceived criterion to bear upon the initiation or modulation of bodily movement, and we also suggested that it is intrinsic to an event's being an action that an agent should in some sense have 'invested himself' in it, that he regards its success as *his* success, its being thwarted as *his* being thwarted, as a blockage of his self-expression. We suggested that in intensional thought the thinker, as it were, points beyond, away from, his self as engaged in thinking that thought. We suggested that in discursive thinking, it is the *thinker* who grasps logical relations holding between the members of subsets of his beliefs. We suggested that if movements simulating an action which fulfils one's current intention were gone through by one's body without *one's controlling* those movements, this would not count as the fulfilment of one's intention.

Since the notions of self and agent appear to be thus central to and ineradicable from an hermeneutical psychology we must attempt some account of them. We shall stick for the moment to the concept of self, for this seems to embrace the concept of agent and something more besides. To be a 'self' something must be an 'agent'; but 'selves' also have passive or receptive sides to which the term 'agent' does not do full justice.

The philosophical and the psychological literatures on the self are both extensive; but unfortunately from neither the philosophical nor the psychological side does much help come towards answering the question of what we ordinarily mean when we talk of ourselves or of others as being or having 'selves'. The best approach we can take seems to be to attempt an account of what may be called the 'phenomenal' side of selfhood, of what, phenomenally, it is to be a self. For doing this will bring us as near as we can get to what people mean when they talk and think of themselves as selves, and as near as we can get to a theory-neutral elucidation of the concept of self. We shall first say a little about what, phenomenally, the self is not, and shall then discuss aspects of what it is under five numbered headings.

First of all, then, let us consider what, phenomenally, the self is *not*. It is *not* a kind of perceptible object (or quasi-perceptible quasi-object). For even if one were able to inwardly perceive some candidate 'object', how, in the notorious absence of any consensus of opinion would one know that the perceptible properties it exhibited were those in virtue of which it could rightly be called a 'self'? And how, as Shoemaker pertinently asks (1963, chapter 3), even granted that one could see a self, would one know that it was *one's* self? Not by observing oneself perceiving it, for that merely shifts the problem back a stage. By observing some of its properties? The only properties which characterize a thing uniquely are relational properties like 'being the mother of . . .'. Then one must perceive it to be uniquely related to just that thing a relationship to which will make it one's self, and one must be able to identify that thing as fitted for the role. And then one's self ceases to be that which is crucial in making one oneself.

How, indeed, could one possibly perceive one's self? The conceptual capacities with which one handles, divides up, the world of perceptible objects one is confronted with, are among one's properties or attributes, are things which *characterize one*. One cannot catch oneself in this network of capacities as if one were a kind of quasi-perceptible object. It would be more nearly true to say that one *is* the network of capacities with which one hopes to catch oneself. The network is one of one's characteristics, and to catch oneself by means of it would involve catching itself by means of it.

We shall discuss aspects of what, phenomenally, the self *is* under the following five headings:

(1) Self as localized enduring source and co-ordinating centre
(2) Self as possessor of attributes
(3) Self as undetermined maker of effective choices
(4) Self as self-determining
(5) Inner and outer aspects of self

(1) Self as Localized Enduring Source and Co-ordinating Centre
This is the side of self where agency lies, and thus the one which is of
particular relevance for the purposes of this book. To be a self is,
phenomenally, in part to be a source of activities, a creator of
actions, activities, plans, chains of thought, speculations. One can
perhaps just about *imagine* an existence which consisted entirely of
being a spectator of events, but such an existence is totally alien to
our own. This source is at once a locus within which these activities
are generated, and a locus from which some of them (one's
'actions'), so to speak, radiate outwards into the external world. To
talk of a locus here is no mere analogy. For the source has or is a
spatio-temporally localized vantage point, or set of interrelated
vantage points, within the world, and from that vantage point it can
operate upon the world.

To be a self is, phenomenally, not just to be a source of certain
sorts of activities; it is to be a source that endures. One regards,
lives, feels, one's various activities *as* successive phases, successive
manifestations, of *something that persists*, something that remains
relatively constant, and that owns or exhibits or produces or creates
or expresses itself by means of the phases or activities. One cannot
observe or point to this persistent something. Its continuity is lived
and not further describable. Yet this phenomenal continuity is not
just a background to our intentions, thoughts and actions; it is
something without which there could *be* no intending, thinking or
acting. For, phenomenally speaking, intentions, thoughts and
actions can only exist and have the relations to each other that they
do have, if they are lived, experienced, as phases of a centre which,
again in a way not susceptible of further description or definition,
actively co-ordinates one with the other.

Take the case of intention and action. Whether or not it is
appropriate to talk of intentions, goals, plans, purposes, etc., *causing* actions, it is at least certain that one cannot stand in a spectator
relationship to one's intentions and one's actions. Any intentions
that one could observe working within one, or any actions that one
could detachedly observe oneself carrying out, would not *be*

intentions or actions, or at least they would not be *one's* intentions and actions. One would be in the same relation to them as to the clouds and the weather. Any causal sequences which one could observe passing through one could not be sequences in which one's intentions had brought about one's actions. If there are any causal sequences relating intentions and actions they have to be of the form 'I intended . . . and that caused me to . . .'. Here the self who intends is assumed, or rather *felt*, to be identical with the self who acts, and is regarded as the link between the two, as that which intends, which co-ordinates intention with action, or translates it into action, and as that which acts. If this were not so, the action would not be a fulfilment of the intention. If one is to regard one's action as having fulfilled one's intention, *one* must have brought about the latter in the light of the former. One lives and experiences as a co-ordinating centre, and could not do otherwise. For, phenomenally speaking, one's intentions and one's actions *are phases* of such a centre, and are related to each other only through its mediation.

(2) **Self as Possessor of Attributes**
People say of themselves, and of others, such things as that they are religious, understand French, are kindly, have high ideals, know all about steam-engines, are patriotic, love music, and so on and on indefinitely. These terms tell us the sorts of actions they can do, and do, given the opportunity, the sorts of things they can think about and do think about given the opportunity, and the principles by which they regulate their thoughts and actions. Now we do not regard these terms as directly describing attributes of people's bodies or of their uncontrolled bodily movements. It is, in one's own case, to one's *self* as localized source and co-ordinating centre that one attributes the tendency to carry out such and such kinds of actions, the tendency to think such and such kinds of thoughts, the tendency to pursue such and such intellectual and practical goals; and when one attributes such tendencies to other people one attributes them not to those people *qua* bodies or sets of moving limbs, but to those people *qua* selves, enduring sources of actions and activities important aspects of which are not publicly accessible. These selves (one's own or other people's) have, in one's estimation, acquired a 'character', have become the *kinds* of sources and centres which do these sorts of things, carry on these sorts of activities. Now it must not be thought that the self is *felt* to possess

these tendencies or characteristics in the kind of way it possesses a lived or felt continuity as source and centre. But on the other hand neither is it the case that these tendencies or characteristics are regarded as properties simply of the overt bodily movements which a self initiates. It is rather that these tendencies or characteristics (thinking of steam-engines, enjoying music, thinking or acting patriotically) often (phenomenally speaking) characterize the self, the source and centre of activities which we have just, however inadequately, tried to delineate. The activities concerned, as it were, phases through which the self from time to time passes. Furthermore the activities concerned recur so frequently because one makes them recur, it is one of one's capacities as source to bring them about, and one does not bring about, or does not generally bring about, activities of an opposite or radically different kind (though occasionally one may act 'out of character' or not 'be oneself').

(3) **Self as Undetermined Maker of Effective Choices**
An important feature of what it is, phenomenally, to be a self is that, anteriorly to any reflection upon questions of free will and determinism, one regards oneself as an undetermined maker of effective choices. One supposes, implicitly, that one's choices determine the future course of events, and that, until one has chosen, the future is indeterminate. If one believed otherwise one could not think of oneself as choosing at all. If the future is determined before one chooses either one's choice is an epiphenomenon, without effect on the course of events, or one's choice is antecedently determined before one makes it, and *one* would appear to have no hand in it. One might still be an agent in the very limited sense that in implementing the choices one brings a conceived criterion to bear in the modulation of one's bodily behaviour. Such an agent would have no initiative, would not be the source of his own actions. He would rubber-stamp decisions antecedently imposed upon him. And none of us looks upon himself as being like that. Phenomenally, at least, some of our choices are our own, they are up to us; the outcome is not felt to be wholly determined by factors outside us.

(4) **Self as Self-determining**
If what we have said in sections 2 and 3 is right, then the following possibility arises, namely that one should appear to onself to be able to alter, by one's undetermined choices, the sort of attributes one

possesses, the sort of character one has; that one should regard oneself as changing and developing oneself. Some people, perhaps most, do thus regard themselves. And of course one might remark that if their belief happened to be *justified* this would be a fact of great importance to psychology. For part of psychology's task might then become to examine the processes and the possibilities of self-development, and to place the means of self-development at the disposal of those who wished to make use of them.

(5) **Inner and Outer Aspects of Self**

It would commonly be held that since the 'inwardness' of a self is not publicly accessible, selves are only known to each other by certain publicly observable 'externals', especially bodily actions and their results, personal possessions and appurtenances, habitual actions, general 'style' of behaviour and so forth. And of course such externals are as readily observable by the self whose externals they are as by other selves. James refers to them as the 'Me' in contrast to the 'I' who observes them. Now we commonly talk of some of these externals as though they *were* the self. One says 'I am ruined' when one's investments collapse, and 'I am humiliated' when caught with one's trousers down. The situation here is something like this. Our 'inmost selves' are centres from which, *inter alia*, our actions and endeavours, as it were, burgeon forth or radiate into the world. These actions are wrought by us in fulfilment of our plans and purposes and very often to make our thoughts, plans, hopes and fears known to others. That is why we refer to them so often as forms of self-expression. In fact it would not be too much to say that normal people have a kind of inner restlessness that can only be satisfied by activity, doing, generally of the public or self-expressive sort. The older terms 'psychic energy' or 'spiritual energy' have often been castigated as embodying inadmissible analogies; and yet they contain a grain of truth at some level or another. For a blockage of any of these forms of self-expression reacts in a direct way upon the self whose 'expressions' they are, and produces the experience we all know of being frustrated, cut off in mid-flow, of a burgeoning of the self that has failed to come to fruition. And the same sort of effect may be produced by the destruction of something in which one has in one way or another invested, as it were, a good deal of one's self-expression and one's psychic energies; for example one's collection of horse brasses or of rare volumes, one's home and family, the business one has built up, and so forth. Damage or destruction here represent the ultimate frustration not just of one's immediate goals and the corresponding actions, but of goals, sub-goals and innumerable actions and activities devoted to attaining them, and of innumerable further actions and activities more or less distinctly envisaged. And furthermore there is a satisfaction in, so to speak, giving a concrete form to one's conceptions so that they have a permanency and publicity and the admiration of others. In admiring what, *salva veritate*, may be called one's brain-children, other people get as near as they can to admiring one's self. One can see why such things should be regarded almost as extensions of one's self. Some of them stand to one in the relation of created to creator, and all of them have been the focal points of divers of one's goals and ambitions so that to cut them off is to cut off, render nugatory, those goals and ambitions, those hungerings of the self. But they are not the self.

In all this one's body is in a somewhat ambiguous position. For only to a very limited extent can one regard it as one of one's creations, and though one applies possessive pronouns to it it is hardly one of one's possessions in the sense that one's house and horse brasses, or even one's wife and children, are. Still one might say that, at the very least, it is one's only instrument in the actions and activities which express one's self, it is the only vehicle of one's self-expression, it is that through which in the last resort alone one's self can become known to others, and through which others will judge it and react to one. Hence its qualities and defects are quite closely associated with other people's views of one, and with whether one 'gets oneself across'. Furthermore, many of the self's plans and activities are concerned with bodily activities and bodily welfare. For these reasons one's bodily characteristics and skills are most intimately linked with the activities of one's self and sometimes one speaks of one's body as though it were one's self. Yet the two are neither phenomenally nor logically identical. For (1) in thinking of oneself *as* a self one thinks of oneself primarily as a source and a co-ordinating centre having a certain essential but not further describable kind of unity; only secondarily, if at all, does one think of one's self as being or having a body. Indeed it is not too uncommon for persons who are apparently normal to have experiences in which the phenomenal locus of the self (source and centre) is altogether outside the body (Green, 1968). (2) The predicates which it is appropriate to apply to bodies are prima facie inapplicable to selves, and vice versa, and there is, at any rate in the present state of our physiological information, no discernible way of bridging the gap. For example one cannot talk, except metaphorically, of selves being muscular or over-weight, or of bodies being *per se* the source of intentions or the co-ordinators of intentions with actions. (3) One could not consistently regard one's continuity as being *just* or even principally the continuity of one's body; for unless one were a continuing and unitary self one could not cognize one's own bodily continuity any more than one could cognize the relation of temporal succession obtaining between an event at time t and another event at time $t + 1$ (cf. pp. 177–8 below). This suggests that those who wish to make bodily continuity the criterion of self-identity are involved in arguments that are ultimately circular.

We have now provided a brief, and without doubt exceedingly inadequate, account of what, phenomenally speaking, it is to be a self or agent. Now when people, uncontaminated in so far as they ever are uncontaminated, with metaphysical theories, talk of themselves as 'selves', what they mean, we believe, is generally that the phenomenal 'appearances' are correct; they mean, that is, that there is some sense in which each of us *is* a localized source of certain kinds of activities, and an enduring centre within which, or through being aspects of which, these activities are co-ordinated; that as such sources and centres we are each the subject of certain individual attributes, have each a certain 'character': that there is some sense in which it is up to each of us, *qua* self and centre, whether or not certain actions or activities shall take place. And we want to end this chapter by claiming that these people are *right*.

We may note to begin with that, whether or not we have or are 'selves' in the relevant sense, we all do possess a concept of self which decisively influences our actions. A lot of one's planning is directed not just to the aggrandizement of the 'Me' but to the maintenance of the 'I' in preferred conditions (free of worries, distractions, out of trouble, bother, fear, etc.). One's plans, expectations, hopes and fears are very often for the future of this persistent something so conceived. Try having hopes or making plans for the future members of a continually changing Humean 'bundle' of sensations and images or for the nth in a series of Jamesian 'passing thoughts' the current member of which is to be identified with 'the thinker'. If the belief which we all cherish that we are persisting selves is an illusion, then it is an illusion which decisively influences much of our lives.

That it is not an illusion is suggested by the following considerations. It is an old argument, derived from Kant and Lotze (1887, II, pp. 168–73, 232–46), that all kinds of relational cognition presuppose a persisting subject who cognizes. Thus Campbell (1957, pp. 75–6) argues that unless the subject to which the *relata* are present is the same, no relation could be appreciated.

> To take the very familiar example of our cognition of succession in time, perhaps the most basic of all cognitions. If event B is cognised as sequent upon event A, clearly A must, in some form, be present to the same subject as that to which B is present. Otherwise A and B would simply fall apart into separate worlds of experience, and no discerned relationship – not even that of apartness, let alone that of temporal sequence – would be possible.

Could it be replied here that it is sufficient that the image or trace of event A persists in diminished form until B is cognized, and then influences the cognition of the latter in some characteristic way? The answer to this is obviously, no! For either the diminished cognition of event A coincides with the cognition of event B, in which case the cognition of temporal succession remains to be accounted for; or else the persistent trace of the first cognition has simply altered the second cognition, and all we have is a single, metamorphosed cognition, in which case the possibility of the cognition of a temporal relationship does not arise. Furthermore, Campbell argues, the subject has to be *conscious of* its identity in different cognitions (1957, p. 77).

> It is a precondition of my apprehending the second stroke *as* the second stroke that I remember having heard the first. But then I do not 'remember' having heard the first (and here is the crucial point) unless I am aware that it was *I*, the being who now hears the second stroke, who heard the first stroke; unless, in other words, I am not merely the same subject, but also conscious of my self-sameness, in the two experiences.

Similar points may also be made when the relations 'cognized' are logical ones. The proposition 'Socrates is mortal' cannot be recognized as following from the propositions 'all men are mortal' and 'Socrates is a man' unless all the propositions are apprehended and kept in mind by the same subject. Again, contradiction cannot exist unless the contradictory propositions are brought (Johnstone, 1967, p. 208)

> within a single perspective. This perspective is the person's self. It is the self that establishes the contradiction by bringing its poles together within a single perspective. This contradiction and self presuppose one another. In the absence of a self, there are no contradictions; there are at best evasive alternations of p and not-p.

Precisely analogous considerations, which we will not spell out in detail, can be advanced in connection with our conative as well as our cognitive activities. There is, for example, and has to be, a kind of experienced but also imposed continuity and co-ordination between the earlier and the later phases of the same simple action. One assesses and directs the present phase in the light both of previous and of projected phases, even though one may not distinctly envisage either. And if one could not keep track of the successive phases and see them, as it were, as parts of a whole manifesting through time, i.e. if one could not relate them temporally and in other ways, one would lose one's capacity to guide and control the whole action in any coherent fashion. When one comes to consider such a complex sequence of events as the fulfilment of a long-term purpose through the implementation of a plan involving the execution of various subintentions the case becomes even more obvious.

It is, as usual, important to be clear what we are *not* claiming. We are not claiming that the self is (or is *not*) a non-physical entity. Let us assume simply for expository purposes that the self in fact *is* some highly complex and persistent subsystem of the brain; it is a persistent aspect of the brain's functioning. What we would then claim is that no account of human intention, action, cognition and conation, can be given independently of a general account of this kind of brain functioning. For intentions, the initiation and guidance of actions, discursive thought, relational cognition, are all aspects of the functioning of this subsystem, and are related together or relatable together through being aspects of its functioning. We would also claim that no account of the functioning of this subsystem could be given in terms susceptible of representation within the GM framework.

We are not claiming that selves possess (or that they do not possess) 'free will'. Indeed we are far from clear what it would be for a self to possess it. In recent years the problem of free will (R. Taylor, 1966; Franklin, 1968; Ayers, 1968; Brand, ed., 1970a, section II) has usually been posed by asking whether it is sometimes or commonly the case that a human agent who did such and such in such and such circumstances ('circumstances' here including his own physical state antecedently to the moment of action) *could have* acted otherwise in precisely those circumstances, 'could have' here having a special meaning not synonymous with 'would have if' or 'it was logically possible that he should have' or any other phrase anyone has yet proposed. Thus posed, the question seems to us unanswerable and very possibly meaningless. For what can it mean to assert that a person who has weighed up all the alternatives and decided how best to act still 'could' act in some other way without circumstances having altered in the slightest, except indeed that it is conceivable that he might suddenly lose control of himself (cf. Whiteley, 1973, p. 86)? Of course if someone says to him, 'Do something else instead in order to prove free will and dish the materialists', or if a new idea suddenly strikes him, he may change his mind. But *then* the antecedent circumstances have changed.

What we do claim is (1) that human agents are the sources of a form or forms of order in the universe which are not reducible to the causal form of order as that has commonly been conceived since the time of Hume (cf. pp. 17–18, 129–30 above); (2) that these forms of order have a limitless number of possible kinds of instantiation; (3) that which of these possible kinds of instantiation actually happens is determined, sometimes at least, by human acts of choice; and (4) that even if 'making a choice' at time t is to be identified with some brain-event (of a kind we cannot as yet conceive), that brain-event could not with certainty be predicted from even the most complete knowledge of the brain's state at time $t - n$ and of its input-history from $t - n$ to $t - 1$. The 'self system', whatever its nature or putative physiological basis, has a certain intrinsic unpredictability, spontaneity, creativity, which render it a true 'source' or agent. If evidence be demanded for this assertion, we can only refer to the biographies of creative people.

12

Experimental Social Psychology in an Hermeneutical Perspective

So far in part II of this book we have devoted ourselves mainly to setting out accounts of certain concepts central to an hermeneutical psychology. But our aim in this has not been to attempt definitive analyses, it has chiefly been to illustrate the important aspect of hermeneutical psychology which, we argued in chapter 6 above, consists in the endeavour to make more clear the meanings of key hermeneutical terms. Indeed, undertaking definitive analyses would, we believe, be misplaced. For there is no reason to suppose that a single, final, detailed determination of these concepts is in fact possible. Their precise form and mode of application, as distinct from their general outlines and interrelationships seem to be a matter of human conventions, conventions which, although by no means entirely arbitrary, may develop in different ways at different times in different places (cf. pp. 8–9, 94–5). It is thus not surprising to find, for instance, that concepts of agency among the Eskimos are different from our own; while we think of ourselves as able to shape natural materials according to our desires, they think of themselves as working in with (embodying) natural processes to reveal what is already present in the materials (Carpenter, 1966). Their concept of agency is, one might say, 'gentler' than our own. Even the most central and ineradicable of hermeneutical concepts have thus a partly 'negotiated' character.

For this reason, among others, our aim in our conceptual analyses must be principally that of illustrating the nature of the endeavour; we cannot urge that any of the particular results we have obtained *must* be adopted *in toto*, we can only offer them as *our* results. Other psychologists engaged in investigation within an hermeneutical framework may find them helpful; to the extent that they live in the same society as we do, at the same time, sharing some of the same goals, values, interests and purposes, then we may hope that they will. But ideally, perhaps, they should begin their psychological investigations with their own conceptual analyses appropriate to their own circumstances, their own aims and interests, and see how their results compare with ours, rather than taking ours for granted.

It remains for us now to bring forward some illustrations of how these conceptual analyses might relate to the conduct of empirical investigations. In this chapter, then, we turn to an examination of some current empirical issues in experimental social psychology. We argue that the conceptual confusions which prevail in these areas can only be resolved when the relevant findings are divorced from the conceptual and methodological presuppositions which gave rise to them and are instead reinterpreted within an hermeneutical framework. In the next and final chapter we attempt to outline the nature of empirical enquiries which might begin and end within an hermeneutical framework. Such enquiries have a different character from enquiries undertaken within psychology conceived of as a behavioural science, for, not being concerned with prediction and control but with the clarification of understandings, they have no set methodology nor any particular theories. They presuppose a framework for the understanding of understanding, an understanding of the way in which different methodologies and different theories may function in the human effort to understand oneself and one's world.

Experimental Social Psychology

Earlier (in chapter 5 above) we mentioned that Argyle (1969) gives as his justification for a 'new look' in social psychology that experimental social psychology has reached something of an impasse: few issues of interest remain for experimental analysis yet nothing very exciting has been discovered. We argued that because he still conceived of his enterprise within the classical framework of natural science, he was simply looking in new places for the same old things – the *causal laws* underlying people's behaviour. While facing a new sphere of application, Argyle's approach still denies the basic fact that people are responsible for at least some of their own actions. Thus, while appearing to repudiate *experimental social psychology* and to prove himself on the side of those committed to studying everyday life activities, he is merely going through old motions in new places. What we would like to do here is to examine more closely the presuppositions that Argyle has translated from one setting to another.

In this chapter we shall first discuss how experimental social psychologists set out their conception of their subject matter, and then consider some of the topics they have investigated – distributive justice (Homans), cognitive dissonance (Festinger) and obedience (Milgram). We shall argue first that these investigations contain a great deal of phenomenology and conceptual analysis disguised as merely heuristic 'asides' and to this extent contain much of value. Second, we shall argue that to the extent that such investigations are held to reveal the 'real' reasons for our conduct, to get 'behind' or 'beneath' common sense, they are being radically misunderstood by those who conduct them.

The Subject Matter of Experimental Social Psychology

Let us begin, then, by setting out the way in which experimental social psychologists conceive their subject matter. The issue is an interesting one as, unlike other areas of experimental psychology influenced by the mechanistic paradigm, in which all talk of thoughts and feelings, etc., must be banished and only talk of inputs and outputs, stimuli and responses allowed, in social psychology the existence of such conceptual things is taken for granted. They are assumed to be 'things' just like any other things and open to the same modes of investigation. Thus Deutsch and Krauss (1965, p. 3) outline the subject matter as follows:

> Just as the animal psychologist who is studying the behaviour of a rat in learning a maze must know the relevant physical properties of the maze to understand or predict the behaviour of the rat in it, so too the social psychologist must be able to characterize the relevant features of the social environment in order to understand or predict human interaction.

In other words, the social psychologist adheres to the principles of Watsonian behaviourism. But how is it that when Watson suggests that it should be possible 'never to use the terms consciousness, mental states, mind, content, will, imagery, and the like', experimental social psychology is still able to refer to mental states, cognitive elements, and suchlike? The answer is quite simple: by using all such 'mental' terminology in a way quite different from the way we use it in conducting social exchanges in everyday life, and by assimilating it to the framework of thought used in animal studies.

Thus it is that, when broaching any topic for study in this sphere, one is not asked to reflect upon what one might have meant when one said one was motivated in a particular social exchange by a desire for, say, justice; one is not asked to show that one understood the implications of one's act and to show why, given them, one felt justified in accounting for one's act that way. Instead of beginning by investigating how one actually does use such words in explaining or justifying one's actions, one is asked to begin by 'seeing' such exchanges in quite other than their everyday terms, as if something else than the attempt to obtain justice was 'really' going on. What is 'really' going on, Homans (1961) asks us to believe, is not the desire for justice, but the desire to have rewards proportional to our costs; in other words, Homans asks us to believe (as also, we have previously pointed out, does Argyle) that in seeking justice, we are not 'really' judging people's actions in relation to moral standards, but are carrying out an 'economic' exchange. But more than simply inviting us to consider things as being other than we ordinarily suppose, such experimental analysts of social life suggest that we *must* abandon our view and adopt theirs, for theirs has been scientifically proven to be 'really' the case.

This claim to be uncovering the 'reality' behind our actual everyday affairs must be challenged. We would like to do this in the course of a discussion of some of the major topics that have occupied experimental social psychologists in recent years.

Distributive Justice
Homans (1961) introduces his discussion of the elementary forms of human behaviour via a discussion of operant conditioning (Skinner, 1938, 1953, 1957, 1959); that is, he proposes that human social exchange can be understood in just the same way as the exchanges that are supposed to go on between an animal and its trainer. Homans takes the old joke – of one rat saying to another, 'Boy, have I got this guy conditioned. Every time I press this lever he gives me a food pellet' – seriously. For he suggests that, 'In the last chapter we might have thought of the psychologist as engaged with the pigeon in an exchange of grain for pecks ... [except that] the pecks reinforce the psychologist not as pecks but as science ...' (Homans, 1961, p. 30).

Well, one can 'see' it like that if one tries, and it can result in some amusing and perhaps important insights. Similarly, when Homans continues, 'With the psychologist the pigeon carries on the same kind of exchange that he does with the physical environment, which is what we mean when we say the psychologist is studying individual behaviour' (op. cit., p. 30), we can again 'see' the situation like that. We can appreciate it as a rather imaginative proposal, poetic even; *but is it actually true* to say that the pigeon carries on 'the same kind of exchange' with the psychologist as with the physical environment? Further, is it actually true to say that such exchanges are what we mean when we say 'that the psychologist is studying individual behaviour'? Observing in a psychologist's behaviour a pattern of events of the same kind as that manifested in a pigeon's behaviour would not ordinarily lead one to say that he was studying individual behaviour; at best, surely, it might lead one to say that he was trying to imitate pigeons, but more likely it would lead one to say that there was no sense in his behaviour at all. Only with a leap of the imagination can one appreciate the force of Homans' approach and 'see' social exchanges as he requests us to see them.

And that is an aspect of this kind of approach, perhaps, not to be discounted, for in the natural sciences great advances often do begin in the imaginative constructions provided by seminal thinkers. Surely there is the same need for such constructions in the human sciences? Well, apparently not. For what makes the study of the human world different from the study of our 'external world' is that, whereas the latter is by definition outside us and the best we can do is guess at what its nature *might be like*, we are in the middle of our human everyday life world, and thus it is not a matter of imagining what such a world might be like, but of getting to know what its nature actually *is* (Berlin, 1976). All of which is only to say, as we have said in other places, that our primary reality is that which is present to us in our everyday lives.

For this reality, however, writers like Homans substitute, by deft moves, another, quite different. In his discussion of *distributive justice* he points out that a pigeon 'expecting' grain and getting none 'displays what looks to a human observer for all the world like anger and frustration' (Homans, 1961, p. 72). But to attribute human thoughts to a pigeon, he points out, would be wrong. 'What the observer *really* refers to when he talks of the pigeon's expectations or deserts is its past history of reinforcement under particular stimulus-conditions' (op. cit., p. 73, our emphasis). Having got us to

accept that pigeons do not really have expectations, only reinforcement histories, he goes on 'In the same way, men express anger,
mild or severe, when they do not get what their past history has
taught them to expect' (op. cit., p. 73). The implication is that men
too do not have expectations, only reinforcement histories. But men
do have expectations, and the move to the discussion of their
reinforcement histories is quite illegitimate. And furthermore, in
making it Homans reveals what the proper analysis should be. He
himself does not fall into the trap of attributing human thoughts to
the pigeon, for he does not say that the pigeon *is* angry or frustrated,
but that it displays what looks '*like* anger and frustration'. And that
is just what one does ordinarily: we describe that which is unfamiliar
to us in terms of that which is familiar. Homans has, however, by
means of subtly discrediting talk of familiar everyday things, turned
the whole process back to front, suggesting that when we talk about
people's expectations, etc., we are *really* talking about something
else altogether.

Now so far we have not outlined Homan's notion of *distributive
justice*. But that is not surprising, for one's understanding of it is
quite independent of all the talk about stimulus-conditions, and
reinforcement histories, and other such terms defined within the
operant conditioning field. And this is the point: when it actually
comes to his proposal for a general rule, Homans states it first in
commonsense terms – 'A man in an exchange relation with another
will expect that the rewards of each man be proportional to his costs
. . . and that the net rewards, or profits, of each man be proportional
to his investments . . .' (op. cit., p. 75). And putting the matter like
this suggests an entirely different kind of empirical investigation
centred around the principle of distributive justice than the one
Homans conducts. Rather than framing our analysis solely in
economic terms, we would want to begin by asking, 'What in different particular circumstances does it *mean* to say that people are
regulating their exchanges with regard to achieving a balance between rewards and costs?', 'What is *meant* in different particular
circumstances by the terms "reward", "cost", "balance", etc.?',
'What methods do people use to come to an agreement about their
concepts in order to make such a general principle as *distributive
justice* applicable in their circumstances?' and so on. These investigations would all be concerned with how people actually do these
things as a part of setting up the framework for the conduct of their
daily lives. Thus our empirical work here would be aimed, not at

providing proof that the general principle of distributive justice was in fact *the* one, single principle regulating social exchanges, but at investigating what is wholly unknown at the moment: the different ways in which people put such a principle into practice.

But we must add, 'Would reference to such a principle as "distributive justice" always clarify what it means to be *fair* in different particular circumstances?' Would it, for instance, clarify the issue in tennis or chess? Surely in competitive games all that one asks of the competitors is that they abide by the rules of the game. We expect the outcome to depend not upon costs and investments, but upon talent – talent being more like a 'gift' than an 'investment'. There is the expectation, not of achieving a balance in the exchange, but of there always being an hierarchy with a 'top dog', else the game is not worth playing.

We could continue, but surely the point is plain: it is logically inappropriate for Homans to try to explain *everything* people do in terms of a few general principles. Such a move fails to mark important distinctions that we really do make in conducting our everyday lives – between acting within guidelines but towards no specific goal, say, and acting towards a goal but within no specific guidelines; and, most importantly, between acts and events, between what people themselves do and what they merely find happening to them. In Homans's world only Homans acts, the people he studies merely behave.

Cognitive Dissonance

Many of the points made above may also be applied to Festinger's (1957) account of *cognitive dissonance*. Festinger, like Homans, introduces the notion of cognitive dissonance in a discussion of particular everyday examples – getting a college education for one's children, smoking, committing crimes, etc. And he points out that what catches our attention is *inconsistent* behaviour: for example, a person may know that smoking is bad for him and yet he continues to smoke. If consistency is 'the usual thing', what happens when inconsistencies like this occur? The answer is not at all straightforward because (1957, p. 2), 'only rarely, if ever, are they accepted psychologically *as inconsistencies* by the person involved'. However, while people may attempt to rationalize inconsistencies, such attempts are rarely successful, and then a condition of 'psychological discomfort' prevails. This is an experience of 'dissonance'. Festinger sets out the basic hypothesis that he wishes to explore,

experimentally as follows (op. cit., p. 3): 'The existence of dissonance, being psychologically uncomfortable, will motivate the person to try to reduce the dissonance and achieve consonance.' And
he then continues, just as Homans did, to invite us to 'see' the social
world with new eyes – 'Cognitive dissonance *can be seen as* an
antecedent condition which leads to activity oriented toward dissonance reduction just as hunger leads to activity oriented toward
hunger reduction' (op. cit., p. 3, our emphasis).

But the trouble is that while we can 'see' certain circumstances *as*
dissonant in some sense, it is not clear even in dissonance theory
what that sense is. What we want to do is to show that from a
commonsense point of view there is no one, single definitive
analysis to be had. And that is why attempts to clarify the concept by
doing yet further experiments only succeed in revealing yet more
senses in which the term may be interpreted.

Dissonance arises, Festinger (op. cit., p. 13) maintains, when the
'obverse' of one 'cognitive element' follows from another. Or, 'to
state it a bit more formally', he says, 'x and y are dissonant if not-x
follows from y'. But just in case we have still not quite understood
what is meant by the terms 'cognitive elements' and their 'obverses',
he gives us some more examples – 'if a person were already in debt
and also purchases a new car, the corresponding cognitive elements
would be dissonant with one another'. But would they? Most people, if they are not already in debt, go into debt on buying a new car.
It is, one might say, 'the usual thing', similarly for buying a house; in
fact, one *is* usually in debt from buying one's house when one buys
one's car. There are certain things people do in our society which
require no justification. They are accepted goals, part of what
everyone normally does who lives out his life in our society. But
going into debt to buy a new hi-fi would be more unusual, and going
into debt to buy a luxury would not be 'the done thing' at all; one's
skills of constructing justifications would be taxed to the utmost.
The task of analysing life's options, and deciding what follows from
what, and what is inconsistent with what, is not at all easy. In trying to decide what we should do next, we fall back upon many
different techniques, heuristics and stratagems; only if we can
succeed in constructing a properly logical framework, and in
forcing our circumstances into it, can we possibly detect inconsistencies.

In introducing dissonance theory, Festinger clearly modelled his
approach upon that current in animal psychology – he thought of

dissonance as a 'drive' to be 'reduced' by the activity it 'motivates' – and in such an approach man is 'seen' as an object caused to move by antecedent conditions. But in recent work on dissonance theory there has been a move away from this view of man towards a view that people are agents who can make choices for which they feel responsible, and for which they might feel called to account. Rosenberg (1970), for instance, has repeated some of Festinger's experiments (Festinger and Carlsmith, 1959) with some slight variations to get entirely different results. Rosenberg compared what happened when he got people to *commit* themselves to advocating an attitude contrary to their own, with what happened when people merely 'went through the motions of' advocating it. People's active involvement proved, as one might expect, crucial – in that situation. Tedeschi, Schlenker and Bonoma (1971), however, consider the case when people exhibit apparent inconsistencies *before an audience*. It is not a matter of whether the person experiences a contradiction, they suggest, but of whether he believes that his audience sees one. Thus his way of acting in such 'psychologically uncomfortable' circumstances is not so much influenced by his internal state as by his skills in 'impression management' (Goffman, 1971).

And so on; and no doubt many more proposals will be introduced each one claiming to give a definitive account of dissonance theory. But, as we mentioned above, the social psychologist's view of man is changing. And as it moves more towards viewing man as an agent who *interprets* his circumstances, such experiments must be viewed as revealing the *concepts* that people are, or might be, using to regulate their actions, rather than as uncovering the *causes* of their behaviour. However, in analysing a concept it is necessary to compare and contrast its use in a great range of particular instances. Thus, although the type of empirical investigations that we would propose conducting in this sphere from within an hermeneutical perspective are already being done, the perspective necessary to make proper sense of the results still seems to be lacking. Thus it is all very well for Secord and Backman (1974, p. 78) to suggest that 'engagement of self' may be important in such issues as these, but if no proper analysis of the concept of self exists the meaning of their proposal remains unclear. They sum up their account of dissonance theory by saying (pp. 81–2):

Both on theoretical grounds and in terms of hindsight it is clear that much of the research has neglected the social nature

of the contrary act and the larger setting in which it is
performed, and that this neglect is in large part responsible
for the fact that a prodigious amount of experimentation has
failed to produce a sufficiently precise theory and an adequate
body of knowledge concerning the effects of behaving
contrary to one's attitude.

We would agree that neglecting 'the social nature of the contrary act
and the larger setting in which it is performed' is tantamount to
neglecting the fact that the way in which an individual experiences
'dissonance producing' circumstances (either in experiments or
otherwise) depends upon how he *interprets* them – 'dissonance'
arising, presumably, not so much out of one pattern of behaviour
being intrinsically incommensurate with another, as out of their
meanings being logically incompatible. We cannot agree, however,
that it is this neglect that is responsible for a prodigious amount of
experimentation failing to produce a precise theory. For, from our
point of view, not only is there no such 'precise' theory to be had,
but to feel that the mere neglect of relevant variables is the reason
why 'experimentation has failed to produce a sufficiently precise
theory' is to misunderstand the whole relation between theory and
experiment.

   To take the last point first: experimental social psychologists
seem to expect theories to grow out of experimental data on their
own. But surely, making observations and doing experiments is
nothing to do with *discovering* theories: experiments are only meant
to put the logically derived consequences of clear theoretical statements to empirical test. Discovering theories is something that
people do either in thought, by themselves, or in dialogue with
others; and theories certainly do not formulate themselves out of
arrays of experimental results.

   Turning now to the question of precise theories: in their search
for the causes of people's behaviour, experimental social
psychologists search for *the* cause of each particular type of
behaviour (*vide supra* the quotation from Deutsch and Krauss,
1965). That is, they expect to discover *the* one fundamental cause of
all happenings of a particular kind. Let us try to show, by outlining
the sort of results we might expect from hermeneutical investigations in this sphere, why we feel hope of a 'precise' theory in this
sense is forlorn; there is both a methodological and theoretical
aspect to our discussion. Methodologically, we would have to point

out that all 'experiments' done should be treated as special cases, revealing solely, not *the* cause of 'dissonance' effects, but merely one example each of how people actually do account to themselves for their own and other people's actions. For, if we are interested in the concepts people use to regulate their actions, and want to understand how they can land themselves in what they see as contradictory situations, and to understand some of the methods they use to extricate themselves, studying just one example is not enough – especially when people are participating in a special form of social interaction known as 'taking part in an experiment' (Orne, 1962). Each different example reveals some of the ways in which a particular concept is used, some of the ways in which it is logically related to other concepts in a person's repertoire. It is necessary to investigate a whole range of cases in order to clarify the network of concepts in which the concepts we are studying play their part. We need to appreciate routine uses and to distinguish them from borderline cases – and where we have trouble in clarifying a concept, we might expect other people to be unsure also and, perhaps, to be confused in accounting for their own behaviour. So, methodologically, we cannot expect an *experimentum crucis* in hermeneutical psychology; we must study a wide range of different cases, and expect, even then, to be able only to arrive at accounts related to particular social groups at particular points in their history. And it cannot be over-emphasized that, although much work done now on 'cognitive dissonance' does view people as agents interpreting their circumstances, they interpret their circumstances in the knowledge that they are 'participating in an experiment' and inevitably their interpretation is going to be different from when they are engaged in a real life decision.

Theoretically, too, our investigations would have a rather different aspect to them. Primarily, the difference would be in the extent to which an attempt would be made to analyse the way in which the concepts featured in any empirical studies were ordinarily used. Without such an analysis it is not at all clear what it is that such empirical studies are meant to be investigating – in 'dissonance' studies, for instance, the matter still remains to be clarified. But even more than this, we would continue the attempt to construct a general account of key hermeneutical terms. For, we would expect any analyses of concepts to involve them in some way (hence their status as key terms). Also, such a general framework could provide a 'yardstick' against which all the different particular accounts arising from different particular empirical investigations could be 'measured' to see if they accorded. So, although the activities of experimental social psychologists may remain in many respects as they are, others of a philosophical kind must be added and be allowed to influence the interpretation psychologists put upon their findings.

Obedience

One of the most remarkable topics of research in recent years has been Milgram's (1974) study of obedience to authority. Essentially, he set up a situation in which two apparent volunteers came into a laboratory to help an experimenter in a study of the effects of punishment on learning. The 'learner's' arms were strapped to his chair, and an electrode attached to his wrist. He was told that he was to learn a list of word pairs, and that whenever he made a mistake, he will be given a shock of increasing intensity by the 'teacher'. The shock machine was graduated from 'slight shock', through 'very strong shock', 'danger: severe shock', to some last positions simply marked XXX. Now, in fact, the 'learner' was always an accomplice of the experimenter, and although he acted as if he received electric shocks, he did not actually do so. The 'teacher', however, believed that he was an ordinary member of the public being paid like himself to participate in the experiment. Milgram's interest in this experiment was to discover at what stage and under what conditions 'teachers' would refuse to shock the 'learner'. In fact few did so. And what made Milgram's result all the more surprising is that *everyone*, when asked merely 'to think' about what they would do in the situation, said that they would break off before the voltage got too high.

Milgram's studies raise some extremely important issues, but while his results might appear clear-cut, their interpretation is not straightforward. Again we would like to suggest that the phenomenological accounts subjects give in these experiments (their accounts of how they assign responsibility for what goes on) and the conceptual analyses involved in setting them up – both of which are 'asides' to the main task of constructing a formal theory to explain obedience to authority – are in fact the results of significance.

Let us begin our discussion by referring to how people say they would behave if they were asked to be a subject in such an experiment. Most people predict that they would not go beyond 150V., where the top shock level is 450V. Milgram lists some of the assumptions that seem to underlie the predictions that people make about themselves: that people do not readily hurt the innocent; that unless coerced the individual is pre-eminently the source of his own behaviour; etc. He arrived at his list by collecting accounts from a fair number of people of what they thought they would do and why in such a situation. But there is something wrong with such accounts. They fail to predict what happens in Milgram's experiments when similar people actually participate in them. What is wrong with them, Milgram (1974, p. 31) feels, is that in giving them, most people 'focus on the character of the autonomous individual rather than on the situation in which he finds himself. With this view, they are likely to expect few subjects to go along with the experimenter's orders.' It *seems* that people fail to take proper account of the nature of the experimental situation and of the subject's commitment to the experimenter.

This, then, *seems* to be the question at issue: why do people, all of whom had the situation fully explained to them, fail to take account of the fact that they will be influenced by their commitment to an experimenter? (That this is not the true nature of the issue will become clear when later we discuss Mixon's (1974) role-playing study of Milgram's experiments.) From an hermeneutical point of view the question would lead to a focus upon people's *accounting practices*, in an attempt to discover why it is that requests for predictions about future behaviour are interpreted as requests only for an account of one's principles, rather than for an enactment, say, of what one would do. For it is not as if we do not understand at a practical level the nature of the commitments we have to one another in various social situations; there is ample evidence of that fact in the protocols of the experiments in Milgram's book. What we do not seem to possess in our society at the moment is a rich and extensive commonsense scheme of accounting for such commitments; the analysis and labelling of them has yet to be undertaken. Possessing such a scheme, people in Milgram's experiments could have said to the experimenter, 'I'm stopping now as to hurt another person in an experiment is not in the nature of the kind of commitment or contract one usually has in these sorts of circumstances'; possessing such a scheme of 'motives' or of reasons for action accepted by society at large, people could *feel justified* in a way unavailable to them at present.

The point we are trying to make here is that in ordinary everyday life people have, if they want to do anything, to be able to justify it to others. If they cannot, then they find themselves in a morally weak position; they are pointed at as fools who do not know what they are doing; others feel justified in restraining them – they have lost that attribute which gives them autonomy in relation to others, the ability to reject criticism and to show that their actions do in fact accord with the values and interests agreed to by all in their society. To be unable to justify oneself is to risk being an outcast, a non-person; it is to lose one's personhood. At any one time a society seems to be constituted by reference to a complex web of 'motives' which function as rock-bottom reasons for why we do what we do. Thus, for instance, getting an education, getting a job, getting married, having children, etc., are the 'done things' in our society, and what is 'not the done thing' is to question them (hence the hostility to those who now are questioning just those activities). And any puzzling, or suspicious, or other untoward activity, can be justified if it can be shown to be properly related to one or another of our agreed ways of going on; our activity can be considered to be *legitimate*. On the other hand, any activity which is not just puzzling, but which is obviously unjustified in any commonsense terms, can leave those experiencing it totally bewildered and confused as to what to do about it, as Garfinkel (1967) has discovered.

Milgram's experiments can be analysed, we maintain, in the above kind of way. And such analyses could provide the kind of explicit justifications for action currently lacking in society in this sphere at the moment. An hermeneutical analysis of commitment, besides focusing upon the problem in a rather different way to Milgram's, could lead also to rather different modes of social functioning.

Let us dwell upon this issue for a moment: in attempting to give his own account of his results, Milgram (1974, p. 125) proposes a cybernetic model of society. He feels that the problem of obedience to authority is not to do with methods of social accounting, but to do with a change that takes place within an individual 'as it moves from a capacity for autonomous functioning to a capacity for functioning within an organisation'. Thus although the principles of the science of regulation and control may seem far removed from the behaviour of participants in his experiments, Milgram is 'convinced' that they are at the root of such behaviour. He attempts to explain obedience as an essential part of man's nature; not, as we have suggested, amenable through greater understanding to self-control, but a part to which man inevitably falls victim. In his experiments, a tendency far more dangerous than man's capacity for anger and rage against others is revealed, he feels (Milgram, 1974, p. 188); it is 'the capacity for man to abandon his humanity, indeed, the inevitability that he does so, as he merges his unique personality into longer institutional structures'. This leads Milgram (p. 188) to the ultra-pessimistic conclusion that, 'This is a fatal flaw that nature has designed into us, and which in the long run gives our species only a modest chance of survival.' Quantitative though his cybernetic theory may someday be, Milgram has not yet calculated what that modest chance is.

In reviewing these three topics of research in experimental social psychology we have tried to show, in broad outline, how an hermeneutical psychology would conduct itself, and what outcomes could reasonably be expected. The matter is best summed up by saying that, whereas the classically motivated experimental social psychologist aims at *replacing* everyday commonsense accounts of human action the hermeneutical approach merely aims at analysing, refining and enlarging upon such accounts so that we know, not only more clearly what we are doing, and why, but also more clearly what else we *might* do instead. The aim is not to provide a *better* basis for social life but simply to enrich what we already have by bringing out into the light of day more reasons for acting as we do, more ways in which people might justify their actions to one another, and thus increase the domain of actions in which they may be self-determining while still acting in accordance with shared interests and concerns.

Experiments in Social Psychology and What is Really 'Real'

Two issues have come up time and time again in these discussions: one is the use of the word 'real' by social scientists, the other is the extent to which experiments are representative of real-life situations. The two are not unconnected. Experimentalists are continually asking us to 'see' what we ordinarily call expectancies *as if* they were 'reinforcement histories', or to accept that 'cognitive dissonance' *can be seen as* an internal state like hunger. In other words, they want us to treat what is in fact going on as if it were 'really' something else. Similarly, they want people to treat the artificial, contrived situations in which they gather their data as if those situations were not artificial and contrived, but were really situations of quite another kind. Let us discuss these two issues in turn.

Now as Stebbing (1937) points out, the words 'real' and 'really' are used in everyday speech without causing confusion. The opposition between a real object and an imitation is clear, as is that between really seeing something and an illusion or mirage, etc. Further, as Wilkerson (1974, pp. 165–8) shows, our use of it in requests for information – are there really adults four feet tall? – is also clear. Our problems arise when the words are not used in familiar everyday contexts but are used in making claims about the absolute nature of things – that tables are 'really' swarms of electrons, that expectancies are 'really' reinforcement histories. But to what exactly is the scientist appealing in making such claims, when the only understandings of the words 'real' and 'really' that we have are drawn from commonsense usage? Clearly the scientist wants us to treat what we feel is real as illusory, and to pattern our future actions regarding tables and expectancies on the basis of his accounts of them rather than upon our everyday accounts. And, of course, we can do this. But we can do it only to a limited extent. If one is going to rigorously uphold the view that all things are nothing but swarms of electrons, a drastic revision of the categories by which we make all our everyday life decisions will be necessary. All the criteria by which we distinguish people from other things would, for instance, have to be changed; but quite by what criteria people-swarms could be distinguished from table-swarms is not at all clear. The fact seems to be that we can only act towards the world and other people *as if* the scientists' accounts were true, because we *already know* from our everyday life dealings with the world and other people how to determine what is real from what is not.

It seems that in talking about the world in everyday language, we are not merely talking about what counts for us as belonging to the world, but are also talking about our modes of commitment for behaving towards it in the future. Thus to say that something is really something else is not just to call the same thing by another name, it is to suggest that people change the whole pattern of action towards it. The world does not present itself to us as full of the same things, irrespective of how we describe it. The world, the real world, is for us largely a function of how we describe it; and the real world of everyday life as we describe it in our everyday language contains an intricate web of related categories developed over centuries for dealing with many problems in an integrated and effective manner.

As the most general-purpose system yet devised it is unlikely to be replaced by a language that proves effective only within specialist enclaves which are both situated within an everyday life setting, and parasitic upon an everyday life understanding of human actions, etc.

We suggest, then, that the claims made by experimental social psychologists to be discovering the 'real' reasons why people do what they do are unfounded. Understanding them *as* the real reasons for people's conduct in puzzling situations is parasitic upon a prior commonsense understanding of the possibly real reasons for people's conduct. Lacking prior possession of such a commonsense understanding, people would not know how, say, to distinguish the scientists' claims from mere illusion; scientists' claims are not illusory, but they are not about what constitutes our everyday reality either; they are merely about what can be seen from a few, special vantage points within it.

In recent years there has been much discussion of the social psychology of the psychological experiment (Orne, 1962; Rosenthal, 1966). Orne has discussed 'demand characteristics' of the experiments. People asked to do five press-ups out of the blue asked, understandably, 'Why?' People asked first to help in an experiment, then asked to do press-ups, simply asked 'Where?' Subjects are only too ready to participate in experiments, believing in the advancement of science and in its contribution to human welfare. Thus subjects attribute great meaning to what they have been asked to participate in, and look continually for clues as to what this meaning is – often finding them in the unintentional ones given off by the experimenter (Rosenthal, 1966). Even when the experiment has no meaning or purpose it is still treated as meaningful, people viewing it as an endurance test or the like. The experimental situation then is a social situation just like any other in which the participants attempt to make sense of one another's actions using whatever clues, assumptions, etc., seem relevant. And one such assumption shared by both subject and experimenter is the belief that whatever the experimental task is, it is important, and that no matter how much must be endured, it is justified by the ultimate purposes of science. Another assumption, clear not from Milgram's experiments but from Mixon's (1974) replication of them, is that as it is 'an experiment', the experimenter has ultimate responsibility for everything that happens. Further, it is clear that subjects, once they have committed themselves to an experiment, want to be 'good subjects'.

Is the experimental situation a real-life situation, then? Well, of course it is. But it is clearly not representative: not in every situation would people be prepared to endure so much, nor would they look to an ultimate authority for protection, nor would they find themselves so puzzled as to what exactly they were involved in, and so on. If people are not simply passive responders to stimuli, but beings who act in terms of the sense they make of a situation, then the sense they make of 'experimental' situations is clearly going to be different from that which they make of real-life situations. The nature of their involvement is quite different – no matter how much they may 'go through the same motions'.

In this respect Mixon's (1974) study of Milgram's experimental set-up is interesting. Mixon transformed the situation into a role-playing exercise. Mixon, along with other helpers, took each role in the 'experiment'. From his own experiences (and those of others) he arrived at a rather different interpretation of Milgram's experiments. Milgram suggests that obedient subjects helplessly perform an obviously immoral act. From the outside the situation seems clear, its definition obvious. But, says Mixon (1974, p. 78),

> It was otherwise to the actors. They were not at all sure what was going on. The focus of much of their puzzlement was the behaviour of the experimenter. They could not understand why, when it looked as if something had gone seriously wrong with the experiment, the experimenter behaved as if nothing had happened.

People, assuming the overall responsibility of the experimenter treated it as one, Mixon maintains, in which despite many appearances to the contrary the usual experimental safeguards still held. As soon as it becomes clear that the safeguards have broken down – as indicated by the agitated behaviour of the experimenter – people will defy the experimental commands, Mixon found. Mixon's result here is corroborated in part by Milgram's own work. In experiment 16 (Milgram, 1974) Milgram had two experimenters run the experiment, one of whom did express worry that things had gone too far. In this experiment, all subjects *did* break off the administration of shocks. Milgram, sticking to his cybernetic model of an hierarchical society, interprets the results as indicating that 'the disagreement between the authorities completely paralysed action' (op. cit., p. 107). Mixon, however, would suggest that such a result called into question the significance of all Milgram's results.

An hermeneutical psychology of everyday life faces the task of understanding the character of an experimental situation but just as one social situation among very many. Its task in this is hardly yet begun. In the next chapter we try to set out an hermeneutical framework for the study of those exchanges in which some form of development takes place, exchanges in which a child, in learning motives and reasons for action, develops into an autonomous adult, able to account to others (and to himself) for his own actions.

13

Empirical Investigations within an Hermeneutical Psychology

We shall now try to bring forward some illustrations of empirical investigations which might be undertaken within the framework of an hermeneutical psychology. Now in one sense the possibilities here are endless, in that, as we have tried to indicate, considerable parts of current psychology could be read hermeneutically. But in another sense the possibilities are very limited, for as yet few investigations of a self-consciously hermeneutical kind have been carried out. What we propose to do is this. We pointed out in chapter 6 that a strong tendency within hermeneutical psychology is towards developmental studies. And among developmental problems is the problem perhaps most central to an hermeneutical psychology, the problem of how, within an extraordinarily brief period, a helpless and superficially inert neonate is transformed, or transforms himself, into a being which acts, has and implements intentions, and desires, is capable, up to a point, of rational thought, and continually attempts to interact and communicate with other beings similarly endowed; a being, in short, whose activities it is possible, or rather essential, to describe and explain in the terms of an hermeneutical psychology. It is upon this problem that we shall concentrate.

Before we begin it is important to emphasize again yet another point which we made in chapter 6, and which received some additional support at the end of chapter 7, namely that the conceptual cannot be derived from the non-conceptual, the intentional from the non-intentional, action from non-action, rationality from the non-rational. We argued that no 'behavioural reduction' of intention, action, concept-possession, rational thought, is possible; no analysis of intention-possession, concept-possession, processes of reasoning, rational action, which represents them as consisting in a system's tending to emit, when in a certain state, certain outputs in response to certain inputs, can survive critical scrutiny. And from this it follows that no 'elemental' analysis whatsoever of the states or phenomena concerned can get off the ground. For any such analysis would be susceptible of formal paralleling on a GM, and our argument has in effect been that no such GM representation is possible. Thus there is no hope of our being able to exhibit the nascent intentions, actions, concepts, communicative endeavours, etc., of the young infant as arising from some synthesis of behavioural or mental elements that are not themselves intentional, conceptual, etc. We have to regard the infant as already possessing the rudiments (*not* the elements) of intention, action, conception, communication, etc. We cannot, of course, say that he *has* intentions, *has* concepts, *can* act, *can* self-consciously try to communicate and so on; and yet we *must* say that he has largely inchoate and unorganized cognitive and conative tendencies which are such that more definite and organized cognitions and conations can differentiate out of them. We cannot by any stretch of imagination conceive what it is *like* to be in such a condition; we can only show by argument and backward extrapolation from empirical findings that the infant *must be in* such a condition.

Thus it is not open to the developmental psychologist to conduct investigations aimed at reductively explaining the origin of intentions, concepts, communicative endeavours, etc. All he can do is (1) observe the unfolding or development in the infant of the abilities to formulate and implement intentions, to communicate with others, to conceive and act in accordance with his conception, and (2), by manipulating the course of development to the limited extent in his power, isolate and assess some of the more important influences upon that development. We shall briefly sketch some recent studies of these aspects of infant development. But it may be said at once that the setting of these aspects of development is the close and reciprocal relationship which in most cases obtains between the neonate and one other adult human being, and that the principal source of influences affecting development is, inevitably, the child's mother.

Although we have argued that intention-possession, concept-possession, and the abilities to act, think and communicate cannot be derived from elements that are not themselves intentional, conceptual, etc., we most emphatically do *not* claim that these aspects of personal development are independent of biological development and functioning. Indeed there is recent work which indicates that the intimate and reciprocal relationship between mother and child, upon which the child's development into a socially functioning human being largely depends, is itself grounded upon certain universally present biological factors. Parts of this work will be touched on below.

We have suggested that the setting within which the infant is thus transformed is that of his relationship with his mother. And we shall further propose that the transformation is effected, or enormously facilitated, by the fact that, whatever the psychological state of the neonate may 'really' be, his mother treats him *as though* he were a person, a being already having, though perhaps unable to express, conscious needs, desires, wishes and intentions. We shall shortly consider some of the relevant empirical findings. But it will, perhaps, help to clarify our interpretation of these findings if we first give a brief account of how we see the potential and the activities of the infant and the role of his mother in developing them.

We asserted a moment ago that, though we cannot conceive what it is like to be an infant, none the less we must regard the infant as possessing a mass of largely unorganized cognitive and conative and communicative tendencies out of which differentiate the more specific and more structured intentions, communicative endeavours and conceptual equipment of the two- or three-year-old. The process of differentiation must not be thought of as something imposed upon the hapless infant. A merely reactive system could never acquire concepts, intentions or communicative capacities, for it would be *par excellence* a mechanistic system in the sense of chapter 2. It would be more nearly true to say that the infant develops himself with a little help from his friends. This, of course, makes the infant's endeavours appear self-conscious ones, and is misleading. It might be less misleading to say that the infant is born *striving* and *experimenting*. By this we mean that however inchoate the infant's cognitive and conative tendencies they involve his striving to subdue the complexity of the world (of whose existence as set against himself he has an inkling – cf. chapter 7) by categorizing its contents so as to handle them more easily; they involve his striving to participate in or to interact with that world, particularly that all-embracing part of it constituted by his mother; and they involve his being prepared in the course of this striving to try out different activities or ploys which he may or may not repeat depending upon their upshots. It is tempting to say that successful striving and successful experimenting are *per se* 'rewarding' to the infant, but one might be thought then to be reverting to a 'reinforcement' theory.

Are we not, in talking of the infant 'striving' and 'experimenting', once again reading things into the putative 'psychological state' of the infant, things which we have no grounds for imputing to it? We can only reply that we feel it is unprofitable to speculate about the subjective side of being an infant. We propose, however, that two things will shortly become clear, viz. (1) that unless we impute to the infant at least some embryonic form of the processes of striving and experimenting, no account of his subsequent development of specific concepts, intentions, communicative tendencies, etc., will be feasible, and (2) that imputing to the infant psychological states describable in the terms of adult psychology *works*. His mother does it all the time, and it appears to be, in large measure, *because* she does it that he comes in the end to act in ways which positively *require* description in these terms, comes in fact to *have* intentions, concepts, etc.

We turn next to consider the role of the mother. Now it seems likely that if an infant were reared totally without contact with his mother or any other human being, and if he were to survive, he would in some degree emerge as a being with intentions and concepts. It is the nature of the infant to strive towards some degree of cognitive and conative competence. What he would *not* have would be any except the most primitive intentions and concepts, and any social concepts or attainments at all. The continual and reciprocal interaction of an infant with his mother not merely facilitates and enormously enriches his conceptual development, and assists him to become a partly autonomous being with complex intentions of his own; it is also that through which he is gradually inducted into the customs and practices of his society, that through which he discovers what is categorically to-be-done or not-to-be-done, what may always or sometimes be done, and which of the events going on in his vicinity are likely to concern him.

How, then, is the mother's influence upon the child exercised? Now we earlier on dismissed as untenable the frameworks of thought within which development can be viewed as a process in which the mother, by selectively rewarding or 'reinforcing' responses to stimuli makes her infant progressively more likely to emit responses from those classes when confronted with stimuli from those classes. We have instead to regard the interplay of mother and child in essentially the same terms as the mother herself regards it. The mother regards her infant as to some extent an intelligent agent, having feelings, wishes, intentions, hopes, fears, thoughts of his own, and in her endeavours to influence his activities she treats him as such. She applies to him, not necessarily self-consciously, simplified versions of techniques one might apply to an adult who did not understand one's language, if one had to attempt to make him grasp the concepts, customs and rules of one's culture. She establishes a 'dialogue'; she seizes upon shared foci of atten-tion; she marks significant events; she likewise marks such of the infant's actions as she considers appropriate to his situation; she discourages inappropriate behaviour; having established approp-riate behaviour, behaviour intelligible to her, she tries to enlarge the infant's grasp of why it is appropriate; and she looks for signs that he is beginning to grasp its significance. Mothers do not just attempt to get their children to complete socially acceptable actions, they 'analyse' the concepts the children are developing by asking what possession of the concept in question would imply for the child's future behaviour. They say, in effect, 'If he knows that what he's just done is significant then he should expect and accept acknowledg-ment from me . . . I will give it . . . he does accept it.' We, like the mothers, understand why these procedures are efficacious in pro-moting the infant's conceptual and social development, because they are at root the sort of procedures which we know might draw *us* out, if we too were projected as aliens into a strange, complex and confusing culture, and because we assume that like us infants are (in however rudimentary a degree) not mere passive puppets but beings with the urge and capacity to conceptualize and participate in what they sense going on around them. And although we cannot usefully speculate about the subjective state of the infant, it must be more nearly correct to describe that state in the terms of cognitive and conative striving than in any others. For if it were not essentially correct to describe it in those terms, we could never explain the transformation of the child, in interaction with its mother, into a little person having socially conditioned concepts, intentions and communicative abilities. And the fact that a mother, by acting *as if* these are the proper terms in which to describe her infant's psychological state, is able to influence the course of his development, as one might expect if her assumption is valid, must surely count as empirical evidence in favour of our proposition.

So much by way of general comment upon the processes of interaction between mother and infant in which the latter (and perhaps the former!) is thus radically transformed, and upon the respective roles which manipulation by the mother and active participation by the infant may play in the matter. It will help to give greater concreteness to our account if we now describe some examples of the empirical investigations upon which the remarks we have just made are based.

That from the very beginning many mothers in our society treat their babies as partners in a personal relationship, is suggested by recent studies. Macfarlane (1974) discusses the way mothers greet their babies after delivery. 'One can observe how the mother verbalizes her inspection of the child . . ., imitates the child and puts her own interpretation on the child's behaviour.' From the very moment of birth the child does things which make him a person in his mother's eyes. And, as Macfarlane remarks, mothers are good observers of these sorts of activities. He notes, for instance, that many mothers comment upon the child's ability to follow the movements of their faces. Again the baby's ability to appreciate the approach of a three-dimensional object is noticed by the mother as the baby 'reaches out' with his lips for a bottle. Mothers, whether or not they would admit it in discussion with psychologists, clearly treat their babies in a personal manner from the moment of birth – they do not act as if they must condition them, and only later turn to treating them in a personal manner.

The obverse of the mother's tendency to treat her offspring *ab initio* as a little human being is the pull which the human face, or indeed anything resembling a human face, has upon the attention of the young infant (Fantz, 1961, 1967; Fantz and Nevis, 1965). More generally, we may say that, *ceteris paribus*, any mobile, three-dimensional, vocalizing object (such as human or animal organisms) will receive far more response from the infant than any other sort of object, however colourful. Thus for the mother the infant is to be treated as a person; and for the child the mother is by far the most interest- and reaction-provoking object in his world.

What form does the infant's reaction to his mother take? Examination of video-recordings of interacting mother-baby pairs suggests, say Newson and Newson (1976),

> Firstly that the different sensori-motor components of the infant's activity are highly synchronised with each other, and secondly that his action sequences are temporally organised so that they can mesh – with a high degree of precision – with similar patterns of action produced by the human caretaker.

Two-month-old infants seem not only to perform a rudimentary form of speaking by moving their lips and mouths ('pre-speech'); they also make many hand and arm movements that are developmentally related to the gestures of adults involved in animated conversations (Trevarthen *et al.*, 1975; Trevarthen, 1974). These synchronized 'communicative' gestures tend to occur in rhythmic sequences (Schaffer, 1974), and the rhythms of one 'communicator' may entrain those of another. Infants are particularly responsive to the rhythms of human speech (Condon and Sander, 1974), and at a very early age may be induced to participate in what may be called 'dialogues'. The infant will for a while listen attentively to the mother, and, when the mother halts expectantly, will 'reply' with the vocalizations, mouthings and gestures of pre-speech.

As Newson and Newson (1976) say, 'observations of this sort add strength to the argument that the infant is somehow *innately primed* to participate in complicated social rituals'. Let us consider some of the ways in which these dialogues may develop and be expanded, and how, in the opportunities for interaction which they provide, a mother may so channel her offspring's cognitive and conative strivings that, by treating him as if he were an intention-possessing, concept-possessing, rule-comprehending and communication-oriented little human being, she helps or induces him to transform himself into one. We may consider first of all direct mother-child interactions or 'dialogues', and, second, 'dialogues' which are 'about' or 'refer' or relate to outside objects and events.

In direct mother-child 'dialogues' one may recognize at least five kinds of interlinked developments which, between the mother's intelligent guidance and the child's cognitive and conative striving, somehow emerge.

(1) A fundamental feature of such mother-child 'dialogues' is described by Newson and Newson (loc. cit.) as follows:

> Within the two-way interaction games which ordinary mothers

spontaneously play with their babies, a very large number of actions which the baby makes are interpreted as communication gestures in the sense that they are incorporated into the dialogue. From the baby's standpoint, these particular actions are apparently rendered significant by the quality and timing of the mother's gestural and vocal reciprocations. The effect is to highlight or 'mark' certain events as having special significance, and hence to *punctuate* the contribution which the baby is making according to a pattern of meaningfulness which is, to some extent, being imposed by the more sophisticated partner. The mother's intonational gestures, often accompanied by dramatic alterations of facial expression, clearly have a powerful effect in alerting the baby's attention to the significance of his own actions.

(2) Once a child has begun to grasp that certain of his actions have a special significance to his mother, his 'experimental tendencies' come into play. In a paper to which we shall refer again, Bruner (1976) says that much of a child's early learning 'is based upon the mother interpreting the child's intent, the child sometimes conforming with this interpretation, sometimes not, but learning, en route, what interpretations his efforts evoke and how these may be modified'. As an example he cites (pp. 266–7)

one of our own subjects, Jon A., and the development of a signal pattern involving reaching outward bimanually while in a sitting position, hands prone. It had usually been interpreted by the mother as a signal that Jon wanted some familiar, hand-sized object. . . . At eight months, one week, Jon used the signal: *M* interpreted it as calling for her hand, since there was no object close by, and performed her 'walking hand' body-game format, with the fingers walking up Jon's front to his chin. He tolerated it. . . . Jon then reached out again. *M* interpreted it as request for repetition. He participates even more reluctantly. *M*, on completion, then repeats game though Jon has not signalled. He averts gaze and whimpers a little. She repeats again and he is totally turned off. Pause. Now, 27 seconds after Jon first reached out, he reaches again, this time pulling *M*'s hands to a position where he can take hold of the ulnar edges and raise himself to a standing position. There is a following sequence . . . in which *M* and

Jon play a game of alternating irregularly between the two 'formats' – *M*'s hand either walking on fingers to tickle position, or *M*'s hands in stand-supporting position. Under *M*'s control, it is made into a 'surprise' evoking, alternating format, with her alternative interpretations of his reach gestures being rendered explicit.

(3) In most early mother-child 'dialogues' it is, as Trevarthen (1974) notes, very common to find the mother 'marking' certain of her baby's gestures by imitating them. Around the age of six months most infants become proficient in imitating some of their mother's actions and, up to a point, her utterances. It is still far from clear how this skill comes about, but it appears likely that it arises, at least in part, through the mother in the first instance stage-managing the infant's actions so as to produce the required result (Pawlby, in press). One can only suppose that after a certain amount of stage management the infant 'gets the idea' himself – we have tried time and again to indicate that one has simply to *assume* that infants are the sort of beings which *can* 'get ideas'.

(4) A child which can imitate can participate in new ways in 'dialogues'. Newson and Pawlby (1973) have studied the development of 'turn-taking' games. Often mothers seize upon opportunities offered by their infants to initiate a back-and-forth sequence of acts, a possibility to which the infants soon cotton on. For example, Newson and Pawlby describe an exchange between Tilly (at twenty-eight weeks) and her mother:

(Following an exchange involving some play with a rattle).
Tilly makes a vocalization (like a cough)
Mother repeats vocalization
Tilly repeats it
Mother repeats it
Tilly puts rattle to mouth
Mother: 'Are you going to eat that one.'

Inserted into the episode with the rattle is a short back-and-forth exchange in which Tilly took her turn and did what her mother expected her to do. Tilly thus manifested, in some small degree, that she could be an agent, that she could *herself* do something appropriate to the social situation, that she could herself make what was interpreted as a sensible response. Perhaps later Tilly will be able to sustain the intention involved over indefinitely many exchanges;

and then we shall find the mother elaborating upon the 'imitation game'.

(5) A step from the 'imitation game' is perhaps games in which mothers and children come to reverse roles. The common game of 'Peekaboo' (Greenfield, 1972; Bruner and Sherwood, 1975) may serve as an example, and so may the innumerable kinds of 'give and take' game. In these games there must be more than a temporal synchronization of the actions of mother and child; there must be some degree of appreciation that the other is a being like oneself, and a certain mutual understanding or conventionally accepted signal as to when roles are to be reversed.

In mother-child 'dialogues' which relate or 'refer' to 'outside' objects or events we likewise find that mother and child between them hammer out developments which may be set down in a rough sequence.

(1) It is fairly easy for an adult to determine which of the objects in a baby's surroundings is engaging its attention. Several recent studies (for example Collis and Schaffer, in press) have shown, by retrospective examination of video-recordings, how closely the mother's line of regard follows the infant's, even when she cannot see his face (Collis, in press). Mothers are thus able to 'mark' objects to which the infant transiently attends by in some way or another incorporating them into the ongoing dialogue. A more surprising finding (Scaife and Bruner, 1975) is that some infants only four months old, and most infants of nine months, can follow the mother's line of regard when she looks at some spot which is not near either of them. How this ability emerges – whether the mother stage-manages it as a form of imitation, or whether it is an intelligent leap by the infant – we cannot say. But once it is established further possibilities are opened up for the mother's 'marking' – even unconsciously marking – objects and events of significance to her infant; and some might see in it the first signs of the infant's nascent appreciation that there are points of view other than his own.

(2) Further methods of 'marking' come into play when the mother wishes not merely to show the child some object or event of potential significance, but to induce him to perform some object-related action. In such circumstances mothers not merely mark the object by looking at it, pointing to it, manipulating it, etc.; they may put the baby through the correct movements, model the required behaviour themselves, etc., and they adjust their endeavours to allow for the infant's current occupation, line of regard, etc. (Wood,

Bruner and Ross, 1976). Furthermore (and this is a vital point) mothers are not satisfied merely with extracting a correct response from their infants. They test the character of the child's responses to see if he has any knowledge of the significance of what he is doing, to see, as it were, whether he did what he did because he understood that that was what he was supposed to do. Shotter and Gregory (1976) describe an incident during an experiment in which a mother was attempting to show her child (Samantha aged eleven months) how to place shaped pieces on a form board. Having just physically helped her little girl to place a piece, Samantha's mother said, 'Oh, clever girl.' But Samantha did not pause in her activity and signal by eye contact and smiling that she knew she had done something socially significant. So her mother leant forward, caught her eye, and repeated her 'marker': 'Aren't you CLEVER.' And then Samantha stopped and smiled. Thereafter her mother was happy to let her proceed. Mothers are not just satisfied with their children doing the tasks that they require of them. The children must also indicate that their actions were based in some knowledge of the socially defined requirements of the situation – the child must indicate that she 'sees' the situation as the mother sees it.

Children fairly quickly come to appreciate that adults expect such signs of understanding, and they develop generalized ways of giving them. For example a directed smile or a moment of shared gaze may serve this purpose. In older but still pre-linguistic children what Bruner (1976) calls 'proclamative' vocalizations may serve the same function. Bruner says (p. 281) that proclamative vocalization

> occurs at two points during joint action sequences: first, at a
> point where the infant is about to undertake his part of a
> jointly attended action, seemingly as an accompaniment to
> intention; second, when the act is complete. The vocalized
> babbling may be coincident with the child looking back at the
> mother or may precede it. The vocalization, in short, appears
> to be initiating or completive with respect to an act embedded
> in a jointly attended task. In this sense, it may be considered
> as a 'candidate-comment' on an implicit topic.

(3) In the work which we have just described, mothers have been asked to induce their infants to attempt some task or game proposed by the experimenter. By and large the mothers have succeeded in getting the children to co-operate. In other words the mothers have

succeeded, by diverse and individually different stratagems, in inducing their (often refractory) infants to develop and implement some short-term and rudimentary intentions. But of course children rapidly become partly autonomous; they develop their own interests and intentions. What influence does a child's continuing 'dialogue' with his mother have upon his own capacity to develop and implement intentions? The only point we wish to make here is this: what may be called 'styles of mothering' are of considerable importance in determining the complexity of the intentions and purposes which a child will himself spontaneously develop. Hess and Shipman (1965) have studied the consequences of the different instructional strategies used by mothers of different social classes. One of the features of the behaviour of working-class mothers and children is, they say, a tendency to act without taking sufficient time for planning. Mothers and children act impulsively; each act seems unrelated to the act that preceded it or to its consequences. The act lacks meaning; it is not sufficiently related to the context in which it occurs, to the motivations of the participants, or to the goals of the task. For example, in a shared task, a mother may silently watch her child make an error then punish him, rather than anticipating his error and warning him, telling him to look ahead and avoid the mistake. In summarizing their findings, Hess and Shipman say (p. 532):

> [The working class] environment produces a child who relates to authority rather than rationale; who, although often compliant, is not reflective in his behaviour; and for whom the consequences of an act are largely considered in terms of immediate punishment or reward, rather than future effects and long-range goals.

Tulkin and Kagan (1972) in investigating whether the class differences discussed by Hess and Shipman also held true in infancy, found that they did, and suggested that one important source of such differences was the mothers' concept of their infants. Working-class mothers tend not to believe that their children can express 'adult-like' emotions or can communicate with other people. Some felt that it was only important for a mother to speak to her infant after the infant began to speak. Furthermore, working-class mothers seemed to feel that they could not have much influence on the development of their children, they saw themselves as somewhat powerless and helpless in this respect. 'Thus', say Tulkin and

Kagan, 'a mother's attitudes are not independent of social and economic conditions. . . .' Mothers are participants in social institutions which have a long history, and they act in a way that seems to them the only 'natural' way to act. And as 'carriers' of the institutional practices they have 'inherited', they pass on their ways of going on.

These reflections bring us conveniently back to our central point. We have proposed that it is because mothers treat their children to some extent *as if* they were purposeful, concept-possessing and social creatures that children come to have concepts and purposes, and to be socialized. And we have proposed further that the mother's assumption, which after all works in practice, though it may not be, indeed cannot be, wholly right, is yet *not wholly wrong*. We have tried, by briefly sketching some recent relevant studies, and arranging them in sequence, to show in a general way how, given that mothers treat their children as though they had intentions, were capable of rational thought, were trying to communicate, etc., and given that there is at any rate something about infants which makes this strategy not entirely inappropriate, the development of infants into relatively rational, purposeful and communicative human beings becomes to some extent comprehensible – comprehensible, of course, basically in terms similar to those in which changes and developments in an adult's concepts, purposes and communicative endeavours are comprehensible. And finally we have cited studies which suggest that to the extent to which a mother does *not* treat her child *as if* he were one term in a personal relationship, that child fails to become a fully autonomous, a fully realized, human being.

We turn next to some methodological and general considerations. The chief methodological point which we wish to make is as follows: the empirical enterprise which we have been outlining in this chapter – that of beginning to describe and understand the transformation of the human neonate into a concept-possessing, intention-possessing and socialized little person – is essentially hermeneutical. We accepted that the infant's actions are 'meaningful', require interpretation, or rather we accepted that the mother's tendency to interpret her infant's behaviour as 'meaningful' is not wholly misconceived. And we described and by implication tried to understand the mother's role in terms of the 'meanings' her actions had for her in the context of her sustained 'dialogue' with her baby. We spoke of her 'marking' actions and events for her infant's attention; establishing shared foci of attention; indicating the completion of a socially acceptable act; conducting a kind of conceptual analysis of her infant's nascent concepts; deliberately participating in and shaping the course of 'dialogues'; responding to the child *as if* his movements and vocalizations were requests, commands, etc.; inducing him to imitate her; and generally encouraging and constraining his activities. It may furthermore be remarked that the behaviour of two mother-child pairs, the 'meanings' of whose actions and interactions we would wish to express in similar terms, may well be physically very different. As Newson and Newson (1976) observe:

> In a sense, it is only possible to chart the course of a communication interchange by oneself engaging in such activity as a 'communicant'. . . . Thus while the analysis of temporal event sequences lends itself appropriately to computer processing, the identification of the significant events must remain the province of the empathic human observer. Indeed it may even be the case that at the pre-verbal level of communication, the mother herself will sometimes be the only person who can identify certain communication gestures which her baby is currently making, because only she shares a history of common communication experience with that baby.   (Newson and Shotter, 1974)

Many workers in this field would probably repudiate with indignation the approach we are proposing. 'Subjective' interpretations of the 'meanings' of actions are not amenable to verification by observation and experiment and cannot figure in the scientific undertaking as that is widely conceived. The answer of these workers has been to conduct experiments on mother-child pairs in which the environment is highly impoverished and only certain gross and physically identifiable pieces of behaviour are taken into consideration. Quantification then becomes easy, and impressive-looking statistical correlations may be established. Now we are far from saying that such techniques may not for limited purposes be of value. But we do not think that any general understanding of the processes of infant development can emerge from them. The whole enterprise smacks of the rat psychology of yesteryear. Few psychologists would be rash enough to claim that studying rats is going to tell us much about the concept-possessing and socialized human being. But some seem to feel that although rat psychology does not help us much with human psychology, and although the experimental methods of rat psychology will not get us very far with those awkward customers, human adults, still, if we apply similar methods to human infants, whose behaviour is often superficially so simple, then we may be in business. *And then*, perhaps, we shall at least have a data base from which to penetrate the complexities of adult behaviour.

A child psychology conceived in these terms is an absolutely hopeless endeavour. We have in effect given the reasons for saying so in the preceding parts of this book and of this chapter. No human psychology having these presuppositions can possibly succeed, at least outside exceedingly limited spheres. And the shortcomings of such an approach are nowhere more readily apparent than in the study of infant development. It will without doubt unearth, in limited contexts, impressive correlations between quantified variables. There is, for instance, as has lately been shown by video-recording (Murphy and Messer, in press) a high degree of correlation between the direction in which a mother interacting with her child points her finger and the line of her gaze as indicated by her eye-movements. Correlations of this kind, i.e. between physically measured classes of variables, may well not hold good outside the circumscribed experimental situation and could only lead to understanding of mother-child interaction if taken in conjunction with the interpretations of 'meaning' provided by an hermeneutical psychology. For, as we have argued time and time again, the intentional and the conceptual cannot be accommodated within a framework of thought which is essentially of the GM kind.

In contrast, hermeneutical interpretations of what mother and child are doing in their 'dialogues' lead, if verified by their accord with further observations and interpretations, directly to the explanation and understanding of behaviour, and they also open the way to explanation and understanding of the processes of development. For we characterized the infant as a being who must be thought of as, however inchoately, striving cognitively and conatively to subdue a world of whose existence over and against himself he has some inkling, and as in a rudimentary way experimenting to further that end. The 'meaning' of some of his actions is thus to be sought not merely in his immediate needs, fears, intentions, etc., but in his overarching striving or 'intention' (though this is a word carrying too much of an overtone of self-consciousness) to enrich the 'meanings' of his own actions, and to enlarge his capacity for meaningful action. And we have to accept as a fact about human nature, very possibly an ultimate fact, that just as human beings can formulate and implement intentions, so they can, especially with help from their friends, as it were, enlarge and transform themselves. The effect upon the child's development, of his mother's promptings, proddings and so forth, can, in general, only be understood as we would understand the effects of such things upon ourselves, as stirring, constraining, educing, diversifying, the goals and capacities of an intelligent and purposeful being. The capacities of such a being, and the process of their diversification, can only be described and explained in terms of the framework concepts of hermeneutical psychology, which, as we have endeavoured to show, cannot be translated into mechanistic terms.

Within the framework of an hermeneutical psychology it may be possible to reach some generalizations about the development of children in interchanges with their mothers. For when actions are characterized in terms of their 'meanings', actions of physically quite different forms may be seen as belonging in the same class, for example there are innumerable different ways in which a mother may 'mark' an action for the benefit of her child, and the mother can be seen to be doing the 'same' thing in quite different circumstances (as may the child). This is not to say that we expect hermeneutical psychology to provide us with a large number of interlinked cross-cultural generalizations. But it may at least provide us with generalizations, some of which may be of importance for practical purposes. For instance we noted a few pages ago that it appears to be the case that in our society middle-class mothers and working-class mothers often pursue different strategies of mothering, and that these differences may be of considerable importance for the development of the child. These differences are of a kind that can only be usefully characterized in the terms of an hermeneutical psychology. Hermeneutical psychology thus provides a framework within which problems of central human importance may be discussed and tackled. In the case of 'strategies of mothering' one of the first moves to be made might be to examine the strategies of the most successful mothers, and this would perhaps involve us in eliciting rules which they held to but could not adequately formulate (cf. chapter 3), in exhibiting them as participating in institutions which they themselves had not fully comprehended (cf. p. 96 above).

Of course many workers in child psychology, and in other parts of human psychology, will continue with unquenched hope to pursue that holy grail, glimpsed by the scientifically pure, an objectively verifiable system of scientific laws. And ever and again they will believe themselves to be in sight of it, for where rational strategies are pursued (as by a mother interacting with her child), certain regularities, certain quantifiable correlations, are likely to emerge. But the holy grail, when grasped, will always turn out to be counterfeit, the observed regularities will never fall into a coherent and comprehensible system. And this will be so not just in the domain of child psychology, but throughout human psychology. We believe that there are two fundamental reasons for this. They are closely linked and ultimately identical. The first is that the behaviour of human beings is not to be understood as a resultant of the behaviour and interactions of innumerable parts or elements of which it is supposedly made up (systems which *are* so made up are preeminently suitable for representation on a GM cf. Sutherland, 1970, p. 98). The parts follow the direction of the whole rather than the direction of the whole determining the directions of the parts. The second is that the behaviour of human beings cannot be accounted for simply in terms of their genetic endowments and personal histories (cf. pp. 178–9 above). Human beings can develop, or can develop themselves, in ways not wholly determined by these constraints. Even those psychological problems which many have thought most likely to yield to a classical, elementarist, approach – let us say the problem of the relation of genes to intelligence, the problem, crucial to 'mechanical translation', of the relationship between the acoustic and the semantic/syntactic aspect of speech, the problem of the number and relationships of our different 'memory mechanisms' – seem to become more rather than less intractable with the accumulation of data. We do not say that it was not worth trying classical methods upon these problems. But surely we can by now begin to see what the upshot has been in these and other problem areas, and why. Substantial areas of human psychology have become graveyards of misplaced ingenuity.

Notes

Chapter 1 Approaches to the Study of Man

1   This of course does not convey anything like a proper idea of the author's or speaker's side of linguistic meaning, a preliminary analysis of which might run as follows. An utterance has a linguistic meaning for a speaker if he believes himself to be utilizing conventionally agreed vocal or related methods to make his hearer conceive or grasp a certain state of affairs already grasped by the speaker, and to make his hearer grasp also that the speaker intends the hearer to grasp that the speaker spoke with the intention that the hearer should grasp that state of affairs and with the intention that the hearer should grasp that the speaker intended the hearer to grasp that the speaker intended the hearer to grasp that state of affairs. If any reader enjoys interpreting texts such as this he should try his hand on Schiffer (1972), long passages of which are more incomprehensible still.

2   The idea that 'phenomenological intentions' are mere epiphenomena inevitably lands, like other forms of epiphenomenalism, in paradox and self-contradiction. For if one states this position, *either* one would not have stated it but for the epiphenomena, and that rules out epiphenomenalism, for the alleged epiphenomena have had an effect on the course of events, *or* one would have stated it anyway, even if *per accidens* the epiphenomena had not accompanied the neural or other processes which they did accompany, and in that case statements of epiphenomenalism are quite independent of the relevant 'phenomenological' facts and can have no bearing upon them. This of course does not show that the 'phenomenological intention' to *x* is in any way responsible for the occurrence of behaviour likely to promote *x*, only that if expressions of epiphenomenalism are to be based on 'phenomenological' facts, epiphenomenalism must be false for those expressions of the 'phenomenological facts'. It is perhaps also possible to show that for some pieces of behaviour it is at least paradoxical to deny that the 'phenomenological intention' to carry out that piece of behaviour plays a part in producing that piece of behaviour, for example suppose one says 'my phenomenological intention to utter the sentence I am now uttering was an epiphenomenon'. Either the intention concerned was an antecedent without which one would not have uttered that sentence, and what the sentence says is false, or else the intention was not an antecedent, in which case the utterance was completely divorced from the fact upon which it was supposed to have been based and can have no bearing upon that fact. And if epiphenomenalism is false in these cases, there is no particular reason for denying its falsity in others.

Chapter 2   The Generalized Machine

1   It should, however, be noted that some Turing machines are assumed to have input tapes of infinite length, a state of affairs which cannot in practice obtain in a computer.

2   Prima facie this suggestion would seem to be ruled out by the fact that Turing machines are non-self-applicable. That is, if they are fed their own rules in coded form they will go on computing for ever. In effect they will never be able to say, 'Yes, these are my own rules' or 'No, they're not.'

Chapter 3   Concepts, Rules and the Generalized Machine

1   It is worth noting and bearing in mind that very many stimulus-neutral concepts, though not psychological, have an important psychological aspect. Analysis of most of them would show that somewhere along the line are involved the intentions, goals, rule-systems and so forth of intelligent human agents. For example notions like property, bargain, justice and game make sense only in the social context of interacting human agents who are themselves capable of consciously following rules – in other words, possess concepts.

2   There are also what may be called 'stimulus-independent' concepts. We have in mind here especially certain fundamental logical and mathematical concepts. While the activities of someone, let us say, extracting a square root or denying a proposition are observable, still one cannot observe square roots or negations. Yet, prima facie, the concept of square root is different from the concept of the activity of extracting a square root and the concept of negation is not the concept of the activity of denying a proposition.

3   Machine-table notation cannot represent structural relationships between different sets of input-output concatenations. Yet as Block and Fodor (1972) point out, there are structural relationships among at least some psychological states, and a successful theory of such states must represent and exploit such similarities. For example (p. 178) there is a relationship between the state *believing that P* and the state *believing that P & Q*

> representing the psychological states as a list (for example, as a list of machine-table states) fails to represent this kind of structural relation. What needs to be said is that believing that P is somehow a constituent of believing that P & Q; but the machine-table state model has no conceptual resources for saying that. In particular, the notion 'is a constituent of' is not defined for machine-table states.

4   A good deal of interest has recently been aroused by a computer model of linguistic behaviour devised by Winograd (1972, 1973). The model is too complex to be described adequately here. It is held to have the following special features: (1) It has a detailed model of ('knowledge about') a small-scale world made up of blocks, pyramids, etc., on a table top. This knowledge is called 'conceptual' and is represented in the machine in the form of the changeable procedures that the machine, if called upon, can go through in manipulating its block world and answering questions about it. These procedures are interconnected (as conceptual capacities are interconnected) in that the sequence of operations corresponding to a given concept may invoke operations corresponding to another concept. (2) It can 'parse' sentences in terms of their syntactic and semantic properties and its own 'heuristic' knowledge of its world, and these kinds of parsing are interrelated in complicated ways, corresponding to the way in which human beings disentangle the meaning of sentences in terms of their grammatical and semantic knowledge and knowledge of the world. (3) It can engage in 'conversations' with an interlocutor about the state of its world, solve problems in connection therewith, etc.

However, it does not seem to us that there is anything here to upset our general arguments against mechanistic explanations of behaviour. For (1) Winograd's model does not in any real sense have a world to interact with. The cubes, pyramids, etc., though displayed on a screen, are not really there or really manipulated. They are represented in the machine by a list of symbols. The machine's operations in effect search through, reshuffle, add to, etc., this list of symbols in various complicated ways. The fact that the machine's different specified operation sequences are interrelated is of no significance. So far as the machine is concerned the symbols could represent anything – or nothing. The interpretation is the programmer's. (2) The test of whether a system understands the (conceptual) meaning of sentences is not its efficiency in sorting through and manipulating strings of symbols in terms of rules imposed by the programmer, but whether in comprehending and responding to these sentences it shows an intelligent and indefinitely varied understanding of the world. Winograd's model does not in any useful sense have a world. (3) The model lacks the whole background against which alone it would be possible to talk of communication with an interlocutor. For the communicative use of language implies an intention to communicate, and appreciation of the possible relations between oneself and another, etc. The message may be indefinitely modified in the light of the interlocutor's sensed needs. (4) Winograd uses some very misleading language in connection with the machine's responses to questions and commands. Here are some examples: 'the program knows that phrases beginning with "the" are intended to refer to a specific object the speaker has in mind' (1973, p. 155); 'By keeping track of selected parts of the original subgoal tree, the system has some understanding of its own motives' (p. 163); 'The system understands quantifiers such as "every", "any", "some", etc.' (p. 165). The introduction here of such terms as 'understand', 'know', 'intention' and 'motive' appears to us to be entirely gratuitous.

Chapter 4   Actions, Intentions and the Generalized Machine
1   Representative books on the subject are by: Melden (1961); Hampshire (1959); Harré and Secord (1972); Kenny (1963); C. Taylor (1964); R. Taylor (1966); Louch (1966); Rescher, ed. (1967); White, ed. (1968); Mischel, ed. (1969); Goldman (1970); Merleau-Ponty (1965); Brand, ed. (1970a); Binkley, Bronaugh and Marras (1971); Bernstein (1972); Langford (1972).

2   The question of whether actions have always causes of a sensory imaginal kind exercised some psychologists in the earlier years of the century much as did the problem of 'imageless thoughts'. See for example R. S. Woodworth's paper of 1906, 'The cause of a voluntary action', reprinted in Woodworth (1939). Woodworth's conclusion is that actions do *not* invariably have sensory imaginal antecedents.

3   It was at one time not uncommon to find psychologists speaking in something like these terms; see for example Stout (1938, pp. 117–19).

Chapter 5   Two Alternative Approaches within the Established Framework
1   Weiskrantz (1973, p. 512) continues at this point by saying, 'Even in physics one can translate from wave into quantum theories of light. Which theory one chooses turns on *matters of preference and aesthetics*, or at the best on grounds of parsimony where it is not all that easy to calculate degrees of parsimony' (our emphasis). Surely he cannot mean what he says. There are very *practical* reasons for one's choice here: one can only have the particular type of effect upon the world that a theory predicts by carrying out the type of manipulations it prescribes. This is the essence of Bohr's 'complementarity principle': a physical system may exhibit two qualitatively different and apparently conflicting properties, *but the conditions which permit their expression must be mutually exclusive*. It is not a matter of preference and aesthetics at all. It may well be that in all the sciences we shall soon have to admit to a multiplicity of views (especially in psychology), each centred on a specific instrumental activity, each involving a different research 'paradigm' to use Kuhn's (1962) term

– the number of such paradigms being quite indeterminate, and with no possibility of a 'neutral' or 'superordinate' view, as there may be no neutral or superordinate paradigm activity, no superordinate way of interacting with the world. Only by centring oneself in human action would all these different ways of going on be seen as different manifestations of the same thing: human action.

2   If one lets oneself go 'glassy-eyed', relaxes one's intention of making sense of the world, one may see mere forms passing before one's eyes. But there are more drastic ways of learning to relax one's intention of making sense of the world. Ehrenzweig (1970, p. 39) discusses the dispersed attention of painters (and musicians) who learn to grasp the totality of a picture which normally alternates between two different views, which is normally ambiguous. Other ways of modifying one's intention to see stable objects may be discovered. One can, for instance, learn to destabilize one's vision by tensing the muscles round the eye in a peculiar way while it is in motion.

Chapter 6   The Shape of an Hermeneutical Psychology
1   We have talked of 'the concepts' of hermeneutical explanation as though there were only one set of such concepts or rather a limited number of closely related possible sets of such concepts, and we have talked further as though we can say *ab initio* that there is only one such framework of concepts, viz. (more or less) the one which is commonly invoked in commonsense and everyday action-explanations. This claim flies in the face of the popular empiricist view that the detached scientist may try out as many conceptual systems as he likes upon his subject-matter, and that he must discover by observation and experiment which one works best. We based our claim upon a mixture of pragmatic and logical reasons, e.g. that it is inconceivable that the intentions and purposes of human agents, as these are commonly thought of, do not critically influence their behaviour; thus no explanation of that behaviour is viable which does not refer to them. Further, the phenomenon of intention is 'intrinsically interrelated' to a whole network of phenomena of other kinds, so that it cannot stand on its own; and the concept of intention cannot be other than the concept of a phenomenon intrinsically interrelated to these other phenomena, so it cannot be characterized without the introduction of concepts of these other sorts of phenomena. There is at least one other set of reasons which points to the same conclusion, though the issue is too difficult to be expounded in detail here. Roughly speaking it is as follows. The phenomena of intention, desire, fear and so on, are, for the most part, not conceptually inert. To intend to bring about a certain state of affairs consists, in part, of conceiving certain things as means to one's end, certain steps that have to-be-taken-by-one, certain preliminary actions that have to-be-done-by-one. To desire something is, in part, to conceive it as having certain intrinsically worthwhile qualities, as if-possible-to-be-sought-by-one-for-its-own-sake (note the overlap with intention here). To fear something is, again in part, to conceive it as dangerous-to-oneself, to-be-fled-from or avoided or suppressed by one (again note the overlap with intention here). Now an agent in the main normally knows what he desires, intends or fears and he also knows that he desires, intends or fears it, and to know these things is, in part, to know the way in which he has conceptually divided the world-in-relation-to-himself. ('Knows' here does not necessarily imply 'can verbally formulate', but only something like 'could work out by means of thought experiments if he had to'.) The agent does not, however, know about his conceptual dividings of the world from his *observations* of them (cf. chapter 10); it would be much more nearly true to say he knows about them because he *is* them. They constitute *how he is* at that moment, and *how he is* has to be stated partly *in terms of them*. It would not be possible to capture *how he is* at that moment without the application of *that* set of concepts. Accordingly these concepts are bound to figure in any true account of his present state, and of his past and future states in so far as he has feared, intended, desired before, or will fear,

intend or desire in the future, and of the states of other people in so far as they are constituted as he is in those respects. But to apply these conceptual divisions to someone's state is inseparable from characterizing his state in terms of the notions of intention, fear and desire, and there is accordingly *no way* of completely describing his present psychological state which does not invoke those concepts.

2   N.B. The question we have been discussing here is the question of whether or not one can give a 'causal' explanation of why an agent with a certain middle- or long-term intention acts in ways which he believes conducive to the fulfilment of the intention concerned, i.e. of why he chooses one action rather than another. It must not be confused with the question, which we touch upon in chapter 9, of whether the relationship between a settled intention as to how to act and overt action which arises out of it can be looked upon as causal.

3   Surely, it might be said, the formal systems of logicians and of transformational grammarians must throw *some* light on our ordinary processes of logical reasoning and grammatical speech. For commonsense logical arguments and everyday spoken sentences can be presented as exemplifying principles derived from these grandiose systems. *Some* light, perhaps, but not because the systems are sets of descriptive generalizations under which the everyday instances may be subsumed as particular examples, or because we all have the propositional calculus built into us somewhere (if we could only put this endowment to full use). It is rather that the formal systems of logicians are built up by the highly sophisticated use of concepts (whatever they may be) which are also embryonically operative in the production of the bumbling logical generalizations of the layman. The concepts are refined and clarified in the analyses of logicians in a way in which they are not in the bumblings of laymen. So a psychologist who wants to study the processes of reasoning in which these concepts are utilized would do well to look at the work of formal logicians. But more than this cannot be claimed.

4   The process of redefinition may pass unnoticed even by the person who carried it out, so natural may it seem to him in terms of the framework which he has accepted. Thus Herriot (1974), who organizes his psychological, though not, he says, his philosophical, thinking around the analogy of 'the human computer', talks of memory (chiefly verbal memory) as a process of reconstruction: 'one cannot conceive of the item as presented being stored with a set of attributes or tags; rather, what is stored is a set of attributes from which the item may be reconstructed when required' (p. 46). This view of memory could not possibly be extended to cover what would ordinarily be looked upon as central cases of remembering, viz. the recollection of particular past events in one's life. For to 'reconstruct' such an event from stored attributes *might* be to relive it, perhaps in some diminished form, but it would not *per se* be to remember it. One could relive the same experience in imagination innumerable times without the later occasions bringing the earlier ones to mind or without one's having the slightest idea that it had all happened before. Does one then reconstruct the past experience from the stored attributes and throw in a dash of another attribute – that of 'having happened'? 'Having happened' is simply not the sort of thing that can be an attribute, any more than 'existence' can be a predicate. Problems crowd thick and fast at this point, and we cannot go into them here. Somewhat similar problems arise even in connection with the recall of stored verbal items. This example should at least serve to show (1) how great is the need in psychology for careful conceptual analysis, and (2) how insidious redefinition can be.

Chapter 9   Wants, Intentions and Beliefs
1   We have not, in general, made any distinction between the closely related notions of 'intention' and 'purpose', but have made the wide-ranging term 'intention' do duty for both. However, there are undoubted differences of emphasis (cf. Austin, 1966).

2   An analysis of the notion of committal is given by Brand (1970b, p. 90) as follows:

> for every person S and every action a, S committed himself to perform a if and only if:
> (i) there is a set of actions such that S performed each of these actions and such that S justifiably believed that this set was the total set of requisite actions for performing a;
> or
> (ii) there is a set of actions such that S would have performed each of these actions if he had had the opportunity to perform them and such that S justifiably believed that this set was the total set of requisite actions for performing a.

These conditions are not sufficient for committal unless one adds that S did these actions *because* he believed them to constitute the set of requisite actions, or would have done them for that reason. But what is the force of this 'because'? It is simply to say that the agent did what he did because he intended to perform a. And this, we shall suggest, involves one in saying that he was committed to performing a.

3   Cf. Castañeda (1971, p. 465n): 'As I see them, intentions are first-person prescriptions, while commands, requests, and orders are embellishments of second-person prescriptions. Prescriptions are, thus, the fundamental units of practical thinking, just as propositions are the fundamental units of theoretical thinking.'

Bibliography

ADLER, M. (1967). *The Difference of Man and the Difference it Makes*. New York: Holt, Rinehart & Winston.

ALLPORT, D. A. (1975). 'The state of cognitive psychology: a critical notice of W. G. Chase (ed.). *Visual Information Processing*' (New York: Academic Press). *Quarterly Journal of Experimental Psychology*, 27, pp. 141–52.

ANSCOMBE, G. E. M. (1958). *Intention*. Oxford: Blackwell.

ARBIB, M. A. (1972). 'Consciousness: the secondary role of language'. *J. Phil.*, 69, pp. 579–81.

ARGYLE, M. (1969). *Social Interaction*. London: Methuen.

ARMSTRONG, D. M. (1968). *A Materialist Theory of the Mind*. London: Routledge & Kegan Paul.

ARONSON, E., and CARLSMITH, J. M. (1963). 'The effect of the severity of threat on the devaluation of forbidden behaviour'. *J. of Abnormal & Social Psychology*, 66, pp. 584–8.

ASHBY, W. ROSS (1968). 'Principles of the self-organising system'. In W. Buckley (ed.). *Modern Systems Research for the Behavioral Scientist*. Chicago: Aldine.

AUDI, R. (1973a). 'The concept of wanting'. *Philosophical Studies*, 24, pp. 1–21.

—— (1973b). 'Intending', *J. Phil.*, 70, pp. 387–403.

AUSTIN, J. L. (1966). 'Three ways of spilling ink'. *Phil. Rev.*, 75, pp. 427–40.

AYER, A. J. (1964). *Man as a Subject for Science*. University of London: Athlone Press.

AYERS, M. R. (1968). *The Refutation of Determinism*. London: Methuen.

BARRETT, C. (1963). 'Concepts and concept formation'. *Proc. Arist. Soc.*, 63, pp. 127–44.

BERLIN, I. (1976). *Vico and Herder*. London: Hogarth Press.

BERNSTEIN, R. (1972). *Praxis and Action*. London: Duckworth.

BINKLEY, R., BRONAUGH, R., and MARRAS, A. (1971). *Agent, Action and Reason*. Oxford: Blackwell.

BLANSHARD, B. (1939). *The Nature of Thought*. Two vols. London: Allen & Unwin.

BLOCK, N. J. (1971). 'Are mechanistic and teleological explanations of behaviour compatible?' *Phil. Q.*, 21, pp. 109–17.

—— and FODOR, J. A. (1972). 'What psychological states are not'. *Phil. Rev.*, 81, pp. 159–81.

BODEN, M. A. (1968). 'Machine perception'. *Phil. Q.*, 19, pp. 33–45.

—— (1970). 'Intentionality and physical systems'. *Phil. Sci.*, 37, pp. 200–14.
—— (1972). *Purposive Explanation in Psychology*. Cambridge, Mass.: Harvard University Press.
—— (1973). 'The structure of intentions'. *J. for the Theory of Soc. Behaviour*, 3, pp. 23–46.
BOHM, D. (1965). *The Special Theory of Relativity*. New York: Benjamin.
BOLTON, N. (1972). *The Psychology of Thinking*. London: Methuen.
BOWER, T. G. R. (1974). *Development in Infancy*. San Francisco: W. H. Freeman.
BRAND, M. (ed.) (1970a). *The Nature of Human Action*. Glenview, Illinois: Scott, Foreman.
BRAND, M. (1970b). 'Choosing and doing'. *Ratio*, 12, pp. 85–92.
BRENTANO, F. C. (1874). *Psychologie vom empirischen Standpunkte*. Leipzig: Duncker.
BROADBENT, D. E. (1961). *Behaviour*. London: Eyre & Spottiswoode.
—— (1971). 'Cognitive psychology: introduction'. *British Medical Bulletin*, 27, no. 3, pp. 191–4.
—— (1973). *In Defence of Empirical Psychology*. London: Methuen.
BROADIE, F. (1967). 'Knowing that I am doing'. *Phil. Q.*, 17, pp. 137–49.
BROWN, S. C. (1965). 'Intentionality without grammar'. *Proc. Arist. Soc.*, 65, pp. 123–46.
—— (1972). 'Learning'. *Arist. Soc. Supp.*, 46, pp. 19–39.
BRUNER, J. S. (1976). 'From Communication to Language: A Psychological Perspective'. *Cognition*, 3(3), pp. 255–87.
—— and SHERWOOD, V. (1975). 'Early rule structure: the case of peekabo'. In J. S. Bruner, A. Jolly and K. Sylva (eds). *Play: Its Role in Evolution and Development*. Harmondsworth: Penguin Books.
BUCKLEY, W. (ed.) (1968). *Modern Systems Research for the Behavioral Scientist*. Chicago: Aldine.
CAMPBELL, C. (1957). *On Selfhood and Godhood*. London: Allen & Unwin.
CAMPBELL, F. W., COOPER, G. F., and ENROTH-CUGELL, C. (1969). The spatial selectivity of the visual cells of the cat'. *J. Physiol.*, 203, pp. 223–35.
CANFIELD, J. U. (1974). 'Criteria and rules of language'. *Phil. Rev.*, 83, pp. 70–87.
CARPENTER, E. (1966). 'Image making in arctic art'. In G. Kepes (ed.). *Sign, Image and Symbol*. London: Studio Vista.
CASSIRER, E. (1923). *Substance and Function*. Chicago: Open Court Publishing House; (1953) New York: Dover.
—— (1953). *The Philosophy of Symbolic Forms*. Three vols. New Haven: Yale University Press.
CASTAÑEDA, H. N. (1971). 'Intentions and the structure of intending'. *J. Phil.*, 66, pp. 453–66.
CHISHOLM, R. M. (1957). *Perceiving: A Philosophical Study*. Ithaca: Cornell University Press.
—— (1960). 'Editor's introduction'. In R. M. Chisholm (ed.). *Realism and the Background of Phenomenology*. Chicago: Free Press.
CHURCHLAND, P. M. (1970). 'The logical character of action-explanations'. *Phil. Rev.*, 79, pp. 214–36.
CLARK, M. (1965). 'Intentional objects'. *Analysis*, 25, pp. 123–6.
CLARKE, J. J. (1971). 'Mental structure and the identity theory'. *Mind*, 80, pp. 521–31.
COLLIS, G. M. (in press). 'Visual co-orientation and maternal speech: looking together, saying and hearing'. In H. R. Schaffer (ed.). *Studies of Mother-Infant Interaction: The Loch Lomond Symposium*. London: Academic Press.

COLLIS, G. M., and SCHAFFER, H. R. (in press). 'Synchronization of visual attention in mother-infant pairs'. *J. Child Psychol. Psychiat.*, 16.

CONDON, W. S., and SANDER, L. S. (1974). 'Neonate movement is synchronised with adult speech'. *Science*, 183, p. 99.

CRAIK, K. J. W. (1943). *The Nature of Explanation*. Cambridge University Press.

CROWELL, E. (1975). 'Causal explanation and human action'. *Mind*, 84, pp. 440–2.

DAWES HICKS, G. (1938). *Critical Realism*. London: Macmillan.

DELGADO, J. M. R. (1969). *Physical Control of the Mind*. New York: Harper & Row.

DEUTSCH, M., and KRAUSS, R. M. (1965). *Theories in Social Psychology*. New York: Basic Books.

DEWEY, J. (1896). 'The reflex arc concept in psychology'. *Psychol. Rev.*, 3, pp. 13–32. Reprinted in W. Dennis (ed.). *Readings in the History of Psychology*. New York: Appleton-Century-Crofts.

DONELLAN, K. S. (1963). 'Knowing what I am doing'. *J. Phil.*, 60, pp. 401–9.

EHRENZWEIG, A. (1970). *The Hidden Order of Art*. London: Paladin.

FANTZ, R. L. (1961). 'The origin of form perception'. *Scientific American*, 204, pp. 66–72, offprint no. 459.

—— (1967). 'Visual perception and experience in infancy'. In H. W. Stevenson (ed.). *Early Behaviour*. New York: Wiley.

—— and NEVIS, S. (1965). 'Pattern preference and perceptual-cognitive development in early infancy'. In P. Mussen, J. J. Conger, and J. Kagan (eds). *Readings in Child Development and Personality*. New York: Harper & Row.

FESTINGER, L. (1957). *A Theory of Cognitive Dissonance*. Evanston, Illinois: Row Peterson.

—— and CARLSMITH, J. M. (1959). 'Cognitive consequences of forced compliance'. *J. of Abnormal & Social Psychology*, 58, pp. 203–10.

FINDLAY, J. N. (1972). *Psyche and Cerebrum*. Milwaukee: Marquette University Press.

FISHER, J. A. (1974). 'Knowledge of rules'. *Rev. Met.*, 28, pp. 237–60.

FLEMING, B. N. (1964). 'On intention'. *Phil. Rev.*, 73, pp. 301–20.

FLEW, A. G. N. (1965). 'A rational animal'. In J. R. Smythies (ed.). *Brain and Mind*. London: Routledge & Kegan Paul.

FODOR, J. A. (1965). *Explanation in Psychology*. In M. Black (ed.). *Philosophy in America*. London: Allen & Unwin.

FRANKLIN, R. L. (1968). *Freewill and Determinism*. London: Routledge & Kegan Paul.

FREEDMAN, J. (1965). 'Long-term behavioural effects of cognitive dissonance'. *J. Exp. Soc. Psychol.*, 1, pp. 145–55.

GARFINKEL, H. (1967). *Studies in Ethnomethodology*. New York: Prentice-Hall.

GAULD, A. O. (1966). 'Could a machine perceive?' *Brit. J. Philos. Sci.*, 17, pp. 44–58.

—— (1972). 'The domain of psychology'. *Bull. Brit. Psychol. Soc.*, 25, pp. 93–100.

GEACH, P. (1958). *Mental Acts*. London: Routledge & Kegan Paul.

GINNANE, W. J. (1960). 'Thoughts'. *Mind*, 79, pp. 372–90.

GÖDEL, K. (1931). 'Über formal unentscheidbare Sätze der Principia Mathematica und verwandter Systeme'. *Monatshefte für Mathemetik und Physik*, 38, pp. 173–98.

GOFFMAN, E. (1956). *The Presentation of Self in Everyday Life*. Edinburgh University Press. Harmondsworth: Penguin Books, 1971.

GOLDMAN, A. I. (1970). *A Theory of Human Action*. New York: Prentice-Hall.

GREEN, C. E. (1968). *Out-of-the-Body Experiences*. Oxford: Institute of Psychophysical Research.

GREENFIELD, P. M. (1972). 'Playing peekabo with a four-month old: a study of the role of speech and nonspeech sounds in the formulation of a visual schema'. *Journal of Psychology*, 82, pp. 287–98.

GRICE, H. P. (1971). *Intention and Uncertainty*. London: Oxford University Press.

GRIFFITHS, A. P. (1963). 'On belief'. *Proc. Arist. Soc.*, 63, pp. 167–86.

GUSTAFSON, D. (1974). 'Expressions of intentions'. *Mind*, 83, pp. 321-40.

HAMPSHIRE, S. (1959). *Thought and Action*. London: Chatto & Windus.

HARRÉ, R., and SECORD, P. F. (1972). *The Explanation of Social Behaviour*. Oxford: Blackwell.

HART, H. L. A. (1948–9). 'The ascription of responsibility and rights'. *Proc. Arist. Soc.*, 49, pp. 171–94.

HARTNACK, J. (1972). 'On thinking'. *Mind*, 81, pp. 543–52.

HEATH, P. L. (1967). 'Concept'. In vol. 4 of P. Edwards (ed.). *The Encyclopedia of Philosophy*. New York: Macmillan.

HERRIOT, P. (1974). *Attributes of Memory*. London: Methuen.

HESS, R. D., and SHIPMAN, V. C. (1965). 'Early experience and the socialization of cognitive modes in children'. *Child Development*, 36, pp. 869–86.

HOMANS, G. C. (1961). *Social Behaviour*. London: Routledge & Kegan Paul.

HOWARTH, E., and CATTELL, R. B., (1973). 'The multivariate experimental contribution to personality research'. In B. B. Wolman (ed.). *Handbook of General Psychology*. Englewood Cliffs, N.J.: Prentice-Hall.

HUBEL, D. H., and WIESEL, T. N. (1962). 'Receptive fields, binocular interaction and functional architecture in the cat's visual cortex'. *J. Physiol.*, 160, pp. 106–54.

HUMPHREY, G. (1951). *Thinking: An Introduction to its Experimental Psychology*. London: Methuen.

HUSSERL, E. (1970). *Logical Investigations*. Tr. J. N. Findlay. Two vols. London: Routledge & Kegan Paul.

JAMES, W. (1890). *Principles of Psychology*. London: Macmillan.

JOHNSTONE, H. W. (1967). 'Persons and selves'. *Phil. & Phen. Res.*, 28, 205–12.

JOYNSON, R. L. (1974). *Psychology and Common Sense*. London: Routledge & Kegan Paul.

KENNY, A. (1963). *Action, Emotion and Will*. London: Routledge & Kegan Paul.

—— (1967). 'Criterion'. In vol. 1 of P. Edwards (ed.). *The Encyclopedia of Philosophy*. New York: Macmillan.

KOCH, S. (1954). 'Clark L. Hull', In W. K. Estes *et al. Modern Learning Theory*. New York: Appleton-Century-Crofts.

KUHN, T. S. (1962). *The Structure of Scientific Revolutions*. University of Chicago Press.

LANGFORD, G. (1972). *Human Action*. London: Macmillan.

LATANÉ, B., and RODIN, J. (1969). 'A lady in distress: inhibiting effects of friends and strangers on bystander intervention'. *J. Exp. Soc. Psychol.*, 5, pp. 189–202.

LOCKE, D. (1974a) 'Action, movement and neurophysiology'. *Inquiry*, 17, pp. 23–42.

—— (1974b). 'Natural powers and human abilities'. *Proc. Arist. Soc.*, 74, pp. 170–87.

LOTZE, R. H. (1887). *Metaphysics*. Ed. B. Bosanquet. Two vols. Oxford University Press.

LOUCH, A. R. (1966). *Explanation and Human Action*. Berkeley: University of California Press.

LUCAS, J. R. (1970). *The Freedom of the Will*. Oxford: Clarendon Press.

LYCAN, W. G. (1969). 'On "intentionality" and the psychological'. *Am. Phil. Q.*, 6, pp. 305–10.

—— (1971). 'Noninductive evidence: recent work on Wittgenstein's criteria'. *Am. Phil. Q.*, 8, pp. 109–25.

LYON, A. (1974). 'Criteria and evidence'. *Mind*, 83, pp. 211–27.
MACALISTER, L. (1974). 'Chisholm and Brentano on intentionality'. *Rev. Met.*, 28, pp. 328–38.
McCANN, H. (1974). 'Volition and basic action'. *Phil. Rev.*, 83, pp. 451–73.
—— (1975). 'Trying, paralysis and volition'. *Rev. Met.*, 28, pp. 423–42.
McCLELLAND, D. C., ATKINSON, J. W., CLARK, R. A., and LOWELL, E. L. (1953). *The Achievement Motive*. New York: Appleton-Century-Crofts.
McDOUGALL, W. (1923). *Outline of Psychology*. London: Methuen.
—— (1928). 'The confusion of the concept'. *J. Philosophical Studies*, 3, pp. 427–42.
MACFARLANE, A. (1974). 'If a smile is so important'. *New Scientist*, 25 April.
MACINTYRE, A. (1966). 'The antecedents of action'. In B. Williams and A. Montefiore (eds). *British Analytical Philosophy*. London: Routledge & Kegan Paul.
MACMURRAY, J. (1957). *The Self as Agent*. London: Faber & Faber.
—— (1961). *Persons in Relation*. London: Faber & Faber.
MALCOLM, N. (1968). 'The conceivability of mechanism'. *Phil. Rev.*, 76, pp. 45–72.
MANSEL, H. L. (1860). *Prolegomena Logica*. Second ed. Oxford: H. Hammans.
MEILAND, J. (1970). *The Nature of Intention*. London: Methuen.
MELDEN, A. I. (1961). *Free Action*. London: Routledge & Kegan Paul.
MERLEAU-PONTY, M. (1965). *The Structure of Behaviour*. Tr. A. L. Fisher. London: Methuen.
MICHIE, D. (1974). *On Machine Intelligence*. Edinburgh University Press.
MILGRAM, S. (1974). *Obedience to Authority*. London: Tavistock.
MILLER, G. A., GALANTER, E., and PRIBRAM, K. H. (1960). *Plans and the Structure of Behavior*. New York: Holt, Rinehart & Winston.
MILNER, P. (1970). *Physiological Psychology*. New York: Holt, Rinehart & Winston.
MINSKY, M. L. (1965). 'Matter, mind and models'. In *Proceedings of the International Federation of Information Processing Congress I*. Washington, D.C.: Spartan.
—— (1967). *Computation*. New York: Prentice-Hall.
MISCHEL, T. (ed.) (1969). *Human Action*. New York: Academic Press.
—— (ed.) (1974). *Understanding Other Persons*. Oxford: Blackwell.
MITCHELL, D. (1962). *An Introduction to Logic*. London: Hutchinson.
MIXON, D. (1974). 'If you won't deceive, what can you do?' In N. Armistead (ed.). *Reconstructing Social Psychology*. Harmondsworth: Penguin Books.
MOUTON, D. L. (1969). 'The concept of thinking'. *Nous*, 3, pp. 355–72.
MUNDLE, C. W. K. (1970). *A Critique of Linguistic Philosophy*. Oxford: Clarendon Press.
MURPHY, C. M., and MESSER, D. J. (in press). 'Mothers, infants and pointing: a study of a gesture'. In H. R. Schaffer (ed.). *Studies of Mother-Infant Interaction: The Loch Lomond Symposium*. London: Academic Press.
NAGEL, E. (1961). *The Structure of Science*. New York: Harcourt, Brace & World.
NEEDHAM, R. (1972). *Belief, Language and Experience*. Oxford: Blackwell.
NEISSER, U. (1967). *Cognitive Psychology*. New York: Appleton-Century-Crofts.
NEWSON, J. (1974). 'Towards a theory of infant understanding'. *Bull. Brit. Psychol. Soc.*, 27, pp. 251–7.
—— and NEWSON, E. (1976). 'On the social origins of symbolic functioning'. In V. P. Varma and P. Williams (eds). *Advances in Educational Psychology III*. London: Hodder & Stoughton.
—— and PAWLBY, S. (1973). 'Imitation and pre-verbal communication'. Paper presented at Brit. Psychol. Soc. Developmental Psychology Section meeting, Nottingham, September.

—— and —— (1975). 'On imitation'. Paper presented at an inter-university colloquium at Nottingham University, 18 January.

—— and SHOTTER, J. (1974). 'How babies communicate'. *New Society*, 29, no. 618, pp. 345–7, 8 August.

NORRIS, S. (1975). 'The intelligibility of practical reasoning'. *Am. Phil. Q.*, 12, pp. 77–84.

NOWELL-SMITH, P. H. (1967). 'Concept'. In P. Edwards (ed.). *The Encyclopedia of Philosophy*. New York: Macmillan; London: Collier–Macmillan. Vol. 2, pp. 177–80.

O'CONNOR, D. J. (1967). 'Tests for intentionality'. *Am. Phil. Q.*, 4, pp. 173–8.

OLSEN, C. (1969). 'Knowledge of one's own intentional actions'. *Phil. Q.*, 19, pp. 324–36.

ORNE, M. T. (1962). 'On the social psychology of the psychological experiment: with particular reference to demand characteristics and their implications. *American Psychologist*, 17, pp. 776–83.

PAWLBY, S. (in press). 'Imitative interaction'. In H. R. Schaffer (ed.). *Studies of Mother-Infant Interaction: The Loch Lomond Symposium*. London: Academic Press.

PENFIELD, W. (1966). 'Discussion comment' in J. C. Eccles (ed.). *Brain and Conscious Experience*. Berlin: Springer Verlag.

PETERS, R. S. (1958). *The Concept of Motivation*. London: Routledge & Kegan Paul.

POWELL, B. (1967). *Knowledge of Actions*. London: Allen & Unwin.

PRICE, H. H. (1969). *Belief*. London: Allen & Unwin.

RESCHER, N. (ed.) (1967). *The Logic of Decision and Action*. University of Pittsburgh Press.

RICHARDS, D. A. J. (1971). *A Theory of Reasons for Action*. Oxford University Press.

RICHARDS, M. P. M. (1974). 'First steps in becoming social'. In M. P. M. Richards (ed.). *The Integration of a Child into a Social World*. Cambridge University Press.

RIPLEY, C. (1974). 'A theory of volition'. *Am. Phil. Q.*, 11, pp. 141–7.

RORTY, R. M. (1967). 'Relations, internal and external'. In vol. 7 of P. Edwards (ed.). *The Encyclopedia of Philosophy*. New York: Macmillan.

ROSENBERG, M. J. (1970). 'The experimental parable of inauthenticity: consequences of attitudinal performance'. In J. S. Antrobus (ed.). *Cognition and Affect*. Boston: Little, Brown.

ROSENTHAL, R. (1966). *Experimenter Effects in Behavioural Research*. New York: Appleton-Century-Crofts.

RYLE, G. (1951). 'Thinking and language'. *Arist. Soc. Supp.*, 25, pp. 65–82.

SCAIFE, M., and BRUNER, J. S. (1975). 'The capacity for joint visual attention in the infant'. *Nature*, 253, no. 5499, pp. 265–6.

SCHAFFER, H. R. (1971). *The Growth of Sociability*. Harmondsworth: Penguin Books.

—— (1974). 'Behavioural synchrony in infancy'. *New Scientist*, 4 April.

SCHIFFER, S. (1972). *Meaning*. Oxford: Clarendon Press.

SEARLE, J. R. (1969). *Speech Acts*. Cambridge University Press.

SECORD, P. F., and BACKMAN, C. W. (1974). *Social Psychology*. Second ed. Tokyo: McGraw-Hill Kogakushe.

SHER, G. (1973). 'Causal explanation and the vocabulary of action'. *Mind*, 82, pp. 22–30.

SHOEMAKER, S. (1963). *Self-knowledge and Self-identity*. Ithaca: Cornell University Press.

SHOTTER, J., and GREGORY, S. (1976). 'On first gaining the idea of oneself as a person'. In R. Harré (ed.). *Life Sentences*. Chichester, England: Wiley.

SKINNER, B. F. (1938). *The Behaviour of Organisms*. New York: Appleton-Century-Crofts.
—— (1953). *Science and Human Behaviour*. New York: Macmillan.
—— (1957). *Verbal Behavior*. New York: Appleton-Century-Crofts.
—— (1959). *Cumulative Record*. New York: Appleton-Century-Crofts.
—— (1972). *Beyond Freedom and Dignity*. London: Jonathan Cape.
SMART, J. J. C. (1963). *Philosophy and Scientific Realism*. London: Routledge & Kegan Paul.
STEBBING, S. (1937). *Philosophy and the Physicists*. London: Methuen.
STEPHENSON, G. M., and WHITE, J. H. (1968). 'An experimental study of some effects of injustice on children's moral behaviour'. *J. Exp. Soc. Psychol.*, 4, pp. 460–9.
—— (1970). 'Privilege, deprivation, and children's moral behaviour: an experimental clarification of the role of investments'. *J. Exp. Soc. Psychol.*, 6, pp. 167–76.
STOUT, G. F. (1896). *Analytic Psychology*. Two vols. London: Swan Sonnenschein.
—— (1938). *A Manual of Psychology*. London: University Tutorial Press.
SUTHERLAND, N. S. (1970). 'Is the Brain a Physical System?' In R. Borger and F. Cioffi (eds). *Explanation in the Behavioural Sciences*. Cambridge University Press.
TAYLOR, C. (1964). *The Explanation of Behaviour*. London: Routledge & Kegan Paul.
—— (1971). 'Interpretation and the sciences of man'. *Rev. Met.*, 25, pp. 3–51.
TAYLOR, R. (1966). *Action and Purpose*. Englewood Cliffs, N.J.: Prentice-Hall.
TEDESCHI, J. T., SCHLENKER, B. R., and BONOMA, T. V. (1971). 'Cognitive dissonance: private ratiocination or public spectacle?' *American Psychologist*, 26, pp. 685–95.
THALBERG, I. (1972). *Enigmas of Agency: Studies in the Philosophy of Human Action*. London: Allen & Unwin.
TREVARTHEN, C. (1974). 'Conversations with a two-month old'. *New Scientist*, 62, no. 896, 2 May, pp. 230–5.
——, HUBLEY, P., and SHEERAN, L. (1975). 'Psychological actions in early infancy'. *La Recherche*, 6, pp. 447–58.
TULKIN, S. R., and KAGAN, J. (1972). 'Mother-child interaction in the first year of life'. *Child Development*, 43, pp. 31–41.
TURNER, M. B. (1971). *Realism and the Explanation of Behavior*. New York: Appleton-Century-Crofts.
UHR, L., and VOSSLER, C. (1963). 'A pattern-recognition program that generates, evaluates, and adjusts its own operators'. In E. A. Feigenbaum and J. Feldman (eds). *Computers and Thought*. New York: McGraw-Hill.
VYGOTSKY, L. S. (1962). *Thought and Language*. Cambridge, Mass.: M. I. T. Press.
—— (1966). 'Development of the higher mental functions'. In *Psychological Research in the USSR*. Moscow: Progress Publishers.
WAISMANN, F. (1953). 'Language strata'. In A. G. N. Flew (ed.). *Logic and Language*. Second series. Oxford: Blackwell.
WARNOCK, G. J. (1963). 'Actions and events'. In D. F. Pears (ed.). *Freedom and the Will*. London: Macmillan.
WATSON, A. J. (1958). 'Some questions concerning the explanation of learning in animals'. Paper 4.6 in *The Mechanisation of Thought Processes; Proceedings of a Symposium held at the National Physical Laboratory*. Two vols. London: HMSO.
WEISKRANTZ, L. (1973). 'Problems and progress in physiological psychology'. *Brit. J. Psychol.*, 64, pp. 511–20.
WHITE, A. R. (ed.) (1968). *The Philosophy of Action*. Oxford University Press.
WHITELEY, C. H. (1973). *Mind in Action*. Oxford University Press.
WILKERSON, T. (1974). *Minds, Brains and People*. Oxford: Clarendon Press.

WILLARD, D. (1972). 'The paradox of logical psychologism'. *Am. Phil. Q.*, 11, pp. 94–100.

WINCH, P. (1958). *The Idea of a Social Science and its Relations to Philosophy*. London: Routledge & Kegan Paul.

WINOGRAD, T. (1972). 'Understanding natural language'. *Cognitive Psychology*, 3, pp. 1-191.

—— (1973). 'A procedural model of language understanding'. In R. C. Shank and K. M. Colby (eds). *Computer Models of Thought and Language*. San Francisco: W. H. Freeman.

WITTGENSTEIN, L. (1953). *Philosophical Investigations*. Oxford: Blackwell.

—— (1958). *The Blue and the Brown Books*. Oxford: Blackwell.

WOOD, D., BRUNER, J. S., and ROSS, G. (1976). 'The role of tutoring in problem solving'. *J. of Child Psychol. Psychiat.*, 17, pp. 89–100.

—— and MIDDLETON, D. (1975). 'A study of assisted problem solving'. *Brit. J. Psychol.*, 66, pp. 181–97.

WOODWORTH, R. S. (1939). *Psychological Issues*. New York: Columbia University Press.

Name Index

Subject Index

Acts, action, human action, 5, 39–61, 154–68; action as movement, 39–41; non-causally related to consequents, 41; conditions for action, 42; acts of seeing, 66; actions to-be-done-by-oneself, 148–50; one's action, 165

Agency, agent, 7, 39, 41–2, 45, 67, 169–79; central, viii; peripheral, viii; agent causality, 41–2; self as agent, 169; self as source of activity, 171–2

Algorithms, 18; Turing machines, 19, 217n

Belief, beliefs, 59, 73, 122, 123, 132–3, 139–53; believing and intending, 59; primitive credulity. 133, 148

Cause, causal determination, 4, 9–10, 11, 17–18, 52, 97, 118–22, 189, 220n; Neo-Humean, 17–18

Coding mechanisms and principles, 63, 65, 66

Cognitive dissonance, 186–91

Commitment, commitments, 44–5, 147–50, 195, 221n; primitive committal, 148; self as committed to action, 150

Complementarity, 218n

Concepts and concept-possession, 21, 22, 23–8, 130, 199, 200, 217n; psychological concepts, 8; object-concepts, 27, 112–16; stimulus-neutral concepts, 31–5, 217n; concept acquisition, 37; a-concepts and b-concepts, 45; of 'ordinary people', 78; negation, 130–2; of something as to-be-done-by-one, 164; stimulus-independent, 217n

Conceptual analysis, 78–9, 98–9

Creativity, 20

Criterion, criteria, 42–5, 155–61; and other minds' problem, 158–9

Culture, 72–4, 95; cultural 'drives', 72; cultural development, 74

Deontic logic, 149

Development, developmental psychology, 83, 84, 199–215; 'developmental' questions, 82, 84, 199; biological factors in, 201; differentiation in, 200, 201

Digital computers, 18

Distributive justice, 182, 183–6

Experimental psychology, 64–8, 92–4; relevance to hermeneutical psychology, 94; demand characteristics in, 196

Formal systems, 220n

Free will, 179

Generalisations, 85–8; descriptive generalisations, 91